DREAMS OF THE ROAD

Sune Le Dromenge

DREAMS OF THE ROAD

Gypsy Life in the West Country

Martin Levinson
& Avril Silk

BIRLINN

First published in 2007 by
Birlinn Ltd
West Newington House
10 Newington Road
Edinburgh EH9 1QS

www.birlinn.co.uk

ISBN 13: 978 1 84158 505 5
ISBN 10: 1 84158 505 X

British Library Cataloguing-in-Publication Data
A catalogue record for this book is available from the British Library

Edited by Katy Charge
Design by Andrew Sutterby

Printed and bound by 1010, China

To Jim, Jessica, Nadia and Miri, and to those who shared their stories.

CONTENTS

ACKNOWLEDGEMENTS

We were fortunate to meet some very special people while gathering material for this book, and we would like to thank all those who generously shared their life stories and photographs with us, in particular (in alphabetical order):

Pat Atkinson
Maggie Bendell Smith
Nellie Danes
Rodney Danes
Diana Hughes
Jim Lee
Jean Orchard
Tom Orchard
Lisa Packman
Dorothy Penfold
Anna Price
Robert Smith
Amy Thomas
Linda White

We would also like to thank those who have granted permission to use text and/or images from other sources. They are:

Katrina Atkinson
Caroline Benson, Museum of English Rural Life, University of Reading
Calico and Jessica at Mr Spot's Chai House, Seattle
Christianity magazine
Gwilym Davies, folk singer and collector of folk music
Robert Dawson, writer, educationalist, Gypsy and Traveller specialist
Simon Evans, broadcaster, photographer, writer
Faber and Faber, publishers of *Everyday Herbs* by Mary Thorne Quelch
Mick Garland, photographer
Emma John, contributor to *Christianity* magazine
Stuart King, woodworker

Milo Books, publishers of *King of the Gypsies: Memoirs of the Undefeated Bareknuckle Champion of Great Britain and Ireland* by Bartley Gorman with Peter Walsh, 2003

John Bearcat Redmond, writer and poet

Routledge plc, publishers of *The Chime Child or Somerset Folklore* by Ruth Tongue, 1968

Routledge plc, publishers of *In The Life of a Romany Gipsy* by Manfri Frederick Wood, 1973

Tim Sandles, provider of a website about Dartmoor www.legendarydartmoor.co.uk

Derek Schofield, Editor, *English Dance and Song* magazine

Stef Bate and the VS team at ValleyStreams UK Vardo Project www.gypsywaggons.co.uk

Carol Wilson, author of *Gypsy Feast: Recipes and Culinary Traditions of the Romany People*, published by Hippocrene Books, 2004

PREFACE

In some ways, this book is a logical outcome of the many years we have spent working with Romani Gypsies. Although we each came to the field from different backgrounds, and with quite separate experiences, it was the convergence of perspectives that generated this project, along with a feeling that Gypsy life in this country is at a crossroads, one at which there is no *drom pukkering cosht* (literally, the stick that says road) offering clear directions towards the future.

I first met Avril while engaged in my doctoral research project at Exeter University, during which time I was investigating the interface between the cultural world experienced in the Romani home-place and that encountered in school settings. At that time Avril was working as a teacher with Somerset Traveller Education Service. Her personality took her beyond the role of supporting Gypsy children in schools; in the case of many children, she had become intimately involved in the lives of their families. This was no easy achievement, as Gypsy Travellers are — and have good cause to be — suspicious of the motives of those working for external agencies. Yet it is also a fact that there have always been exceptions, and some have gained admission to the home world; both of us have found Gypsies to be very astute at 'reading' people, identifying very quickly qualities such as honesty and integrity.

Meanwhile, we were both influenced by stark images of home life, which affected us in powerful ways, especially as visual milieus have been salient features in each of our lives. Avril is a trained artist, particularly well known in the South West for her work with stained glass, while I spent a number of years working as a photographer, travelling across countries such as India, China and Mexico, collecting ethnographic images recording diverse cultural worlds. The Romani landscape, as seen by each of us, revealed a home world very much hidden from the mainstream population, a universe in which people survived on the margins, facing physical privation and, not uncommonly, danger. This is the reality of officially allocated sites, a terrain most of us prefer not to see — a situation not altogether unacceptable to a people who have often preferred to remain invisible.

The emergence of large sites contrasts with the past memories of a picturesque landscape, and as David Sibley has pointed out in *Geographies of Exclusion* (1995), one that is often romanticised by Gypsies and non-Gypsies alike. It seemed to us that we could not really comprehend the current situation for Gypsies without gaining a fuller understanding of that past world. The tracks leading to that world are winding, difficult to follow, and require guides in the form of those who lived that life as children. These guides are not always reliable, as at times – quite justifiably – they elect to conceal aspects of their childhood. It is as if they suddenly vanish from the path along which they are leading you. Moreover, they often grew up with secrets kept from them.

Nevertheless, as it evolved, this book became a shared project – between us and our 'guides'. As far as we can, we have tried to separate fact from fiction, presenting the former for the reader, but as you will appreciate, this is not always a simple task, and for all of us, memory is capricious. Meanwhile, it is composed through the eyes of those who operate outside the spatial and temporal norms of mainstream society, regularly moving between places, and allowing natural rhythms, rather than clocks and calendars, to dictate decisions about time.

A common feature amongst those who contributed seemed a sense of self as a link in a chain, and for that reason, this book is not presented as a series of biographies. Indeed, gradually, during the course of the composition, the life stories of those speaking to us, and those of their parents and grandparents became a narrative not so much about themselves but about their world. And as we came close to the end, we began to appreciate that the story was not just about what Romani Gypsies may have lost, but what we have all allowed to unravel, both from the fabric of their existence and our own.

Martin Levinson
February 2007

Gypsies in the West Country

An Introduction

The word 'gipsy' in the village was usually spoken with slight contempt. Gipsy girls, the sun and the wind, golden brown faces, plaited coils of hair like ripe wheat, strong and supple figures – my thoughts were my own, and alas must remain thoughts.

Henry Williamson, *Life in a Devon Village*, 1945

Truths about Gypsies are rather like the making of a campfire stew: throw in your well-trusted ingredients – some facts, a few myths; then, in no particular proportions, add whatever comes to hand – some tales heard in distant places, a few downright lies; garnish with a few spices and half-truths for extra flavour, and give it all a good stir, then serve.

As with information about modern Gypsies, the truth about their origins in Britain is rather shrouded in mystery; according to one early Romani source, there are probably about ten thousand books on Gypsies, less than a dozen of which provide any new facts or throw light on their subject whatsoever. One reason for this lack of clarity is that Gypsies were sometimes confused with indigenous roaming bands. Traditionally, they have always passed on accounts of ancestors by word of mouth, leaving their forebears located somewhere between story and history – and indeed this oral tradition is reflected by the fact that there are such huge discrepancies in the spellings of names and locations, and little importance is placed on precise dates. As such, throughout this book the preferred spellings employed by our sources have been maintained. For facts we have often been left to rely on Gypsy folklorists, such as George Borrow, who finished writing his *Romano Lavo-Lil* in 1874, some three centuries after the Gypsies first arrived in Britain:

> They roamed about in bands, consisting of thirty, sixty, or ninety families, with light, creaking carts, drawn by horses and donkeys, encamping at night in the spots they deemed convenient. The women told fortunes at the castle of the baron and the cottage of the yeoman; filched gold and silver coins from the counters of money-changers; caused the death of hogs in farmyards, by means of a stuff called drab or drao, which affects the brain, but does not corrupt the blood; and subsequently begged, and generally obtained, the carcases. The men plied tinkering and brasiery, now and then stole horses, and occasionally ventured upon highway robbery.

There remains some debate as to the precise origins of Gypsies, though linguistic evidence (see, for instance, Gjerdman & Ljungberg, 1963; Paspati, 1870; Sampson, 1926) has been perceived as indicating origins in the Indian sub-continent. Other than references to an infestation of Saracens or Moors in Galloway in the mid-fifteenth century, the first official record of Gypsy people in the United Kingdom came with the arrival of 'exotically attired Egyptians' in Scotland in 1505, as cited in W. Simson's *A History of the Gipsies* (1865). In England, in 1514, during the reign of Henry VIII, Thomas More reported the appearance of a Gypsy, or an 'Egyptian', woman, who could tell marvellous things simply by looking into a person's hand. Perhaps it was to hear his fortune, along with other entertainments, that a William Cholmeley paid a group of these people forty shillings at Thornbury, near Bristol, in 1521. However, the vogue for such 'outlandish people, calling themselves Egyptians' was short-lived, at an official level, at least, with an act being passed in 1530, by which Henry VIII forbade the transportation of Gypsies or 'Egypcyans' into England. The fine was forty pounds for a ship's owner or captain; the Gypsy passengers were simply hanged. Further acts were to follow. In 1547 Edward VI passed a law requiring that Gypsies be seized, branded with a 'V' (they were doubtless lucky to have avoided the full term 'vagabond') on their breast, and then enslaved for two years. Captured escapees were branded with an 'S', and made slaves for life. A further act was passed during the reign of Elizabeth I in 1562; death and loss of lands and goods being decreed on all except for those who 'quit their idle and ungodly life and company'. Despite such legislation, the Lord Lieutenant of Dorset managed to find a way round the instructions of the Queen's Privy Council to make an example of a large band of Gypsies in his area – this group was spared from execution on the grounds that they had not been transported and conveyed into England, but had come overland from Scotland.

Apart from acts passed specifically against them, Gypsies were also prone to suffer from such statutes as that of 1572, which allowed for the children of 'rogues and beggars' to be seized and put in service. Nevertheless, over the following two centuries, Gypsies somehow survived in England as a group, generally through their wits, sometimes through the use of counterfeit passports, and quite often, with the collusion of local people. That they were established in the West Country from early times is evident from contemporary records. For instance, in 1558, Joan, 'the daughter of an Egiptian', was baptised at Lyme Regis Church. In 1650 the Churchwardens' Account for Uplyme records one shilling and sixpence being given to '12 Egyeptiones' brought in by the local constable.

At the same time, over the ensuing centuries English Gypsies remained in a vulnerable situation, as is reflected by a famous West Country case of the mid-eighteenth century.

At the edge of Chedington, perched in the West Dorset chalk hills along a wooded ridge, is a cutting known as Winyards Gap, from which point the road winds down into Somerset. Nestling beneath an ancient earthwork is Winyards Gap Inn, formerly known as The Three Horseshoes. Long associated with legend and intrigue – Charles I's army marched by this windswept, solitary spot in 1644, during the

Civil War, and generations of innkeepers have told tales of smuggling and highway-men – the place is also integral to an eighteenth-century incident that led to a famous Old Bailey court case.

On 1 January 1753, Elizabeth Canning, an 18-year-old girl who lived and worked in the city of London, went missing. She returned home, almost a month later, bedraggled, saying that she had been abducted in the Moorfields area, which was a notorious haunt for highwaymen. She claimed to have been imprisoned by a brothel keeper, Susannah Wells, in Enfield, just outside London, where a gypsy called Mary Squires had removed her stays and the two women ordered her to work as a prostitute. After Canning's escape, Wells and Squires were arrested on the orders of Henry Fielding, the local JP (and famous novelist). A girl called Virtue Hall, a prostitute at the brothel, at first claimed never to have seen Canning but, under pressure, changed her story.

At the Old Bailey trial, Gypsy Squires claimed to have been travelling in Dorset at the time. During the crucial period she said was with her family at The Three Horseshoes. Three witnesses came from Dorset to corroborate her alibi, but a mob outside the courtroom, baying for the blood of 'the Gypsy', blocked their entry. While Fielding stirred up a good deal of sympathy for the 'poor girl' Elizabeth Canning, others, such as John Hill, the pamphleteer, hack writer, botanist, apothe-cary, charlatan, and peddler of bogus medicines, took the opposing side. Ultimately Wells was subjected to branding; Squires was sentenced to be hanged.

A family group alongside their Brush wagon.

Dissatisfied by the outcome, the Lord Mayor of London, Sir Crispin Gascoyne, conducted his own investigation, gaining a subsequent pardon for Squires, and a conviction against Canning for perjury. Canning was transported but did not, however, leave on a convict ship. Supporters arranged for a trip in comfort. In America, she married a great-nephew of a Governor of Connecticut and had five children. She died in 1773, aged 38, taking the secret of her missing month to her grave.

During the course of the eighteenth century a number of English Gypsies found themselves transported as slaves to the New World colonies, but in general, there was a relaxation of laws against them, and their situation was better than that of many of their counterparts in Europe. In the early 1800s in Germany, for example, Gypsy hunts ('Heidenjachten') were a common and popular sport, similar to fox hunting.

Despite restrictions, such as the Turnpike Act of 1822, by which fines were handed out to those found camping on the roadside, a recognisable Romani lifestyle was developing, and during the 1830s the first Gypsy, wooden, horse-drawn, covered wagons began to appear. Charles Dickens described a wagon or 'vardo' thus:

> One half of it…was carpeted, and so partitioned off at the further end as to accom-modate a sleeping-place, constructed after the fashion of a berth on board ship, which was shaded, like the windows, with fair white curtains…The other half served for a kitchen, and was fitted up with a stove whose small chimney passed through the roof. It also held a closet or larder, several chests, a great pitcher of water, and a few cooking-utensils and articles of crockery.
>
> Description of Mrs Jarley's van from Charles Dickens's *Old Curiosity Shop*, 1840, ch. xxvii

According to F.G. Huth, writing in the *Journal of the Gypsy Lore Society* in 1940, there were five types of Gypsy-living wagons in the nineteenth century: the Bow-topped, the Ledge (or Cottage-shaped wagon), the Brush, the Showman's (straight-sided wagon, or Burton), and the Reading wagon.

The Reading is often considered to be the most advanced design, although some wealthy owners opted for the Showman's, many of which were constructed according to individual preference, and tended to be particularly elaborate, decorated with features such as gold leaf, cut glass, angel lamps and wooden carvings. However, they were not designed to travel particularly long distances. Less ornate was the Brush wagon, a somewhat unwieldy creature that lumbered along the highways, with racks and cases attached externally, carrying brushes, brooms, baskets, furniture, and other assorted items. Used by general hawkers, as well as by Gypsies, it was effectively a store on wheels.

Bow wagons. (By courtesy Valley Stream Uk Vardo Project)

The Gypsy perspective of the contemporary landscape is implied in the Romani names for English counties and towns, as recorded by George Borrow in *Romano Lavo-Lil*:

Romane Navior of Temes and Gavior / Gypsy Names of Counties and Towns

Baulo-mengreskey tem	Swineherds' country, Hampshire
Bitcheno padlengreskey tem	Transported fellows' country
Botany Bay Bokra-mengreskey tem	Shepherds' country, Sussex
Bori-congriken gav	Great church town, York
Boro-rukeneskey gav	Great tree town, Fairlop
Boro gueroneskey tem	Big fellows' country, Northumberland
Chohawniskey tem	Witches' country, Lancashire
Choko-mengreskey gav	Shoemakers' town, Northampton
Churi-mengreskey gav	Cutlers' town, Sheffield
Coro-mengreskey tem	Potters' country, Staffordshire
Cosht-killimengreskey tem	Cudgel players' country, Cornwall
Curo-mengreskey gav	Boxers' town, Nottingham
Dinelo tem	Fools' country, Suffolk

Giv-engreskey tem	Farmers' country, Buckinghamshire
Gry-engreskey gav	Horsedealers' town, Horncastle
Guyo-mengreskey tem	Pudding-eaters' country, Yorkshire
Hindity-mengreskey tem	Dirty fellows' country, Ireland
Jinney-mengreskey gav	Sharpers' town, Manchester
Juggal-engreskey gav	Dog-fanciers' town, Dudley
Juvlo-mengreskey tem	Lousy fellows' country, Scotland
Kaulo gav	The black town, Birmingham
Levin-engriskey tem	Hop country, Kent
Lil-engreskey gav	Book fellows' town, Oxford
Match-eneskey gav	Fishy town, Yarmouth
Mi-develeskey gav	My God's town, Canterbury
Mi-krauliskey gav	Royal town, London
Nashi-mescro gav	Racers' town, Newmarket
Pappin-eskey tem	Duck country, Lincolnshire
Paub-pawnugo tem	Apple-water country, Herefordshire
Porrum-engreskey tem	Leek-eaters' country, Wales
Pov-engreskey tem	Potato country, Norfolk
Rashayeskey gav	Clergyman's town, Ely
Rokrengreskey gav	Talking fellows' town, Norwich
Shammin-engreskey gav	Chairmakers' town, Windsor
Tudlo tem	Milk country, Cheshire
Weshen-eskey gav	Forest town, Epping
Weshen-juggal-slommo-mengreskey tem	Fox-hunting fellows' country, Leicestershire
Wongareskey gav	Coal town, Newcastle
Wusto-mengresky tem	Wrestlers' country, Devonshire

An established Romani circuit was emerging, allowing for the growth of a distinctive cultural and economic tradition, involving activities such as peddling, seasonal farm work, fairs and races. With regard to the latter, the Gypsy attendance at the Taunton racecourse in the early nineteenth century was recorded in Edward Goldsworthy's *Recollections of Old Taunton* (1883):

> The town on the days when the races were going on looked as quiet as a village, but as soon as they were over it appeared full of life. The race-course itself presented a very animated appearance. There was the Grand Stand with a row of carriages, phaetons, gigs and carts on each side of it. On the other side of the course stood booths, shows, timble-riggers, tumblers, sword-swallowers, gypsies and 'Punch'.

The colourful Gypsy presence at fairs across the West Country, such as Stow, Bampton and Bridgwater, is well documented, though a rather less well-known contribution is that of the nineteenth-century dancing booths. These seem to have been a historical fad, an offshoot of barn dances sometimes located on village greens. It would appear that such booths were initially large tents, though some became quite grand in design. George Broadis, a hawker and fiddler, would set up one such booth each August at the fair at Bampton. In 1860, one newspaper correspondent observed that: 'The booths devoted to the lovers of the mazy dance were, as usual, well patronised, and the partakers of this exhilarating exercise indulged themselves with a gusto quite amazing to those who were witnesses of their enjoyment.'

Another observer described Gypsy performers at one such event:

> … seated on raised platforms, and elaborately dressed in long, black coats, brightly coloured plush waistcoats, velvet knee-breeches, and smart top-boots, [where they] fiddled for the dancing from early morning until dark, whilst the tarni cais in their feast day attire – turban felt hats with long, amber feathers, gorgeous multi-coloured shawls, red, or blue … white satin dresses, and black high-heeled, brogue shoes – collected the money in the tambourines which they occasionally played…
>
> Thomas William Thompson, *Journal of the Gypsy Lore Society*, 1910

Despite this apparent celebration of Gypsy exuberance, there was also ambivalence towards this group who have come to represent the largest minority in the South West. They enticed the settled population; they also inspired apprehension and fear, feelings that are reflected in the following two extracts from Henry Williamson's account of life in a Devon village, published in 1945:

> At the back of the booths we had glimpses of a jumble and congestion of motor and horse caravans, tents of faded grey canvas, cooking fires, unwashed brown-limbed babies, children with bare legs and arms and matted hair, lurcher dogs with long legs and narrow heads… A fat woman with rouged cheeks, black plaited hair, earrings, neck and arm bangles, and the name of Madame Montana, beckoned us to come into her tent to have our fortunes read…

> As I passed through the people on my way to the booths and stalls lining both sides of the street, I had to run the gauntlet of the gypsy girls who were in charge of the rifle ranges. For any youth or man under seventy years of age it was embarrassing to glance at their eyes; for then they darted forward with a lithe and seductive motion, holding out a small rifle for him to take.
>
> 'Come, my fine gentleman! Try your luck, my gentleman! Only sixpence for four shots! Come along, my gentleman. I've had a hard time, my gentleman, and only taken a shilling all the morning.'
>
> Many words were poured softly in my ear. I tried to be firm, and avoid the tigress-eyes and tongues…
>
> Henry Williamson, *Life in a Devon Village*, 1945

From the agricultural depression of the 1880s onwards many Gypsy families have moved to shanty areas on the outskirts of towns and cities. At various times over the past century, there have been fluctuations in the attitudes towards them among the settled population, according to variables such as the need for agricultural labour. Along with economic change, the traditional Romani lifestyle has been restricted by legislation, the underlying purpose of which has often seemed to concern the regulation of an alternative lifestyle: the Moveable Dwellings Bills of the late nineteenth century, the Children's Act of 1908, the 1944 Education Act, the Caravan Sites Acts of the 1960s, the Criminal Justice and Public Order Act of 1994. In many cases, Gypsies have demonstrated remarkable resilience in their resistance to pressures to conform, reflecting the strong desire to retain a separate identity. And quite often, this has been mirrored by nostalgic (and often, romanticised) yearnings on the part of the mainstream population that Gypsies should continue to symbolise our desire for freedom, and remain as mysterious nomads who alternately appear within and vanish from the wider consciousness.

An early twentieth-century image of Gypsies on Epsom Downs racecourse.

THE ROAD

I really loved travelling about from place to place – going on to a new stopping place. We had three wagons – the boys in one, the girls in the other – nice round barrel wagons...

We love step dancing, a few drinks and a good singsong – all the Romani songs, and country and western. The old travelling men and women used to sing them around the fire... They told a lot of stories...

Diana

As soon as Gypsies appeared in Europe, myths gathered around them. Early Christian legend taught how, in common with the Jews, Gypsies had to atone for their role in the death of Jesus, both groups being condemned to a wandering existence on the margins of society. Whether, in fact, Gypsies chose the road, or whether the road chose Gypsies is immaterial: the road came to crisscross the Romani landscape like veins, arteries and capillaries, linking body to mind, and somehow, without charts or maps, without any of the means by which others have navigated between one location and the next, they have always managed to move from place to place, as if following some ancient call.

Members of Diana's family.

Djelem, djelem, lungone dromensa	I was going, going along the roads
Maladilem baxtale Romanse	I met happy Gypsies…
Sah Romale katar umen aven	Ah, Gypsies where do you come from
E charensa baxtale dromensa	With your tents on the happy roads
Ah Romale, Ah Chavale	Ah Romale, Ah Chavale
Vi man sas tu bari familya	Like me you had a big family
Mudardasla e kali legya	The black legion killed them
Aaven mansa sah lumiake Roma	Come with me Gypsies of all countries
Kaj putayle e romane droma	Then we'll take the Gypsy way
Ah Romale, Ah Chavale	Ah Romale, Ah Chavale

The above was selected as the Romani anthem at the first World Romani Congress, held in London in 1969. The words were composed by Jarko (alternative spelling, Zarko) Jovanovic to fit a traditional melody. According to the Patrin Web Journal, this was based on a Gypsy song, originating in the Balkans.

In the West Country certain roads are held with particular affection, though precise routes differed between families.

Robert:

I was born on the side of the road in a horse-drawn wagon and travelled the nomadic way of life until my brother was killed in 1950, when he was seven. From that moment on my mother lost the heart for travelling.

Going back to the romantic notion about Romani Gypsies, it was a hard life. It was a persecuted life. It's all very well nowadays for *gadjes* to look back and say, 'That's the real Romani Gypsies!' but it was a really hard life – living in tents, sleeping under wagons through all kinds of weather, moving from one place to another. As a child I loved it. I can remember that was the best time of my life. I loved the actual moving on, going to different places. We'd go hop picking, pea picking, following the A38 route down to Devon and back [to the Bridgwater area] – meeting up with different relations – cousins usually – at different times of the year.

We wouldn't stop in a place more than a few weeks. That would only be for work like pea picking and bean picking round the Bridgwater area. Usually the farmer would have a plot of land that you could stay on. Your relations would gradually come. Wake up the next morning and there'd be another wagon parked there with your cousin the next one up…

We'd stay three or four weeks then be off somewhere else, making a living – a livelihood. Pea picking, then peg making, or flower making. My earliest memory of that is by the outside fire – sat down, I don't know, three or four – watching my father shape the flowers with his peg knife, like the chrysanthemums. I've never seen anything like it. I've seen other Travellers and *gadjes* try to make them – they couldn't make them like him. Because when you're making them for a living you get the skill that's handed down to you. They

Often more than one wagon would choose the same stopping place; family groups loved a good get-together.

used to dip them in coloured stuff and put the green round them. Fantastic! One of my first recollections...

I remember we went to Devon, Wiltshire and Herefordshire. That would be our route. It was at a time when Travellers didn't go so far generally – they travelled in their own area. I always associate my people with the Mendips. We stopped on the Mendips a lot round those roads, to such an extent there's a big iron trough up there, and they used to call it Dannal's Basin. My grandad was called Dannal, and obviously he must have stopped there a lot, met up there a lot – 'We'll meet at Dannal's Basin'. A big trough in a field. I can remember us stopping on Ember Pond too – a traditional stopping place.

Maggie:

We went down as far as Maiden Down and Wellington. Romanies lived in that common for hundreds of years... We went down to Kennford...

People used to say that Gypsies wander aimlessly, and that is entirely untrue, because we lived by the seasons of the year...start in February... From there we'd make a few picks and wait until June. Then down to Bridgwater, hop picking, fruit picking... Some went off round Evesham...

Anna:

We travelled down here when we were little, me and Jim. We used to stop at Plymouth. Even before us, our grandads and grandmas came down here. Gypsy people have got their own run. Two main roads, the A38 and the A5 are the main Gypsy roads. Every generation of Gypsies...

When the wagons moved on, the only way we'd know the way – 'cos none of us could read or write, none of us – when the men was driving along in the old wagons and the flat carts, they would drop a bit of stick or grass to show the way.

Such a 'patteran' was left to allow others to follow – that is, when people wanted to be followed.

Diana:

> When we used to travel around with the horse and wagons we'd never use the signs 'cos nobody couldn't read nor write. There'd always be a marker. We'd come to a four-cross road; they'd always put a piece of grass, or break a stick off, to tell the rest of them which way they went. If you didn't want nobody to know which way you went, you wouldn't bother.

Diana's parents, Priscilla and Walter Cooper and family.

Rodney:

> We used to have the Bluebird caravans you'd tow behind the old Bedford lorry, but me Uncle Bill and Aunt Tilly had the horse-drawn wagons. We used to visit them regularly. Uncle Bill would come back with some scrap on the back of the wagon. I was eleven or twelve at the time. You'd say, 'Oh, they've been this way!' You could see the tracks of the iron wheels of the wagon. You could see the scratch marks on the tarmac. We used to follow it. One day we followed these tracks round these lanes – 'They've got to be down here!' – and it was a tractor pulling a binder behind! Then they changed over to rubber wheels. They used to put out loads of grass from the bank in the road where they'd turned. All the kids used to say, 'They've moved there!' There was always some kind of sign. Might have been a stick – an old, dry stick. Or stones. Nobody else would take any notice but you would be looking for it. Most of the time you had some idea where they could be – a nice, big, wide verge, with half a dozen wagons or more. Everyone got together. It was fantastic. They used to cry when they had to leave one another.

Despite the fact that they could not follow maps or read road signs, there seem to have been few occasions on which people got lost:

Plenty of firewood was needed when a large family got together. Maggie's and Robert's grandparents are pictured here with their Aunt Emmy during the mid-1940s.

Dorothy:

The policeman was inside the room – me father was the only travelling man, all the rest was outsiders – and he [Dorothy's father] said to all these men, 'If you was going along the road and you come to a crossroads and the sign was down, how would you know which way to go?' Nobody didn't know, so my father said, 'Well, you'd know the way you'd come; point the signpost the way you'd come, then you'd know which way to go!' My father was like a lawyer.

Diana:

The problem is getting around. Reading signs. One of my boys went all the way from Taunton to St Austell the other day. How do Gypsy boys get around? You tell me. Going all over Britain. How do they read the signs? I tell you, 'e can look at maps; 'e can't read them, but 'e can understand them.

It is easy to slip into cosy nostalgia about the old ways on the road, but in reality, there was a volatile and precarious quality to life.

Maggie:

Me dad was one of those people that wouldn't conform. He stayed travelling until he wanted to give up. He used to put bags on the horses' hoofs to go through some villages so the kids couldn't hear the horses. We knew if the kids was out the horses might be frightened in the shafts – [the kids] might throw stones. We did go through purgatory. We've been kids sitting round a fire – and it was never a little fire because of all the cooking and everything; it was a good fire – and we'd get the policeman come up and give you five minutes to shift. You couldn't catch your horses in five minutes – couldn't harness them – but we had to be gone totally when he said. If we wasn't gone, we kids many a time had fire kicked all over us. He'd put his boot in the fire and kick it over us…

Farmers would set about our men when we pulled in a lane. We had lanes and grass verges all over the country because the men knew where all the springs and water was. There's springs dotted all over, and we would pull in where the fresh water was. Sometimes we'd have to knock on doors, and might have to knock on six doors before you'd get a kettle of water, so they'd go where the springs in the ground was where they could dip the water out. If it happened to be near a farm, the farmer would ask you to move, and if you didn't, he'd send a couple of farmhands up to fight the men to make you move. It wasn't an easy life. It was good for the children. Me and Robert have always said we had the best childhood that any kids could ever have. Grown-ups suffered. They suffered for us.

There were also the hardships of an outdoor life, without the conveniences that most people take for granted, though it should be added that most of those concerned recall it as a healthy lifestyle.

Linda:

Me mother and father, when they first got married, they had a tent and a horse and cart. Me mother would have curtains around the tent. They'd have a new tent every year. That was like a kitchen. They'd have floorboards and curtains all around it and a little fire and a gas cooker. These days they have towing boxes – like a horsebox. They have a real kitchen in it these days. I've had tents…fire…the wind. Then you've got to put them up and put them down. The bowls – even now there's one for washing up, one to wash your face in and one to do your washing in, and you always had a can to get your

Nellie's family setting off on an outing.

water. You can have them made of stainless steel with your name on it. You'd never wash your face in the same bowl that you'd wash your dishes in. Years ago there was no toilets. You had to make your own, sort of thing. My family, we used to have a little toilet tent with a toilet bucket and the men would go and do it. Very rarely you done that! Very rarely. If you had to, you had to, but you always found somewhere where they had toilets.

Dorothy:

Everybody's got one dirty habit! People! Years ago, the woman used to go to work, come back, change, wash, get an apron and always wash the food. Loads of people do it now. The caravan – they used to leave the children home to clean and brush. When the people used to live in the tents besides the hedges, they'd go to toilet away from where they was living. They'd always dig a little hole and the children always learned that. You was brought up to it! Frosty mornings, with snow on the ground, you'd have to dig through it, or get a shovel and put it over the hedge!

Lisa:

It's lovely in the summer. In the winter it's not! The caravan would be rocking – oh, my God, it's going to go over in a minute! You get used to that. There's no hot and cold water in the trailers. You'd have to go out. You'd go to a house – some people would say yes, some people would say no. Or you'd go to a garage. There was no baths, no toilets. You had to dig a hole or go over the hedge! You had to go wherever you had to go.

Anna:

We never had running water – I cannot understand for the life of me why people say you can get diseases. We washed in a brook, we washed in a ditch, we drunk out of a ditch, and we never ailed with nothing; just ordinary things – mumps, measles, chickenpox.

Amy:

We were always on the move – never had a place to live. We'd stay in one place in the winter for a couple of months when the bad weather was on then we'd move along – everything was worn out by then! Because we weren't the only people in this area.

There was always barter, and conflict – who was going to have this, who was going to have that – but it was quickly solved. You might get a couple of men out there and have a fight but it would be solved at the end of the day. They might go to the pub in the evening and shake hands or they might go to the pub and have another fight! Who knows! Life on the road was very hard.

Of course, social hierarchies did exist, some people living in greater comfort and style than others, though when looking back, most speak of being content with a fairly rudimentary existence.

OPPOSITE: A chance for a chat; the women and children gather round the fire.

Maggie:

It was the only shelter that they had when they was travelling. Twelve months of the year that was all the shelter they had and they had to make their own rod tents – very much like the benders the Native Americans have: a half-moon – like an orange cut in half – and the sheet come round to tie and beds of straw. Come the forties, you could find places where they could make the square bow tents and they would have floorboards – that was like millionaires! In those days you could buy a good horse for nine, ten pounds, which was a lot of money when you'm only earning sometimes two shillings a day and you had to eat out of that two shillings as well as save. They were wealthy people that had the tents, and then we progressed to the wagons. Most families with mixed children would have a wagon and a tent 'cos when we got to eight we were never allowed to sleep together. They were segregated. As we got older, the girls that never got married would end up with their own wagon entirely theirs. That was their home with their mum and dad – they had their own wagon to sleep in.

The 'square bow tents' of which Maggie speaks were square-shaped tents, approximately ten by twelve feet, in green or brown, with four poles meeting in the middle at the top to form a pointed roof, supporting a sheet above. They were one of the early types of framed tents and had a 'dolly' or 'bell' at the top of each pole and were the next tent on from the benders, appearing in the late 1940s. They came with two-piece wooden floors and one part of the roof could accommodate a chimney.

Anna:

The old wagons are making thousands of pounds now. They were only our homes. They were nothing extra special to look at. And before the wagons, it was the old rod tents. And when my mum and dad got married, honest to good God, they never had no things. Me dear old dad had a flat cart; me uncle gave him a horse; me other uncle gave him a green sheet. He got the hazel out the hedge, bent them over, chucked the sheet over, and that was a brand new wagon to them.

There was ten of us fetched up in that old wagon. It was lovely. The boys would sleep outside, and the little girls would sleep inside underneath the bed. We learned to tickle the trout – only for food, never for sport.

We had no fridges – on the side of the road you ain't got no fridges. Me dear old dad's home-cured bacon was hard as a board – that wouldn't go off. All they had to do was put it in a net and hang it on the back board of the old wagon. Then you could cut that off. The animals wouldn't go into it because it was rock hard. A few bacon bones boiled in the pot with a few potatoes

Making a kite wagon. First published in Open Air *magazine in 1923. (By kind permission of Robert Dawson)*

Driving a kite wagon. First published in Open Air *magazine in 1923. (By kind permission of Robert Dawson)*

*A family group set up camp
and cook alongside their kite
wagon. First published in
Open Air magazine in
1923. (By kind permission
of Robert Dawson)*

and cabbage; some bacon hock, a few breasts of mutton; some sausages… lovely meals. Not like today.

Rodney:

These were barrel-top wagons and the ordinary loaf-of-bread shape and ones with a tarpaulin over. Uncle Nor had one with the big wheels on. He was the only one with a wagon like that. A man over Langport way used to make wagons. They used to moan because he'd make it out of green timber and sometimes the wagon was so heavy!

They used to carve them. On the front they had the wide beading coming down the front. They had bits tooken out – blue, red, blue red, or yellow red. I would love to restore one. Something I've always wanted to do. I remember me Granny Anna's Queenie stove. You'd have a fire when you're outside of the night time. You'd have your old overcoat on, and sit back in the brambles – pretty comfortable! Just push back into the hedge by the fire. When you'd finish, just shovel the coals up, chuck 'em in the stove – about ten minutes and it was all lovely and cosy. Two big double beds, top and bottom.

Dorothy:

We lived in a tent and caravan, and me mum and dad would sleep in the caravan and me and me sister would sleep in the tent. There was all curtains around the tent – floorboards and a little Queen stove. We used to have this little stove and the piping – the chimney – going out through the top of the tent. That old fire would be roaring away. You'd toast bread or cook a stew on top of the little Queen stove.

Lisa:

That was a lovely life. We lived in a rod tent — a bender with a bed in, kitchen, everything. Plus Mum and Dad had a big tent she'd lived in when she was single, and they used to put the floorboards in, the curtains, beds, everything. You could stop and live anywhere. That was a good life.

Most of those who experienced this sort of life recall a strong sense of togetherness. In the days of horses and carts, if someone needed a new harness and was having problems finding the money for it, there are memories of others helping out. Such customs even continued in a motorised era.

Anna:

If a man's motor 'ad gone, if the engine 'ad gone, or 'e needed tyres: 'Oh, come on', me dad'd say, 'we'll go out together today.'

Sometimes you'd be dying to go away, dying to move, but if one of them were broke down, they'd always say, 'Well, it's all right around 'ere.' We never leave anyone behind.

Indeed, most recollections are of a harmonious existence, entailing friendly relations with the outside world.

Nellie:

It was a bit lonely — you made friends but you couldn't keep in contact. I used to love to go to the pictures and we had parties — gramophone records, trumpets, accordions. Dancing and singing. Old policemans used to come up, ask how long we were staying. 'That's fine,' they'd say. People used to stop and look inside the wagon.

Diana:

I was born in Beaminster, Dorset, in a wagon. They couldn't go no further. Me mother came in labour and she had to pull on the grass verge. My parents, Walter and Priscilla, were proper, true Romanies — always on the road. We used to go farm to farm, fruit picking, pea picking, swede cutting — anything to go with the farm. We travelled every area in Somerset, Dorset and Devon. There were twelve — seven girls, five boys. I was number six.

People were very friendly. People remembered us. When we used go on to a village, they'd come up and say hello to us; they know'd all our names; give us food.

It was a lot better then than what it is now. It wasn't so crowded. There weren't so many cars on the road and you could pull off anywhere. But now you can't, see. People were friendlier. You could always walk in a back door. You'd never see a back door locked then. You could always go in. If you went and asked for anything, if they had it, you could have it. But not now, you

*Priscilla and Walter Cooper
and family.*

can't. They'll slam the door in your face or call the police. It was a lot friendlier then – we know'd a lot of farmers, and when we pulled in, we'd get plenty of fresh vegetables and milk. It did change.

I really loved travelling about from place to place – going on to a new stopping place. We had three wagons – the boys in one, the girls in the other – nice round barrel wagons.

We love step dancing, a few drinks and a good singsong – all the Romani songs, and country and western. The old travelling men and women used to sing them around the fire. They'd always get a piece of board out and dance. They told a lot of stories. My mother used to tell we bedtime stories.

With the advent of motoring, there came new challenges and, sometimes, it was more than the emotional connection to the traditional horse-drawn lifestyle that caused obstacles. Maggie recalls her uncle, Jimmy, a man who never quite mastered the conventions surrounding the new means of transport. On one occasion, when he was stopped by the police, Jimmy attempted to transfer the blame for his misdemeanour onto his wife.

Maggie:
It was in Newton Abbot, somewhere they wanted to go there, and he didn't halt. There was a halt sign, and so when he got across, the policeman pulled him in, and he said, 'Jimmy, that sign means halt; you should stop.' And Uncle Jimmy said, 'It wasn't my fault, sir; it was her – she didn't change the gears, so I couldn't stop.'

As it happens, he was not telling a lie. Jimmy viewed the motorcar as a form of transport that required a driver and co-driver. While he took responsibility

for the steering and the clutch, his wife would organize gear changing, and most of the time, it worked pretty well.

A wagon stuck in the snow. (By kind permission of Robert Dawson)

For perhaps a decade after the Second World War it seems Gypsies were able to continue their roving across the South West counties. However, times were beginning to militate against such an existence and changes were occurring both from the outside and from within. Local farmers were no longer in need of seasonal workers; the drift towards urban areas in search of work had intensified; land across which Gypsies had traditionally roamed was sought after for development; more and more Gypsy families were replacing horses with cars; and local populations were no longer viewing these people as 'picturesque' remnants of some idealised rural past.

FAMILY AND COMMUNITY

A STRONG BOND

I've got cousins up in Gloucester. You go to them – they open their arms, take you in, feed you, bed you, put a roof over your head and set you right or find someone that can help you better than they can, or give you some money and send you on your way. That's the way it is. That is the truth of Travellers. Travellers are one.

Amy

Traditional images of Gypsy communities depict close-knit groups, consisting of extended families. Such an image is reflected in the account of Cornelius Smith, born in 1860, who in his autobiography, *Gipsy Smith: His Life and Work* (1911), described his childhood as moving from county to county, sleeping in a tent, playing in the woods with other Gypsy boys while his father repaired cane chairs and made baskets, pegs, tin ware and items sold by the women. Members of the community 'found' what they could not buy; they stuck together through times of hardship and ease; they never abandoned one another.

Such picturesque and colourful portraits persist in the memories of some of those contributing to this book.

Anna:

Me grandfather was John Gaskin of the East Midlands. They all bought their bit of land and pieces of places. Father – he was a Smith. Me granny was a Price. I'm what you call a mongrel! We're all into one! When you check back, one's a cousin, one's an uncle. They say that when we used to go to Epsom and Doncaster when we was little, the Lees would pull that side with their wagons, the Prices would pull that side, right, and the Smiths would pull there. It was one big field – you'd be in your own group. We were all relations. The Lees'd wear red – that was their favourite colour. What they'd call flying the flag. The Prices'd wear yellow. Me grandad was a Gaskin, and every colour of the rainbow they'd wear. We'd say, 'You can tell he's a Lee, 'cos he's got a red shirt on. You can see she's a Price, 'cos she's got a plaid skirt on – a yellow plaid skirt.' I've still got my old yellow plaid skirt. They'd put plaid shawls to decorate it – in between the wagons. Jim'd be out with his dad, scrapping, hunting the rabbits and the hares to feed the children at home. The girls would be cleaning…

It's a bit like the Stone Age with the Gypsy people. We're still living in the

ABOVE: Members of Dorothy's family. Back row, left to right: Laurell Penfold (b.1886, daughter of Ned, married Leonard Small), Harriet Penfold (daughter of Ned, married Willy Small), Ned Penfold (son of John and Harriet née James, married Rachel Holland), Charlotte Penfold (daughter of Ned, married first Joe Roberts and second Leonard Hughes), Becky Roberts (daughter of Joe Roberts, married Mike Penfold), Jimmy Penfold (son of Ned, married Sarah Connors), Caroline Penfold (daughter of Joe Penfold and granddaughter of Ned), Cal or Connor (Caroline's boyfriend at the time), Trainett Penfold (daughter of Fred and Rebekka Roberts, married Joe Penfold, son of Ned) Caroline Orchard (married Cold Pudding Jack Penfold – also a son of Ned and Rachel but is not in this photograph). Front row, left to right: Eddie Small (son of Willy and Harriet née Penfold), Christiana Penfold (daughter of Cold Pudding Jack), Joe Roberts (married Charlotte Penfold and brother to Trainett), Leonard Small (married Laurell Penfold) or Tom Penfold (son of Ned, married Sophie Birch), Sarah from Wales (married son of Ned Jimmy Penfold), Joe Penfold (son of Ned, married Trainett Roberts), Bob Penfold (son of John and Harriet née James, married Fiance Smith), Edwin Penfold (son of Cold Pudding Jack and Caroline née Orchard). Ned and Rachel had twenty-two children – five of whom were off fighting in the First World War when this picture was taken. They were: Mosey, Thomas (?) Christopher, Edward and Cold Pudding Jack.

past. The men are still the bosses. We wouldn't have it no different. The men would make the pegs at home and the elder flowers and the baskets. And the women, in the morning, would get up and the men would fry the breakfast outside – I've still got the chichy irons and the old cast-iron pots. You can't cook in aluminium on a fire…

My mam never used to wear make-up. All she'd use was soot and salt to brush 'er teeth. And she'd get a bit of dye from out of the flowers, and she'd make a bit of rouge. And I've seen me mam get soot from out the fire, put 'er finger like that, and wipe it on 'er eyes…

When the women got home, they'd put the baskets down and fry a bit of dinner, and the men would probably walk off for a bundle of sticks for the fires. The women would do the washing; the men would start all over again making the pegs and the flowers. It was a lovely way of life.

Included in this picture are: Harry White, Diney, Betsy, Andrew Bowers, Liberty, Dousher, Liza, 'Cripple' Dousher, Rhodi and Prissy.

Robert:

All Gypsies are related. Where we're sat now in the shadow of the Glastonbury Tor – just down the road, half a mile, there's my cousin. He's got a little bit of land and moves on every year – just round the corner again is the Ayres – relations. Next to them is the Isaacs family – relations. We're going round the Tor now! We've got another Ayres family on the other side of the Tor. We're all related – intermarried years ago because they wouldn't marry out of the family – or couldn't! Who wanted to marry a Gypsy generations back? It couldn't happen both ways. We know the mixed blood ones – *diddikois* we call them…

A *petulengro* was a horseshoe maker. That means 'smith' – who we are. They'd know everything to do with the horses to make them work, to make them useful, part of the culture that they had. The Smiths are a big family – all the brothers and cousins and relations. We're disintegrated now – spread out all across the country.

Linda:

You'd never, very rarely travel on your own – me mother used to travel with just one lot, maybe two lots. When I travelled, I travelled with dozens. You could pull on a site where there were fifty or sixty…

There's a loyalty among Travellers – a Traveller won't hurt another Traveller… I could send my girls from one end of the country to another and they'd be safe.

Amy:

I've got cousins up in Gloucester. You go to them – they open their arms, take you in, feed you, bed you, put a roof over your head and set you right or find someone that can help you better than they can, or give you some

Robert and Maggie Smith's great-grandparents (seated right) with their family in front of their Reading wagon in 1910. Also pictured is their grandfather, Jimmy Small (wearing the cap) with his first wife.

money and send you on your way. That's the way it is. That is the truth of Travellers. Travellers are one.

I've got Travellers living over the hedge there. We hardly see each other. But if I was in need, or they were, the first place they'd come is here, or I'd go there. Everything else, feuds – whatever – doesn't matter. There are some feuds – if it's not near family – where you don't get that kind of connection, and there are some that never forgive. So you've got to go round the back door then. If the wife is related to you, but there's been a fight with the husband, you go to the wife, or vice versa. At the end of the day there's a way in.

Indeed, there appear to have been times when a harmonious situation existed, but apart from its tendency to encourage stereotyping, the persistent (usually nostalgic) portrayal of Gypsies as forever part of a group, winding down country lanes in horse-drawn wagons, denies them their existence as individuals, while glossing over the rugged individualism of Romani culture.

Children were brought up to be part of the group, yet at the same time, independence was encouraged from an early age.

Linda:

My father was born in 1912. He was one of ten children. They used to live in tents and had horses and carts. They used to travel around Cornwall. My father told me a tale that when he was about fifteen or sixteen, he and his brother and his cousin, his father gave them a fiver between them and sent them up to Somerset to pick ferns – 'cos that's what my grandfather used to do. They had a tent and the fiver to keep themselves. They pinched a chicken each and cooked their own chicken round a fire.

Where groups existed, they were often loose-knit alliances made between and within

Members of Diana's family.

families, as easily broken as forged. Moreover, there were situations when it was not in a family's interest to be tied too closely to others. In such cases, far from leaving a patteran by the roadside for other Gypsies to follow, individual families would do everything to cover their tracks, such as travelling through the night. This was especially likely when a family had negotiated a local deal that could be threatened by others.

Maggie:

When I'm writing it down I'm back – I go right in those copses. I'm in they copses picking they daffodils, and you're hearing things and seeing things and listening out because of the gamekeeper – he had so many families he'd let go in that wood. He had favourites and you didn't want any other Travellers to come in that copse and upset that mush 'cos he was our friend. He'd let us in if we was quiet and crept about; we could stay all day until we'd had our fill, and we could go in the next day until we'd had our fill. But then you'd get other kids runnin', screamin', fightin' where they was breeding these pheasants and partridges – their main food supply – and they were upsetting it. You couldn't take dogs in there. Our dogs were trained to sort out the rabbits, pheasants and partridges. So we had to be careful. We felt privileged, and me dad got really upset when that other family come and upset the man. He never forgot it. In fact they fought about it when they met up at a fair. It come up. It was a livelihood then that was gone from that little area.

You can't mend it because they say, 'You're all the same.' You get good, bad and ugly in every group. It's just nature. They've got wild kids and their kids can do whatever they like. This was the main problem in travelling. This is why we travelled on our own, unless we was with me dad's brothers or sisters, we would very rarely travel with anyone with wild kids, 'cos they could do what they liked, but we wasn't allowed to do what we liked.

On other occasions, feuding was the reason for divisions.

Dorothy:

A lot of Travellers row and argue and don't talk for years. I haven't talked to my brother for nineteen years. It was something stupid. We was up Evesham, picking plums. Me husband, because he's a roofer, he was on the top picking the plums, putting them in chip baskets. Me brother and his wife was down the bottom of the row. We finished our row. We was counting up the chips. Esme said to us, 'You're touching my plums on my row.' I said, 'I'm not!' Their branches came right out. They got up the tree, and started pulling the plums at me and me husband! We haven't talked since and that was over plums! He never give anything to my children or anything to my grandchildren. They never gived 'em a squeak. And they's millionaires! If I could save his life with a spoon of blood, I wouldn't do it.

Lisa:

You do try to get on. You try to help each other. But if they get rowing, that fight goes on and goes on and goes on right through the years and don't get forgot. These days it don't happen a lot. It did years ago with older generations. You just try to get on with everybody.

I can remember my dad fighting years ago. Over kids. 'Don't do that to my son, mate. Let's see you do it to me.' Then it would cause a great big row, a great big fight. It would go on and go on. And you don't insult people's parents. It's bad.

Anna:

The Gypsy men would be walking with big bundles of wood on their backs – the women would be saying about the men been rowing or whatever. That was always the same. Still I say it now, 'That man's useless. He can't do a thing.' That's our way. We're blind with rowing!

Yet, in most cases, the feuding was never sufficient as to break the essential shared feelings of unity, a spirit that has sometimes been most strongly affirmed in times of sorrow.

Tom:

You can get a bad *gadje* and a bad Gypsy, but they're not all tarred with the same brush. If you get one bad person, everyone says, 'The whole lot's all the same', but that's not right. You get good and bad in all. There was a bloke I fell out with years ago when he was going too fast. I said, 'Look, my son, you pass this road, I'll put a stop to you and give you a good hiding.' When the boys died [Tom's two sons], lo and behold, he was the first person to come to the door. The man couldn't do enough for us. He lost a son in a car accident. I didn't know that and I look at things differently now. Everybody's got a bit of good in them somewhere, and for some reason, it comes out when there's a tragedy. It shouldn't do – life's too short to fall out.

It is inevitable that amongst people depending on relationships – both with other Gypsies and with non-Gypsies – for their livelihood, the actions of individuals have a wider impact. In such cases in the past, the convention was for a meeting involving older family members, along with respected community elders, during which there would be extensive negotiation. Effectively, this was a court session, and in such instances, a close family member might argue for leniency towards the offender. Where the offender was a child, parents were deemed to be responsible for their actions. Some offences, however, were considered to be indefensible, and if an adult was discovered to have committed acts of indecency against a child, he was liable to suffer extremely rough justice prior to banishment. One woman who spoke to us recalled her uncle having behaved 'inappropriately', all the sisters in the family being too scared to tell their parents for fear of the repercussions. Indeed, they kept it secret for years, coping with the situation by giving one another sweets. However, most people say that such acts were exceedingly rare within Gypsy communities, and there was little tolerance of any sexual misdemeanour. There are accounts of young men being maimed for sleeping with a married woman, while the woman was whipped and spent the rest of her life in shame, virtually a servant to her husband. To as great an extent as possible, such events were concealed from children. Years later, they might discover that the father of a family member or close friend was not the man they had thought.

Not only were some relationships convoluted, they were made still more confusing through the custom of passing on names.

Amy:
They used to have a railway carriage over there on that piece of land, and when my mother was fourteen years old she used to walk up to her grandfather's on Sunday to have Sunday lunch with him. My great-grandmother had left him and gone away. She went to Southampton. She was called Angeletta. She was a woman to be reckoned with. Angeletta had a sister, Maria – she had a big business with loads of horses and shires. She'd show them. She had a load of men working under her and she'd horsewhip them! She cracked the whip – men who didn't work, even her own relatives – they'd get a beating.

My grandmother had a sister called Maria, after Angeletta's sister. That's how it went – as you go back down, everyone's called the same name! My brother's got a son called Nelson and he's got a son called Nelson. My grandmother on my dad's side was called Harriet. I wasn't called Harriet, but I was called after her first child, my Aunt Amy...

Going back to Angeletta – it's a big old story. She went away from here for thirty years. She ran away with a man. Angeletta and her husband, Henry, had had eight children. Her youngest daughter was only seven when she ran away. She took her with her. My grandmother hadn't seen her mother for thirty years, then the man died. When the man died, she came back. She had nowhere else to go. She had nobody up there, none of her family. Some of them had died. She'd never come back 'cos Henry would have threatened her – 'If you ever set foot in Cornwall, I will kill you. I will shoot you.' She never had contact with her children. Nobody even knew she was still alive. Until, when it was time for her to come back, she contacted her eldest son Henry – called Henry, after his father! She got in contact through the police – very clever! She couldn't read or write but she was very clever.

Henry, he was going to shoot her when she came back. He went down there to do it. She was petrified. But he couldn't. They never made friends, but they made a pact. He went there with a shotgun and his britches and leggings on. She never divorced, so she never married again. All those thirty years, back then – it was a sin. Although people did it all the time – they ran off with everybody! Half of them ran away and they never did get married, but that man you were with, that was your man, and that piece of paper made no difference. It's only lately that the piece of paper made a difference for financial purposes. Angeletta fell in love with the man, ran away, stayed there for thirty years, and when he died, she buried him, and she came back like a lady. Her children were all grown up. My mother's mother had looked after all the children Angeletta left, and did all the business looking after her father.

Henry never found anybody else. It wasn't done. He ruled with a rod of iron, but he was a wonderful man – he looked after his children – he cooked and cleaned and did everything for them. My mother, being a grandchild, at fourteen years old, could walk up for Sunday dinner. Nobody else had an oven to have a roast dinner!

Henry lived to a hundred and one – she was a hundred when she died.

In altercations between families, any accusation would be made in a public place, so that all should know. If the rest of the community took the side of those who were complaining, and the offence was sufficiently serious, the offending family would be ostracized: a place round the campfire would be denied to them; they would work alone, eat alone, and in some cases, they would be driven away. Feuds between families were liable to be passed down from generation to generation, a mere family name being sufficient to spark off a fight over some hurt or insult a century old.

All of this meant it was far preferable to seek a resolution as quickly as possible.

Robert:

If you talk about fights – our people can get a few drinks in them and they do fight at fairs over a horse and who's done what in the family, but to deliberately kill someone is an isolated thing.

Afterwards [after a fight] they would shake hands and it would all be forgotten, or they may carry on a feud in the family but nothing would be done about it: they'd never speak to each other or go near each other. They'd isolate each other. Because we're all related – we've got a bush telegraph up and down the country…we'd know about any deliberate acts of aggression.

Isolation does happen. If a family does things like going around conning old people, taking advantage, trying to earn money by deception in one form or another, stealing even, the only weapon we've got against them is isolation. Don't have anything to do with them. Don't badmouth them. You don't do anything. You just ignore them. They're not part of your family any more. That even happens in the same family where one or two do that kind of thing. They just become isolated, disowned. That's the only weapon there is in life. Generations back, they'd be banished from the tribe, from that particular group. That was my grandfather's generation.

The Gypsy sense of justice did not necessarily coincide with that of the State. The wife of one man (known as 'Long Jack') used to like to stop off for a few drinks on her way home after selling her brushes and china. One day, Long Jack went off to meet her and an argument ensued on the road. Grabbing a brush out of her basket (one they used for cleaning banisters), he gave her an 'unlucky' blow on the temple and killed her. In the eyes of Gypsies, this was a crime of passion, and after a sixteen-year prison sentence, it was felt that he had served his punishment – especially as he had, by all accounts, adored his wife.

The preference has always been to resolve problems without recourse to *gadje* authorities. In a group of such inter-dependencies, there was clearly a distinction between stealing from other Gypsies and pinching from *gadjes*. Though there was often a fine line to be drawn in terms of acceptability, acts of petty theft against the latter might be viewed as an act of cunning, warranting some combination of notoriety and respect.

Maggie:
With this particular family…they were well known for picking up bits while your back was turned out of your home. Well that's not, that's never known amongst us, so it hits you hard and you don't forget it. So every time I see that family I think, 'Yeah, I don't trust you.' So you're paying them back in the same way but differently; your trust has gone. That's how it used to be: you wouldn't have them round your fire if somebody pinched anything off you, or if you'd known them…I mean, thieving years ago…bad thieving was hay, or stuff out of the fields like cabbages and swedes, and then lead off the church roofs. That was big-time thieving, and pinching from the coops. Christmas we would have they 'cos we had our own chickens we carried with us all the year round; we had Gypsy banties, they lived the Gypsy life, but at Christmas you could bet your life my dad would know where the coop

was to go and get a hen or a duck or a goose or whatever; he would know where to go and do his shopping. That was life.

There was such a myth about Gypsies in those days: all we lived on was stealin'. So when we pulled up near a farm, the farmers would automatically think we'd nick their eggs, their chickens, their hay. We probably did a good amount of that, but you must remember that in those days, if you was arrested, you went to prison... My father done a calendar month for stealing a bale of hay. An' pinchin' lead! Me dad's brother, Jim, he was a devil for doing that. He was called Jimmy Longtoe, and the church would never know he had it until it rained and it leaked, and it could be months or weeks later... I've seen him with it; it wouldn't be no wider than that! He'd roll it up – I suppose it was in the joints, and he would go up there and roll the lead up and drop it down. And it weren't until they got a leak they knew they'd been robbed, but he was famous for it, literally famous for it. He was a devil! He was famous for taking lead off the church roofs, me dad's brother, and me and me mum used to say he was wicked, 'cos although we don't go to the church – we go for weddings and funerals – but although we don't go to the church like people do, it don't mean to say that we don't believe in God, because, believe you me, we do.

Despite his alleged fame, it does not seem to be the likes of Jimmy Longtoe who have become the most revered among Gypsy people. That honour seems to be reserved for those who have been seen to do good for family and community.

Amy:

In our culture you've got the men and women – but mostly the matriarchs – who are the head, and they're the ones, if you're ever in need, that you call to.

It is true that a few people will refer to 'Gypsy Kings' and 'Gypsy Queens', but in general, the accounts provided by most people suggest an eschewal of any situation that would confer certain individuals with authority over others. Status is not granted lightly, and where hierarchies exist, those afforded respect are often perceived to have earned it through action. Above all, respect was never a commodity to be bought.

Amy:

You can't make a silk purse out of a pig's ear. It cannot be done. If you see a lady and a gentleman – a *rawnie* and a *rai* – they could be poor as paupers but because they talk posh they are a gentleman and a lady. Because money doesn't make a gentleman – or a lady; it's breeding.

Robert:

There's thousands of Gypsy Kings and Queens! If a Gypsy lady or a man lives to a fair old age and they keep their faculties, can talk about so long ago, in the Gypsy circles, the person would become well known and liked, and loved, the status would be given... The Lees, the Boswells – the old names, like the Francombes, the Bowers, the Isaacs, the Coopers – they've all had their Kings and Queens.

Most people, especially the men, had nicknames, some deriving from physical characteristics, such as 'Jimmy Longtoe', 'Cockeye Joe', 'Cripple 'un' and 'Half a Yer', the last of whom had lost half his ear. Others gained nicknames for obscure reasons that no one could quite recall. There was 'Harry One Dog', who would officiate at fights, with his insistence on fair play ('One dog; one bone'), who subsequently became 'Harry One Dog Two Bones' after a few glasses of cider, as it took two men to handle him. There was 'Kipper', 'The Magpie', and 'Hard Times Joe', so named because, throughout his life, he was never known to have begun a conversation with the word 'hello'. Instead, he would approach with the line: 'Hard times innit? He'm 'aving 'ard times.'

Sometimes, the incorrect use of a nickname could lead to trouble.

Maggie:

I had an uncle called Squeaker, but his proper name was Henry and he hated it, he hated to be called Squeaker... And we had a real big tragedy up in London when we had these four kids die in one trailer fire, and his wife was me dad's sister, this Squeaker. And we'd all rushed up to London and I was coming back and we, with bereavement, we use white sheets to cover everything up, apart from where this person is going to be brought home to. And she said to me – her nickname was Tui, her proper name was Jane – and she said, 'Maggie are you going back tonight?'

And I said, 'Yes.'

She said, 'Call in to my Henry, and ask him for the sheets.' They'd never been used; they was antique sheets but they had to be the ones for these kids you see up in London.

'Call in and ask him for the special sheets.'

'Right.'

'You won't forget?'

'No.'

Well, I'm driving back, I'd come off the motorway at Bath, and I'd driven back...and all I'm thinking along the road is, 'Oh I must stop in to old Squeaker and ask him for these sheets; got to go in and see old Squeaker; mustn't drive by, it's important.' And I stopped outside, and I knocked on the door, and I said, 'Uncle Squeaker, Tui said...'. And bang went the door. He wouldn't answer the door to me no more.

So when I went back up to London the next day she was waiting for the sheets, and I said, 'I haven't got them.'

'What do you mean, you haven't got them? Wouldn't he give them to you?' she said.

'No', I said.

'Why not?'

'He slammed the door in my face,' I said.

'Whatever is the matter with him?' she said. 'The old so and so! What did you do?'

So me mum said, 'Well, you'd better tell her what you've done.'

So I said, 'Well, I must tell you, Aunt Tui, I forgot myself. I knocked on the door. He opened it. I said, "Uncle Squeaker, Tui said…" and bang went the door.'

'And serves you bloody right! No respect today, serves you right,' said Aunt Tui. It happens, you forget, you really do forget.

In fact, once people reached a certain age, around fifty, they were usually called 'uncle' or 'aunt' as a mark of respect. In some instances, people would refer to others younger than themselves by those terms. As for nicknames, they were less common among women, but then when people possessed names such as 'Defiance', there was little point in creating anything else.

Members of Diana Hughes' family pea picking at High Ham in the 1950s. Adults, left to right are: Uncle Joe, Cousin Caleb, Aunt Betsy, Cousin Freedom, Cousin Rhodi. The children, left to right are: Violet, Freedom, Willy, Liza, Jean, Diana.

CHILDHOOD

Nane chave, nane bacht.

(If there are no children, it is bad luck.)

Romani proverb

Nearly all the Gypsies involved in this book remembered their childhood as a happy, special time. Although many remembered working hard from a very early age, the sense of freedom, the absence of school and the closeness of family generated many warm, positive memories. Robert Smith and his sister, Maggie, remember the pleasures of meeting up with other children.

Robert:

For us children it was fantastic. We'd go off playing together. We didn't work when we were small. We started work at seven or eight when you get to the age when you know what you're doing. We weren't made to, we did it out of choice, just to do something and be with our parents and the cousins out in the field. The adults would be working all day but the children would probably be laid down sleeping somewhere or sneaking off somewhere! Before that, you'd be out playing or with a gang and the older children would look after you.

There was eight of us in the family, and cousins. After work we played. It was a wonderful time. The whole world was our playground. The world was different. *Gadje* children, as well as us, could walk up the road and go off across fields. You can't do it now. It's sad. Then, a stick could be a magic thing. In our travelling days we made friends with different children in different villages – or the farmers' children.

My mother said I never should play with the Gypsies in the wood.
If I did she would say 'Naughty little girl to disobey.'
The wood was dark, the grass was green,
In came Sally with the tambourine.
I went to sea – no ship to get across,
I paid ten shillings for a blind white horse,
I was up on his back and was off in a crack,
Sally, tell my mother I shall never come back.

Taken from R.F. Kilvert's diary, 1840–79

Older girls take care of the younger children as they work in the hop gardens, early twentieth century.

Like Maggie and her playmates, this boy looks as if he is no stranger to mischief! (By kind permission of the Museum of English Rural Life, University of Reading)

Sometimes the children's love of adventure and exploration led them into mischief, as Maggie ruefully remembers.

Maggie:

We used to ramble, ramble away for miles. You could ramble five or six miles in a day, playing there and playing back, and we had some *gadje* kids with us. We always had *gadje* kids you know, they used to come and want to play with us because I suppose we was a bit different and bit more – yeah, daredevil. We wandered and wandered and wandered and we found this caravan, and the door weren't locked, but we'd looked through the window and they'd had it set up for a meal. What had happened was, we found out after, that these people had come to wherever we'd found them, like, for a holiday. There wasn't many holidays back then. They'd set their tea up and they'd gone off in their car, and they thought when they'd come back they could just get out the car, go in and put the kettle on and they'd got a meal, but they didn't because we'd ate it; we'd got in and ate it. And there was a packet of washing powder called Omo, and I thought, 'Well I'm going to have that for me nan, I'm going to take this back for me nan!'

And we'd walked miles for this Omo, and I got back and I was so pleased that I had something, and I had the biggest hiding of my life because my nan said, 'I hadn't sent you to the shop, where have you got it from?' She hadn't paid for it so she knows how I've got it. Nobody's going to give you a box of washing powder – sweets, yeah – not washing powder. And we told her because we didn't think it was that wrong; we'd got in this trailer, we'd ate the cakes and the bread and butter and the lemonade '…and I brought you back this Omo out of the trailer.' So she called me dad and me dad beat me, and the boys took off and got away. He made me go back inch by inch, every step of the way, and he was clouting me with his hat all the way, and believe you me, to get hit with a trilby is not like being hit with anything else, and he took me back to the trailer and the man's there waiting. He could see from my face I'd had a hiding. And then my dad told him straight, 'This was one of them! Well, they ate the food.' He said that he was upset at the time but nothing, how can I explain it, nothing personal was took out, no clothes or personal things. It was silly, what we did.

What would I have been? Eleven or twelve. And he made me give the powder back and he made me say sorry and then he gave me another hiding in front of the man to show the man that he'd punished me. The man hadn't seen him beat me at home or clout me all the way down the road, but that man had to see us being punished, so you'd get two punishments.

The others had it in the end when they come home; they had to come home some time. That's what my dad would say, 'They can run but they'll come back.'

Despite the punishments Maggie wasn't put off playing. She always felt excited to pull up at the next stopping place and meet up with a new set of playmates.

Maggie:
We stopped on Melksham Common, and because we'd been travelling all these months on our own, as soon as we lot looked out the wagon and seen all these wagons round the Common and all these kids playing – we were in seventh heaven! We got kids to play with!

However, on one occasion, Maggie's excitement was short-lived. Her vivid memories of a terrible accident are still fresh after half a century.

I must have been so excited, running and capering and I wanted a drink. Well, instead of going to the can, I went to the kettle and the kettle's singing on the fire, and I swallowed it. Many an old Gypsy will tell you this story. They took me to the hospital – today they could cure you easily but in them days they had nothing. Their knowledge was very low to what it is today. The doctors used to tell me mum there was nothing they could do. They had to keep bursting these bladders down me throat. It wasn't looking too good at all. They left the other kids being looked after by the other Travellers 'cos her and me dad was sitting in hospital. They went back to check on 'em and feed 'em and wash 'em. When they got back, there was this *gubb* – an old woman. (A *gubb* is what I've become, that I can scuss – curse – you.) She heard about the child in the hospital and she was a greedy woman. Me mum had never seen her before. She went up to the fire – a few of the other women was there – and said to me mum, 'You've got trouble on your hands. If you give me a piece of soap and I want a pair of your prettiest plates, you'll have good news about that child.'

Me mum she was a bit sceptic. She'd laugh in your face, she would. Anyway, the others told her, 'Don't laugh at her. She's an old *gubb*. Better give

Diana's Aunt Priscilla with various family members. She was a wonderful cook and kept everything spotlessly clean.

her what she wants. Because she can put the curse on you.' Anyway, me mum did it. She gave her best pair of plates and all the soap she had. They stayed there then and me mum was upset that she'd give her good plates away. When they was getting ready to go back to the place where I was, the policeman came up and told 'em to get back to the hospital, and they thought I was already dead. But the hospital said they could bring me home the next day. I'd made a change for the better. They took the credit. I reckon she left something in me, that old woman. I inherited something from her. Because she saved me life, I believe I can do it. I know I can do it. I've done it.

For many older Gypsies, schooling was at best intermittent. Some, like Diana and Nellie, came to regret their lack of formal education when they had children of their own and took steps to make up for lost time. Others, like Lisa, started at a new school whenever the family pitched up, but it is not easy to be forever starting afresh with different teachers and fellow pupils.

Diana:

I never got to school. I was working ever since I can remember – from about eight till I was twenty. We used to get up in the morning. Mother used to get us out of bed, at the peep of daylight. I used to go with my mother. We used to work all day then come home to the wagons. We had to fetch the water and fetch the wood to make a fire. We used to do a lot of calling – in the season, it was the fruit picking and the pea picking – in the winter we used to have to call; knock on the doors. We sold paper flowers, pegs, lace – Nottingham lace. The men made the wooden flowers, with the old peg knife. The women made the paper flowers.

Defiance Smith (seated, centre) with a group of pea pickers.

We'd all help – we'd all do our own chores. Cooking was always out on the fire – the old pot.

I really loved travelling about from place to place – going on to a new stopping place. We had three wagons – the boys in one, the girls in the other – nice round barrel wagons.

Nellie:

I was working all the time, really. We'd go down North Petherton every year then. I used to do land work; work in the fields on the machines; riddling potatoes and a bit of pea picking. I was round about nine or ten, probably younger than that. I used to get up in the mornings about six o'clock and go out in the pea fields working, then stop for a bit of tea, like – out on the fields. It was a lot of hours. Longest journey we did? To Minehead.

Lisa:

I was born in Abergavenny. We lived over Chepstow for fourteen years. That was a lovely life. Me dad was a car dealer and scrap dealer – whatever he could earn a shilling out of. He always kept bread on the table for we children. Mum and Dad had four children. We never wanted for nothing. We always went to school, but we couldn't settle in a school, not for very long; it would be a week or fortnight, the police would come and tow us away. That's why we never had a lot of education.

Although there might have been little formal education, nevertheless a huge amount of learning was going on, as parents and older relatives showed children the skills they would need for life as a Gypsy.

Jim Lee's relative, Nighty Lee.

Anna told us how shrewd the older generation was in ensuring that the children were learning – invariably presenting a new skill as a game, or a challenge. Her father would bet that his child could pick more than another man's child.

Anna:

They'd say, 'Come 'ere, child, le me show you 'ow to do this.' Or, 'Let's go for a walk. Come with me to get this wood.' Well at the end, we'd end up carrying it, anyway. It wasn't so much of asking me to do it. You wanted to show them 'ow you could do it, anyway.

Fishing was only a game, but it was a skill. We learned to tickle the trout – only for food, never for sport. We only ever takes what we need. We don't kill for pleasure. That's how they used to teach us – they'd put it to us like a game. They'd say, 'Sit here child now, by the fire, sit here and sit quiet now.' And you'd sit and watch and observe and all the time they'd be teaching you. You'd see the peg man doing a few pegs, and the elder flowers, then they'd use the dye and dye the flowers; they'd look lovely, but if it ever rained… your hands were plastered! They never lasted as long as that.

Anna's uncle found her a ready pupil when hunting for rabbits for the stew pot.

Anna:

Then I'd go and meet me uncle and set the slings up at night to cetch the rabbits, and 'e'd stand up there, and I'd be thinking, what's 'e looking at? Then 'e'd set the sling – 'e'd find the entrance and make the loop round it. Next day it would be, 'Come on! Are you coming to have a look at what I've caught?'

Well, other children would be squeamish about seeing a rabbit dead, but I knowed it'd be feed-time, and I'd say, 'Oh look, Uncle Eddie! Oh, you've caught one 'ere!'

'Where else did I put it, then, child?' 'E'd make me show 'im where we'd put 'em, but it was learnin' me where the runs was.

Anna's uncle also taught her a thing or two about horse sense.

Anna:

'Oh come on, then child, the 'orses need to be watered.' Well, you'd walk up to the horse. He'd be tethered. Me uncle'd take this bucket. There were always ditches, and then 'e'd sweep it, not touching the water, just the end of the bucket in the water. So then, when 'e'd cleared away the twigs and rubbish, 'e'd dip it in sharp and the water would be clean. Uncle always make sure as the 'orse would come to 'im first.

'Well', I'd think, 'well, take the water to 'im', but 'e wouldn't. He made sure as the 'orse was at the end of the tether as the bucket wouldn't get kicked and go over, so I learnt that…

When it came to motivating her daughter to help with the washing up Anna's mother was a gifted psychologist…and if psychology failed, well, there was always the old, hard brush.

Anna:

When me mam wanted you to wash up, she'd stand you up on a stool, and she'd say, 'Watch 'ow yer mam can do this.' And I'd say, 'I can do that.' And it was like a game, and every day it was learning.

I can remember me mam saying to me, 'Clean the corners, and the middle'll do itself.' Well, I got on me knees with the brush – 'cos we never 'ad 'oovers or things like that, just the old 'ard brush, and I done every corner.

So she said, ''Ave you done all the corners?'

'Aye,' I said. 'I've done all the corners.' She gave me such an 'it with that brush.

'Well', I said, 'Mam, you said "do the corners and the middle'll do itself." I done that, but it ain't.' Smack I 'ad it with the brush, but I made sure as I brushed up then.

Me mam'd get the old bath out…the old tub, with a piece of blue in it.

Defiance Smith, and possibly Maggie, sometime in the 1940s.

Then she'd wash up. The carpets; she'd get them in the bath, then she'd make you stamp on them. Then the mangle was one of them old-fashioned ones; if they got stuck in the cogs, me and me brother Jimmy'd 'ave to go back again, but it was just like you were playin' a game. You'd be manglin' for 'ours.

When Anna's mother was working she put the baby in a sling, made from a shawl, and carried it around while she worked, so the baby was always close. For the girls, caring for small children would be the most natural thing in the world. The roles were very traditional; mothers showed daughters how to care for the home and family and fathers taught boys how to make a living.

Anna:

The minute them children can walk, then they start teaching 'em, like a puppy. Children was brought up sensibly: they knowed 'ow to clean, they learned to go out; they knowed 'ow to cook. The boys learned to look at scrap and judge it, look at metal, look at a good 'orse and judge it.

Take the men's dealing – the boys are there by the fire, listenin' to their dads. The girls are listenin' to their mams. When me mam is making puddin', she's talking all the time how to do it.

I remember selling the first time. I was about eight at the time, but I'd been running around with Granny since I could walk. I thought these people's going to shout at me, 'ow can I do it? I knock at the door. This nice man answers, and buys lace for 'is wife. I was so proud.

Jim told us that his favourite childhood possession was his sling, enabling him to hunt rabbits and pheasants. Like all children, he made his own sling, and he remembers that his cousin was able to catch 'anything that could run; anything that could fly'. He learned how to follow animal trails, and decipher different tracks.

Diana's brother, Wilfred, with Dunny.

Jim:

> With a rabbit the run is bald, and the same with rats. The old 'edge'og now, well 'e leaves bits of grass, a few leaves, and you can find the nest.

> Jim loved to be with his uncles and grandfather as they pursued their traditional activities – poaching, selling horses and betting on dogs when they were raced on a Sunday morning. He enjoyed seeing how many rabbits they could catch. He must have felt on top of the world when he was carried on the shoulders of his grandfather, Grandad Saley, or his uncle, Wiggy, on poaching expeditions. He recalls going for walks, picking 'blue stalks' (mushrooms), then going home and cooking them with rabbit they had caught.

Jim has many memories of poaching – for rabbits and fish, particularly. The evening was the best time to catch fish. There were numerous occasions when he and other family members had to run away from farmers, and police. Throughout, he remained undeterred.

Jim:

> I recall running across fields, through rivers, being dragged through rivers. Me and me brothers we were up that big river fishing, and when we were there, we went up to the top, and by the second bridge… I was fishing with me brothers, and I looked to the top, and there was all the bailiffs. One of them beckons. 'Come 'ere!' Well, 'e took me rod off me and 'e said, 'You've got to have a licence.'

> 'I didn't know, sir,' I said. So I lost my rod that time, but I went up again; we just took a bit of stick, and a bit of line, and I fished it again.

Jim emphasises that his father always told him to only take what they were going to eat. No-one saw any harm in pinching a few potatoes or trout just to eat.

Many of the aspects of childhood that the settled community takes as given, did not apply to Gypsy children. One of the reasons toys did not feature a great deal was

Jim Lee's parents, Darkis and Jim.

because there was nowhere to store them. Not only that, there were more important things to do than play. Nevertheless, Maggie did find herself longing for a particular toy.

Maggie:

We couldn't have toys. We couldn't carry toys. We could go to the tip and take toys off the tip and play with them but we had to chuck them back to move on. Ever since I can remember first knocking on doors, I seen this dear little house this girl had and I used to keep on and on.

'Can I have one of they dear little houses?'

'No.'

I had one when I was sixty. That is my pride and joy. I even went back to get one from that era. I went to an antique place up at Shepton Mallet and I found one and it had all the furniture in of that period. I got all old dolls I've collected 'cos we wasn't allowed to keep 'em. I've even got a doll's pram out in the shed – things we never had – so I go back to me childhood. Me grand-daughters will end up with [them] one day. I've had to own it to say I've had it.

Every time a toy was chucked out the wagon 'cos every space was allotted, it used to upset me. I used to cry at the door. Me mum used to say, 'When you gets older you can have them.'

Lisa:

I never was a toy person. We had toys like dollies and prams – we'd play with them for five or ten minutes, but I wasn't interested 'cos as soon as you got them out Mum would say to us, 'Right, go up and clean the trailer up!' Then we could play with our toys but if we didn't help we wouldn't have no pocket money. We was never allowed to be cheeky to anybody, or be brazen. We did what our parents told us. We didn't believe in answering your parents back. You only got parents once. I hope my children do the same thing and appreciate me.

The ingenuity that characterises Gypsies is evident in Anna's description of the toys she remembers making. She had a big old overcoat with a huge button. She passed a bit of cotton diagonally through the two holes and then she'd spin it round. It would make a whistling noise. She would play with this for hours.

Anna:

I'd get a piece of wood from a tree, an old branch that was thick at the bottom, put me leg over it, and that was me 'orse. And we'd 'ave a piece of string and make swings. But we never 'ad time to play much, as we were always learning. We never 'ad nothin', but we was 'appy. We never 'ad any of these toys, or things like that. We lived out of a ragbag. The clothes what the 'ouse-people gived, we weared. When they chucked their rags out, what they called them, that was our clothes. There was ten of us: what other choice did we 'ave?

As long as we 'ad dinner, and a clean bed to sleep in, that was enough for us. We're proud people but we can eat anything. We're not afrit.

Dorothy, too, had very few toys. She remembers her childhood with some reservations, and has been at pains to bring up her own children with kindness and affection.

Dorothy:

There's happy memories and there's sad memories. When I was five years old me mum went around with a basket and I was playing with a doll, and this woman said, 'Oh, you can have that doll!'

But me mum said, 'Oh no, she don't want it.' But I saw me mum put it in the bag and I had it for Christmas! He had one leg!

Different Travellers had different bringing up. Really and truly, we had a poor bringing up. We always had plenty to eat and drink but we were never treated right. Me mum and dad would be gone to work and we would go to school. We had to come home and me sister wasn't very old and had to make a fire. One would get the wood and one would get the water and start dinner. I was seven then. We was always brought up what we calls rough and ready.

For Christmas we used to have an apple, a few nuts, an orange and chocolates. And for me birthday I always had Black Magic. And I can't stick Black Magic! We was served rough. We was brought up rough. I'm there for mine, but me mum and dad was never there for us. Anything for me children and me grandchildren! We all do get on well.

Thinking about her maternal grandparents, Dorothy observes that even the strictest parents cannot control their children forever.

Dorothy:

They were very, very strict. Years ago Travellers weren't allowed to marry outside. The girl was always told, 'If you brings back trouble, you've got to go.' They couldn't go out with young boys until they was about seventeen or eighteen years old. As soon as my mother was let out, she was married at seventeen and a half!

Diana's parents were also strict, but very kind, and she wishes her children could have some of the advantages that she took for granted whilst growing up. Nevertheless, she was aware that some other Gypsy children were not so fortunate.

Diana:

Back then you had to do what you was told. My parents were very kind, but a lot more stricter than I am. They wasn't a cruel family, not a rowing family. A lot of Travellers do have strict punishments. If the older travelling men and women told the children to do something, they expected them to do it. If not, no supper. Simple as that. You'd have to go to bed. No coming and saying, 'Oh, you'd better come out and have your tea.' That was it. You had to stay there till the next day. They were very, very strict, the older Travellers. It's only in my time that they've been lenient. If they went off in the morning, my parents, to weigh a load of rags and scrap and drop bills, and they left me and me sister and the little ones, they'd say, 'You can have that, but don't touch that until we come home.' We wouldn't touch it. It would still be there when they got home. We'd have what they told us to.

I'd love to have brought my children up like I was brought up. It's too dangerous now, in my eyes. You find drink and drugs everywhere now. I never know'd a drunken man back then – Father might go and have a few pints, but he was never a heavy drinker. What it is now, they've got the money too easy and they get bored. They've got nothing to do. When we used to have the old travelling wagons, the horse and wagons, you had to do everything on foot. You couldn't waste four or five hours in the pub. You always had something to do. You had to look after your animals, earn your money – no social – no income at all unless you got it yourself. If you didn't get it, you wouldn't eat. Time goes on so quick now. Everything's so fast. It's too easy. They want to be on the fast lane all the time. They're forgetting where they came from.

It would be understandable if the constant moving on, the dramas of life on the margins and coping with hostility resulted in very insecure Gypsy children, yet somehow, then as now, the adults created a loving environment, and a sense of warmth and safety. The extended family, at its best, offers children a profound sense of security and belonging, and many people spoke warmly of the role that older relatives played in their lives. Grandmothers are often remembered with particular respect and affection.

Anna:

We were dressed in plaid – Granny used to go to Scotland to buy it, in big rolls. She'd make the plaid skirts. Years ago Gypsy women didn't show their legs – they were called dirty if they did. So me mam, and me granny and me, we'd sweep the roads ('cos our skirts were so long). We'd wear thick petticoats underneath, little flannelette petticoats with a bit of ribbon – they'd last for years, with the extra hem to let them down. Granny made her own pinnies.

The old flannelette was very thick. She'd warm up one of them old cast irons on the little Queenie stove so the seams were easier to sew and she'd measure a yard, like this, from 'er nose to the tip of 'er hand. Granny would cut it up to make clothes and napkins. She'd put ribbons round the corner of the nappies.

We'd always have ribbons for special occasions, like visiting family. Posh clothes – we 'ated them! We 'ad a nice cloth skirt, or a nice little cotton frock, a white pinny, a little bit of ribbon in our 'airs... Gypsy children 'ave always got long 'air.

The large families enjoyed by many Gypsies ensured plenty of caring adults to keep an eye on the children, and lots of other youngsters with whom to play. The memory of safety in numbers, and constant company still evokes a sense of thrill in Anna.

Anna:

To be honest, I've 'ad no sad days. Every day was an adventure, and an 'appy day.

The children never used to stop in the wagon. They'd run behind. They thought it was fun to run behind. I've done it many a time. Our toys when we was little, was a piece of branch… 'Gee up! Gee up!' We'd play all day up the road. The road'd be as clean as a brand new shilling. We'd play pitch and toss – they won money off you! And we'd play horseshoes. We was all happy.

Away from the circle of the campfire there were fears, however. To house dwellers who remember the old rhyme about never playing with the Gypsies in the wood, it may come as a surprise that Gypsy children were brought up to be afraid of them.

Diana:

When we used to stop in the villages, me mother used to say to us, 'Don't never roam off down the village, or the *gadjes*'ll chor you, chor the chivvies.' That means to say the people in the houses will take us away. My parents used to say it to us in Romani. We were never allowed to leave the wagons. I've found out since that a lot of the people in the village, when the Travellers used to travel around with the Gypsy wagons and the horses, they used to say, 'Don't go down with the Gypsies – they'll steal you away!' Wasn't that funny! It was just stories.

Anna:

When I was little– and when you're brought up to it, you've got to accept it – my dear old granny, Sally Price, would say to me, 'The house people, child, will take you away' and I was a-fritted. Granny wouldn't leave me going up the doors; she was always frit of someone ripping you in the houses. We don't go in houses. Being in a house, it feels like you're suffocating, which is why the windows and doors is always open. I'd sit on the doorsteps and tell the fortunes. Also another thing why we wouldn't go in the house was because of them blaming you, 'You've pinched out of the house.'

Adults often use scare tactics to keep children safe and to encourage good behaviour. Jim never knew whether the following was a cautionary tale, to keep him out of trouble, or whether it actually happened.

Jim:

I remember me mam telling me this story of two little Gypsy boys. Well,

they was comin' 'ome, one day, and they was very, very thirsty. And they
knocked on two or three doors; they asked for a drink of water. There was
no one in. Well, when they went to this other 'ouse, and again there was no
one in. Outside, there was a bottle of milk – the old bottles – and one of the
boys picked it up and drunk it. Well, when they was walking 'ome, this
woman 'ad been in the 'ouse, and she said afterwards, they had never come
to the door, but she's seen 'im, this one boy, take the milk. Well, they took
the boy – 'e was ten or eleven – and they locked 'im up until 'e was a man.
And unless they said that there to scare me – well, I do not know – but she
always would come up with that story.

Certainly Jim's parents were very strict, and he may not always have liked that, but
he did respect their wishes.

Jim:

If me dad said, 'You're not to go to the pictures', there were no ifs and buts
about it: I would just sit down. If I were going to a dance, and they told me
I was not to go, I'd just say to my friends, 'I don't want to go.' I did want to
go, and I didn't know the reason why I couldn't, but I wouldn't go against me
dad or me mam. I wouldn't go over their 'ead. That was it.

Maggie can understand why parents could be strict and anxious about their children.
Looking back, she sees that things were not so easy for the adults and realises that
the carefree existence she remembers was special.

Maggie:

It was good for the children. Me and Robert have always said we had the best
childhood that any kids could ever have. Grown-ups suffered. They suffered for
us. It was terrible when we were children. The biggest fear we had was me dad
being locked up. Because they would take him. Even if it was one policeman
on his own, on a bike or on a horse, if he said to me dad, 'You've got to come
with me,' he'd have to go. That's why we had so many names. They had to
change their names when they went back to those villages where they'd got
arguing with the police. The police told them to go, and they scarpered, and
the women moved the wagons. The next time we had to go that road, they
would be another family. They had to change their names so they wouldn't get
locked up for answering back. They weren't allowed to answer back. If you
went in a shop and you said, 'That bread's stale,' they'd say, 'Take it or leave it.'
They'd have the new bread for their people, but they'd have yesterday's or the
day before's bread that they'd sell us.

As Maggie remembered how hard life was for her mother and father, she recalled a time
when her parents were particularly frightened following a conversation with a farmer.

Maggie:

It was coming back from hop picking. I couldn't have been no more than three or four years old. I can picture us coming down the road and I can remember meeting up. We was excited because we were meeting Leilee and Jimmy, the children. They hadn't been hop picking so we hadn't seen them for some time.

I can remember pulling on the Common with all the other Travellers. Then it was straight into the farm work – we did shift off the Common onto the farm. I can remember me mum keeping on about the woman. We'd been there before, and she wouldn't never have nothing to do with us. This particular year she'd come back to the fire and say how good the kids were and how lovely the kids were. Stuff like that. Then, of course, the farmer went across the field and asked if he could have [me brother] Alfie. It all blew up. It got so frightening. 'That child's going to go. If we don't run and hide him, they're going to take him.' And he was [me parents'] oldest child; he was the oldest, Alfie. The farmer only wanted to adopt him but it put my mum and dad ten years back. They didn't understand that that man could not just walk to the fire and take that child because he wanted him. We never ever went back to that farm – that was me dad's winter work for many, many years.

They lost the work. I can hear them now, when we slept under their bed, and they would talk half the night and both of them would cry because they thought they were going to lose their child. It was horrendous. We lived with that fear.

Even though we know that life on the road must have been incredibly hard, it is clear that precious memories of working together as a family – girls out calling with their mothers, sons helping their fathers collect scrap – or playing together with friends and relatives while learning how to survive – have created resilience, humour and resourcefulness in the Gypsy population. And somehow, adversities, both large and small, were negotiated and overcome.

Linda:

My father told me his father gave him a half a crown for his first wage, and he went and bought himself a little boat with a wind-up handle and he put it on the water and it went out and it never came back!

They used to go to see the pictures – Charlie Chaplin and Buster Keaton. They always had a bag of chips between them and walked home from Plymouth to Ivybridge. My mother – the first pictures she went to – she went with one of her cousins – whatever the film was, there was a train. She'd never been before – the train came towards her, she thought it was going to knock her down, so she fainted!

Get an Education, and Lose Your Mind

I'm not a very good scholar – I can read a bit but not all that well. Where we used to travel about so much, me and me sister went to about fourteen schools. Every village we went to me parents would put us to school. If the police come along and said, 'Oh, you've got to move on!', me mum and dad would say, 'Oh the children's to school – can we stay here for a week or two?'…then the policeman would come again and say, 'You've got to move.' And we'd go to the next village.

Dorothy

Many Gypsies still strongly believe in the old saying, 'Get an education, and lose your mind.' As evidence of the futility of schooling, people will reel off the names of the wealthiest Gypsies they have come across, telling you that between all of them, they had never experienced more than a few days of formal education. Conversely, they will recall dozens of highly educated Gypsies with hard-luck stories; individuals who never acquired the traditional skills that have ensured the survival of generations.

One of the biggest challenges is to negotiate the differences between contrasting worlds.

Diana:

I'd been using my own Romani language to get by, and I had to go strictly to English. My Romani language kept cutting in. I use it a lot. All my generation do. My children – not so much. But they know what I mean. My parents used it all the time; it was the only language they knew.

Maggie:

I think it [school] ruined us. To be perfectly honest I think it took a lot away from us 'cos we had to lead a double life – we used to sit all the time all day in that school and when we was talking to the teacher and the kids it had to be in English. But it's so easy to go back into Romani. If we lapsed talking to them they'd go, 'Eh?' 'What?' 'Pardon?' 'What do that mean?' It give us a lot to worry about.

However, the more people we spoke to, the more equivocal the responses. It is not uncommon to hear someone asserting in one breath that education is the worst thing that can happen to a Romani, and then talking wistfully about acquiring standard literacy.

Diana speaks with pride about the manner in which her sons have managed to get through their lives without formal literacy skills.

Diana:

My boy came out of school not reading, but great at arithmetic. 'E's learnt more now; 'e can read now. The other day he read this sign on a bottle, a great, long, complicated word… But what I'm saying is, 'is problems with English never stopped 'im from making a living.

At the same time, she speaks of a need to acquire standard literacy.

Diana:

It's more important now, to my opinion, for the youngsters to learn. My lads need to get work. It's different. All these motorways and signs, and forms to fill in. I keep telling them you keep at it. I say you need it for jobs now. Lots of jobs you've got to read and write. Not so much the boys who go out in their vehicles. Maybe it's getting equally important for the boys.

I get letters. Me daughter, reads 'em to me. I'd just love to be able to read and write meself. Only a few older ones can read and write. I mean I can tell figures, ones and thousands, but if you give me all the money in the world I couldn't tell you what it says on the bottom of my shoe.

Diana has her own secret.

Diana:

I've gone back to school. I'm learning to read. I go twice a week. It's very confusing, having to push one language back; you need two brains. It 'elps you get through more in town [with] signposts, shopping. All food's marked different these days. Then there's letters from schools. I can read papers and magazines. I don't read nothing about sex!

Others would concur with the value of a formal education, even one gained belatedly, acknowledging the ways in which formal literacy is connected to empowerment.

Robert:

It was a very rare thing, generations back, some of our people could read and write. How they got that, where it came from, I don't know. They'd never gone to school. Maybe missionaries. The most famous one used to go round in a wagon converting, in the New Forest — that little tin church. If they knew somebody could read and write, they'd go to them. It's only recent history the ordinary *gadje* could read and write. It was kept from them. Even scripture was kept from them and the Latin – they did that on purpose, kept the scriptures in Latin so nobody could learn to read it. All that was to keep control. But it's not the be all and end all to be able to read and write. I'd say nowadays it's an asset, but maybe not in business terms – I think we've all got hidden parts of our brain that we don't use and perhaps not being able to read and write brings out something. Maybe being able to read masks off something.

I can see now where my mother was coming from. She didn't want to travel any more. It allowed me to read and write because I was made to go to school. I became more associated with *gadjes*. I was forced to be two people. When I was home, I was who I was, but in the daytime, I had to be part of the mass, the settled population. I had to be both things and I learnt the ways of both. Not a bad thing. I didn't lose my identity but it gave me, slowly, more opportunities. With the UK Romany Council I know both sides. I'm not coming at it bull at a gate. I know what the problems are with our people. I know how the general population view our people.

Most Gypsies avoid *gavvers* (policemen), but when she was a little girl, Nellie approached a policeman, telling him that she would like to go to school. Decades later, she still feels acutely aware of her lack of formal education.

Nellie:

A pity the teachers didn't come round then like they do now. My brother used to go to school. I don't think they bothered about me going to school. I would have given anything in the world if the days had been like it is today, then I could have been educated like my brother. All my relations, all the younger generation, can read and write. At college – you'd never believe it – they got a lady coming there about a hundred and one!

In Maggie's case, learning to read and write was more an outcome of her father's curiosity than any formal, pedagogical practice.

Maggie:

The schools never learned us to read and write. We never learned no reading and writing in those schools. The person who learned us to read and write was Dad. He used to draw his name – his signature was like a painting – like you'd look in a mirror. But he was nosy. When we bought the first bit of land at Peasedown, if any of our lot got locked up for anything, he'd want to read about that in the papers. He'd go to the shop and ask the woman, 'Is our so and so in your paper today?' He'd say, 'Which one?' and he'd bring that paper, and it might be just a bit and it might take me three hours but I'd break it down one way or another until I could read it to him and he'd know what happened to that person. He was amazing. He could learn you without you knowin'.

For most Gypsy children in the past, school experiences were partial and fleeting. The school careers outlined below are very typical.

Dorothy:

I'm not a very good scholar – I can read a bit but not all that well. Where we used to travel about so much, me and me sister went to about fourteen schools. Every village we went to me parents would put us to school. If the police come along and said, 'Oh, you've got to move on!', me mum and dad would say, 'Oh the children's to school – can we stay here for a week or two?' We could stay there for a week or two all the time we was going to school, then the policeman would come again and say, 'You've got to move.' And we'd go to the next village.

They'd always call you 'Gypsy'. 'Fleas, fleas!' they would say. Give 'em a bloody good hiding!

I went to a convent school, a primary school and a secondary modern school and always had friends. I would like to meet me old school friends.

Lisa:

My last school was at Congresbury, near Weston-Super-Mare. I left there when I was eleven. Our parents didn't believe in it. My dad said, 'As long as they can get by, that's the main thing.' Girls at fifteen, sixteen going to school – we don't believe in it. They're too old.

I did like school – P.E., football, netball. I loved doing that. I was really interested in that. Me and me brother used to do it. You'd meet other people – it was nice and friendly. Yet when you start going into school, these kids say, 'Oh, there comes the Gypsies, the Gypsies!' We are not dirty people. I said to this girl, 'You don't hear [of] Travellers with nits in their hair!' Which is true.

When I was eleven the teachers used to come out to me mum and say, 'Where's your daughter, Lisa?'

'Oh, she's gone away.'

'Do you know where she's gone?'

'Couldn't tell you. She's gone with her grandma.' Which I was, which was no lie.

A common practice was to hide children away during visits from education officers, sending them off hurriedly into fields, or to neighbours' wagons. Children's ages would be changed for the benefit of visiting officers. Jem recalls being five years old until he was ten, at which point, he suddenly passed his fifteenth birthday! Others were not so lucky.

Linda:

I left school at eleven and we came back here and I got rounded on, and I had to go to school again at fourteen. It was bad, believe me. I thought I was a

woman in my eyes and I had to be a child again. I'll never forget: they wanted me to play piggy in the middle. I can't play piggy in the middle! I ain't
used to such things. I don't think I went a full week. The only thing I really
liked at school was cooking.

Early on the persistent efforts of her parents to get her brother to school seem to
have been destined for failure.

Linda:

Me brother can't read or write. Me mother and father would take him to
school – take him into the school. 'Here you are, John.'

'Yes.'

'In school.'

'Yes.'

As soon as they was gone, he was gone. Who knows what he done. I know
one time me mother said – they were stopping here down a bit, and me
father was going out ferning, and John was supposed to be going out to
school. Me father said to me mother, 'What have you been doing?'

'I've been doing so and so,' she said.

And me brother said, 'No, you haven't.'

And she said, 'What do you mean, I haven't? How do you know what I've
been doing?'

And he's been up in a tree looking at her! They went mad to think he hadn't
been to school again. But he can't read and write – nothing at all. He's got a
son who went to playschool – went to two schools – all the lot – and he can't
read or write either!

There were certain advantages in sending children to schools. In the case of families
such as Dorothy's, as we have already seen, it was a useful strategy to gain a little
more breathing space before being moved on. For others, it provided the means to
stay in touch with relatives.

Maggie:

Mostly why they wanted us to read and write was for communications
between themselves. It wasn't for your benefit. The families were split up.
Mother came from Plymouth an' Newton Abbot, and she married in
Wiltshire/Somerset. She would go and knock on your door, going out callin'
in the day, and she'd always have a bit of writing paper and a pencil and she'd
knock on the door and say, 'Could you write to my sister and let her know
that we's all right?' And that kind woman would write it and address it to the
post office at Newton Abbot where her sister would go and collect it. It was
always the same! 'My Dear Ellen, Hope this letter finds you the same as it
leaves us.' That was it. It was a communication. To them, being a hundred

miles apart was like you being over in Spain from here, because there was no way of contact – only in an emergency, which would be the police.

Schools themselves were not always as keen as education officers to facilitate the inclusion of Gypsy children. There are a number of memories recalling the collusion of schools with regards to frequent absences.

Ralphie:

Teacher used to say to me, 'Ralph, you coming in tomorrow then?'

And I used to say, 'I don't think so, Mr T. No, I'll probably be helping me dad and Uncle Ted.'

'Good idea, Ralph', teacher would say. 'You'll probably only get up to no good if you do comes up 'ere.'

Duke:

I learned to buy and sell 'orses and cars from my uncle. I'd skive school three or four times a week. Pea picking, apple picking, currant picking. They let us 'ave time off from school. They weren't bothered.

There are also recollections of neglect.

Rodney:

I found school 'ard. All the moving around. People know you're a Traveller or Gypsy and call you names. School was a nightmare for me. I went all the time, from the age of five, wherever we was to. I never really learned to read or write properly…

At school we had to keep this diary, and every day I used to copy out what I had written the day before, very slowly. I wrote out that day over and over, the same old thing. They didn't realise what problems I was having.

When I got to my next school in Taunton – I can remember I was about twelve, and I still couldn't tell one letter from the next. I'd 'ave gone a lot further if I'd been able to. I was better than I seemed. I never really seemed to have a chance.

The negative aspects of schooling cited most frequently are the interruption to a travelling life, the unnatural incarceration of children in buildings, and above all, the bullying from non-Gypsy children.

Linda:

I didn't go to school till I was seven and stopped when I was eleven. I don't remember a lot about it really – I know I never liked it because when you travelled about it wasn't so good. Every county did different things and of course you got called names. The dirtiest person in the school would call you a dirty Gypsy, and believe me, that was bad. Then you'd fight back. You'd call them a green ass *gadje*.

As well as name-calling, those who attended school recall numerous incidents involving physical bullying. Not many Gypsy children were inclined to turn the other cheek.

Maggie:

I nearly killed a boy in Peasedown St John. He was a miner's son. When me dad bought this bit of ground, Alfie wouldn't go to school no more so it was just me and Robert. He was way down where the other classes was, so we were both on our own, and the first week in that school I had the hiding of me life every day. I was bit, kicked, punched, thrown down the stairs – me plaits tied to chairs. Ink from head to toe. They treated me cruel. The ringleader was one boy. I made up my mind. 'I'm gonna 'ave you. Whatever happens, I'm gonna 'ave you. You're gonna 'ave the same as what you gives me.'

If I went back crying to my dad he'd give me a hiding and tell me to go and give him a hiding. He'd give me a hiding for going home crying.

I waited until I learned, when they started to fidget, that school was nearly over. I left the class one day in that first week and I went out. I went out and got me coat and I stood out by the gate and when he come out he didn't even know I was going to do it. And I clocked 'im straight between the two eyes and he went down and I beat his 'ead in the wall and it must have went on for some time 'cos it was the teachers that got me away from 'im. Now he was a big lad. On the night his father come up to me dad, straight from the pit, and all you could see was the whites of 'is eyes – the coal dust – and 'e 'ad 'is boy with him and he wanted to fight me dad because of what this person had done. He was looking at me but 'e didn't know I'd done it. I'm only 'alf the size of 'is boy.

Me dad said, 'I'll fight you, but you've got to give 'e a hidin'. There she is there, what give your boy a hidin'.' The man was ashamed that I got the better of his son.

I'll tell you what – I never got bullied no more in that school. Only by the teachers – not by the kids. In fact I turned into a bully. It turned me into a bully. We had to leave that school and go by coach to a place near Radstock and all those kids that had done me wrong in that school, I put off that coach. I had me mum up there – their mothers up there – she'd give me a hidin' in front of the mothers and when we got to the next stop I'd 'ave them off again. It was revenge. You wouldn't believe how Gypsy children years ago was treated.

Anna had just a single day of schooling. She was aged ten at the time, and her family had stopped in a village.

Anna:

Me mam thought I were dressed nice, with like, a party frock on and a bow ribbon, but I always 'ad curly 'air, masses of it, and I looked really, like, when I think about it, like I was going to a party. And I stuck out like a sore thumb, anyway, never mind being a Romani child. These children come runnin' in the schoolground, and they call me 'Gyppo'. The only thing I've ever knowed in me life is to stick up for meself, so I automatically 'it 'em. This was at dinnertime. The 'eadmaster there, 'is name was Mr Wright. So they said, 'Mr Wright wants to see you,' and 'e's got this big stick, and 'e was bending it, and the children said, 'You're going to get ten of the best,' and I didn't know what they meant, I thought it was a good thing…but when I see this big stick, I knows it's not good.

And I made sure I've got the swing door to my back, 'e's coming to get me, I've slammed the door right in 'is face, knocked 'im over. I runned all the way 'ome to me mam and me dad… The man was riding behind me with a bike, I cut over the fields, the short cut over the bridle… I says to me mam that the man wants to beat me with a stick. Just then my dad's pulled up with a lorry. I'm crying. I tells me dad that man wants to beat me with a stick…

So, anyway, my dad said, 'What do you want to 'it 'er for? I've never 'it any of my children in my life.'

'She's 'it the children.'

'Well,' me dad says, 'She must 'ave 'it those children for something.'

Well, when I explained, this man hasn't taken my word. He's took the other children's word, 'cos I was a Gypsy child. So after I told my side, my dad says, 'Well, if you're going to give my child ten of the best, I'd better give you just one of the best,' and 'e's 'it the man over the gate. Mr Wright's ended up in a worse state than what I did.

He says, 'I'm going to send the local policeman down.'

Well, the policeman used to drink with me dad in the pub, so he ain't going to listen to him, anyway. So the policeman's come riding down on his bike, and said to me dad, 'I've had reports about you from Mr Wright.'

My dad says, 'I'm not sending my children to school to get beat, so you won't see me in the pub tonight – I'm leaving.'

And he tells us, 'No more school, where you'll be fetched up like *gadjes*…'

So, about ten o'clock that night, me dad 'ooked the trailers up and we moved away, and I never went to school again in my life.

Schooling and education have never been synonymous with the Gypsy way of thinking and generally, for Anna and children like her, to have spent only one day in school would not have been perceived as a disadvantage. Indeed, it would have allowed them more time to get 'proper learning' at home, while protecting them from values considered

Children of all ages helped with work in the fields, 1940s.

anathema to the 'Gypsy way'. For example, it has always been thought inappropriate to teach children about sex.

In this regard, daughters were brought up in a vacuum. Parents avoided any reference to the subject in front of them, and sought to limit opportunities for any 'informal' learning. And when they were not there to do this, other family members assumed responsibility.

Anna:

I 'ad a brother, 'is name was Fred. He was seven years older than me. Oh, I used to cry to go to the dance. Me mam would say, 'Take 'er, but look after 'er.' Well, that was the worsest thing she could ever say. You'd get in the dance, you'd 'ave a coca cola, because we never did drink. And you'd be talking to the lads. Obviously, boys would come up to dance with yer. Oh, 'e'd say, 'Sit back down, little woman. You're thinking yourself too much of a woman now. I'm going to tell me mam and dad.'

Well, I was frightened. So then you'd sit down. You see, virtually, you may as well 'ave stopped at 'ome. Then 'e'd go 'ome and say, 'I'm not takin' 'er no more. There was boys all around 'er.'

So that would be me, and I'd say, 'Well, I never done nothin'.' But 'is word was better than mine...

Me other brother was alright. We'd say, 'We're going to look for some wood. We're going to look around 'ere.' And we'd go to the pictures on the bus. But we'd 'av to be back before me dad got back from the public house, nine dead on the dot. So you'd get to leave 'alf the picture, miss it every time, gets the bus, and run.

But me dad always knowed some'ow – 'e'd know we'd been to the pictures.

'E'd say, 'There's a man in the village said such and such.' But we'd go and admit to it. See me dad was so serious that we 'ad to give in, 'cos if we were caught out, it was worser. And to tell me dad a lie, I don't think I could.

Similarly, when Maggie went out to the cinema with a boy, her brother would be sent with her as a chaperone. She recalls offering her brother a few shillings to be left in peace, but though he would accept the bribe, he would still sit with them, watching out for any improper behaviour, such as handholding.

Rather unusually, Maggie did acquire some formal education through a boyfriend.

Maggie:

When I was sixteen I had this *gadje* boyfriend, and he spent his life teaching me to read and write, and adding up. I suppose he thought, 'If ever I marries her, I can't have somebody ignorant, like she is.' Instead of taking me out nicely, he'd come with books and paper. He wanted me, but he didn't want me as I was. I had to know things, and it was hard, because I didn't want to know. I used him terrible; my mum and dad accepted him, so it meant I could go to the pictures without being escorted, once they got to know him. He did make an oath to them that he'd never get me any trouble and he never did. He had his mind set on learning me to read and write. There was no love there – he was more like a mate, but I could use him to go places. I think they thought he was safe – he wasn't good looking – he was down to earth – they could shout at 'n and he wouldn't answer back. Me dad did shout at him. You wasn't allowed to kiss – you wasn't allowed to hold hands, you wasn't allowed to sit next to each other. That was your courtship. But you was allowed to sit with pen and paper. They accepted that.

It was wicked what I was doing but it was either having him or having me brother Alfie, and you couldn't look at another chap when he was around 'cos you'd have a black eye. He took it as his life role to protect me and that stemmed from them schools: from that first school he started protecting me, and he never gave up till the day he died, even though I was married. He never stopped protecting me.

WEDDINGS AND CELEBRATIONS

One of the best weddings was Lovey Hughes and Roy Hardwich [during the 1970s]...We were doing the potato picking at the time. We all left in the back of the lorry to go to the wedding. They had everything on the side of the road — all these cakes! Thick slices of bread and meats and cheese...You had the fire going if you wanted to warm something up. The custard was extra thick. Wedding cake. Lovely!

The old record player was going. They'd get a piece of board out and do the step dancing. I had a go!

Rodney

Stories of life on the road for Gypsies in the South West make it clear that the hard times went hand in hand with a rare ability to create a celebration almost out of thin air. A zest for life, spontaneity and a sense of fun shone through as people talked about the times when they gathered together:

Dorothy:

I got married down Barnstaple — we invited sixty or seventy — and loads come! People always give money at a Traveller's wedding. Better than toasters and kettles! You can get a lot of toasters and kettles! When I got married I had towels — enough to fit this room — and Marilyn, she had drinking glasses. If you put twenty quid in a card people can buy what they need.

People used to travel a long way to weddings and fairs — when they gets there, see, they'd enjoy themselves — eat, drink, dance. They used to have a bit of board and tap dance on there — make their own enjoyment. If there wasn't no music they'd make their own amusement — tiddle eye ti ti, tiddle eye ti ti! Then they'd get and dance. Mouth tuning. Tiddle eye ti ti, tiddle eye ti ti. [Mouth tuning is accompanied singing, giving the beat for step dancing.] Then somebody else would stand up and tap dance.

The benefits of music and dancing were not just confined to parties. Nowadays the therapeutic value of music is being explored in hospitals and other institutions. Travellers always knew that music could heal.

Dorothy:

When Tom Orchard was in hospital — he had to have an operation — the son went in. He was playing the accordion, the woman was playing the clappers, the daughter was singing! Another one came and tap danced! The nurses said, 'You can't do this in here!'

'Well', they said, 'We wants our father to get better!'

Tom's wife, Jean, showed us a very early wedding photograph (see below) showing members of the Orchard family, and sure enough, one member of the wedding party is playing the melodeon (a type of small accordion).

Jean:

> The wedding took place in Clawton, just outside of Holsworthy. The father of the bride (the man with the bowler hat next to wagon wheel) was 'Farrier' Joe Orchard who lived in Bridgerule and was a great-great uncle to Tom, brother of Tom's dad's grandad. The bride (his daughter) was Amy Orchard and the groom (big watch chain) was Alfie Penfold, who was also a great-great uncle to Tom, the youngest brother of Tom's dad's granny. The boy in the wagon with the melodeon was Farrier Joe's son, Billy Orchard.

Incidentally, Farrier Joe was well known for curing afflications such as warts, shingles and eczema. Tom's dad has got Joe's old pill machines and several letters from people who wrote to him asking him for 'repeat prescriptions' and letters of thanks for successful treatments.

A wedding celebration, thought to be that of Alfie Penfold and Amy Orchard at Clawton, near Holsworthy in 1910.

Although some wedding celebrations were formal affairs, stories abounded of high spirits and shared happiness.

Rodney:

One of the best weddings was Lovey Hughes and Roy Hardwich [during the 1970s]. They had the reception on the side of the road at the Drifts, off the A30 near Chard. We were doing the potato picking at the time. We all left in the back of the lorry to go to the wedding. They had everything on the side of the road — all these cakes! Thick slices of bread and meats and cheese. There was bacon. You had the fire going if you wanted to warm something up. The custard was extra thick. Wedding cake. Lovely!

The old record player was going. They'd get a piece of board out and do the step dancing. I had a go! It's the older generation really — they'd make the tune with their mouth. 'Mouth tuning'. You had your groups. You could be up there with the music, or you could get down the road a bit if you just wanted to have a talk, or you could go and have a kip in the wagon. It was ideal.

I got drunk! I wasn't supposed to drink — I was fifteen! Georgie Hughes had these crates back in the wagon and let us have a drink. Little bottle of brown. He wasn't supposed to — Mum and Dad would've gone mad!

It was a lovely summer day. We were jumping this rope and I fell over in a bunch of stinging nettles — that stinging nettle bite lasted for days! We all went back in the back of the lorry — made it more fun. Just like the Waltons!

Another Traveller wedding was completely different. Tommy and Alison got married in Chard. Proper church wedding. We went back; it was a sit-down meal. We were served with everything — whatever you wanted — it was spot on. Superb. They wouldn't serve me any alcohol there! But wild by the side of the road was alright for me!

Rodney's mother, Nellie, shared her son's love of a good get-together, but her long and happy marriage had a rather difficult start.

Nellie:

I used to love to go to the pictures and we had parties — gramophone records, trumpets, accordions. Dancing and singing. Old policeman'd come up. Ask how long we were staying. 'That's fine,' they'd say.

I was twenty on my wedding day. The family weren't happy about it. My mum made my brother and a friend put my clothes outside by the door. Later, when I came back, my mum wasn't there, and my granny had a go at me as well.

We lived in a house for about five years. I loved it. If it had been a different house I'd probably have been there now. It was a smallholding but it was damp and that — if you put a pair of shoes in the cupboard they'd come out white. My husband — he was a local person — was brought up in a house, but he loved the caravans! We 'ad a showman's wagon once. He loved the life. He was a very happy man. He wasn't like some men going down the pub and throwing his money away. Quite contented, like.

Nellie's marriage to a 'local person', or *gadje*, met with family disapproval, and that was often the case for those who stepped outside tradition, as Maggie recalled.

Maggie:

I'm lucky that I married Terry. I can live your life and I can live me own life. I had to forge me dad's name to get married. I'm a forger! The man give me a form at the registry office to take back to me parents – you had to be twenty-one then and I was twenty – I took it up the road, signed it and took it back. Then they wouldn't come to the wedding. Then Terry was interrogated something terrible. It was like he'd done a crime. What me dad put my man through – oh, it was horrendous. In fact, they'd never met him until the wedding day, the morning, because no-one was going to come... He was given long lectures on how to look after me. And keep me in order! I mean, they told him straight, he wouldn't get a good talking to, he would get a good hiding if I turned up bruised and battered. Although me dad could half kill me mum, I couldn't be beaten.

Terry was a gambler. I didn't know what a gambler was. He'd bet on two flies walking up a wall. We got into some trouble. We didn't have any money. He said to me one day, 'What are we going to do?'

I said, 'Well, I'll give you one chance, that's all you're getting, then I'm going back to me dad.'

I would never have gone back to me dad! The day I got married, he told me in front of everybody that was there, 'You've made your bed – lay on it. If it gets rough, shake it up and get back on. You don't come home. You chose your way.'

Having chosen her way, and discovered that, indeed, there were rough patches, Maggie found her own special way of shaking things up to make her marriage work.

Maggie:

When we had a house at Shepton Mallet Terry got in with this crowd up there, playing cards. They'd stay in the pub and they'd never come home for their dinner. So this Sunday I put his dinner out, put it on the back seat of the car and I took it up. The landlady wouldn't give him a knife and fork.

'I hope you enjoyed that.'

'No,' he said.

A few weeks later he said he'd come back and take me and the boys out. He never come back. What we had in the yard was a horse-drawn hearse. They phoned up and said, 'You'll have to come and fetch him. He's had too much to drink. He can't get home. He can't drive home.'

A happy couple in the late 1930s. Maggie's mother is seated second from the right.

'No problem', I said. I don't know whether you've ever stood by a horse-drawn hearse but they are high! We didn't have a horse, only a pony – I put a pony to do a cob's job. I put the hoss in the shafts, the two boys up on the front and I drove up to the pub.

I went in and I said, 'Bring him out.' They pleaded with me. They pleaded. They went on their knees.

'Don't do it to him, Maggie.'

I said, 'Put 'im in. I'll learn 'im.'

They been and put 'im in and half of them was drunk as hand carts and they're following me and I went through three villages with this pony flat out, sweat pouring off the hoss. You've never seen nothing like it. I pulled straight back up in the yard and I unhitched the hoss and I blocked the door so he can't get out and I left him there all night and for months the drivers used to go by and raise their hats and pretend I'd killed him. They used to do it to be respectful 'cos he's dead! I had him in the horse-drawn hearse and he woke up and thought he was in a nightmare. I tell you what, he was always home on time after that.

It is a tribute to both Maggie and Terry that, over forty years later, they remain happily devoted to each other! Although neither would say that marriage between

Gypsy and *gadje* is easy, times are changing:

Dorothy:

Marrying out was frowned on years ago, but they don't take no notice today. Loads of people marry *gadjes*. My daughter married a *gadje*. Travelling boys today – they're mad and wild.

Running away to get married was not unusual – in many cases parental opposition melted away after the wedding.

Linda:

My father's first wife was my mother's sister – they had a son and she died in childbirth and my granny looked after the baby. Me father came up to see him every weekend and he and me mum got together and they ran off and my father's sister and my uncle, they ran off at the same time! They only had horse and carts. All my uncle had in his pocket was five shillings. They got married on the same day. They were each other's witnesses. They went and had bread and cheese. When my mother was expecting me sister they made up with the rest of the family.

Maggie:

Well, in my family it was a runabout; they run about for a day and a night and then they knew they could be together, so they, the youngsters won in the end. I mean, it happened last year with my nephew; the parents wouldn't let him see the girl. He wanted to take her out so they ran away and the wedding was arranged two days later, and they was happy as pigs in muck; she's expecting her first baby. It's a way of forcing the hand.

In effect, couples took a calculated risk when running away together. Subsequently, they could return safe in the knowledge that they would be permitted to jump the broomstick.

Anna:

They'd run away… If you went out for the night, and didn't come back, that was it: you were as good as married, then, that was the end of it. You made your bed; you slept on it.

Well, the women would help the girls, with, like, a few bed sheets, or a few things; the men would help the lads with a bit of money to buy a wagon…or a harness and a bit of something.

When they got back, after running away…well, the next morning, the old people would say, 'Well, we'll do a bit of a do' – and a bit of a do was just like a few sandwiches…and they'd be proud to have a new daughter-in-law or a new son-in-law.

They'd all dance, then the two of them would both jump over the broom…the broom would be on the ground…and that would be the marriage. You'd always know the new couples, because they'd pull the wagons away from the older people…

Robert:

There's still quite a gathering now for funerals and weddings but nothing like it was in the old days – they're not so romantic now, obviously. When you're young everything's romantic and gorgeous. When you look back on it you see things that are all strange to you like jumping the broomstick. That was quite common – literally doing that – jumping over the broomstick and that was the wedding vows – the solemn thing that they were going to carry on through life.

Jumping the Broomstick

If a chap is in the hop field, or is in the fruit country and he sees a young girl he takes a fancy to – he looks at her and she looks at him – he'll either talk to her the first chance he gets or he'll give her his dicklo – the scarf he has around his neck. Now, when he sees that girl again and she is wearing his dicklo as a headscarf he knows that she will go out walking with him. Well, then they go out walking for a time and then they will decide on a day to go off together.

Well, they go off together – jump the broomstick, as they call it – and they live together for several days. They'll build a bender – that's a tent – he will buy a cooking pot; if he hasn't got a kharvisaster – that's a kettle-iron – he will make one and they will live together for several days to see if they suit; and if they suit each other they'll come back to the tribe and are first married in the Romany tradition, or some part of the old ceremony anyway and there will be a great wedding feast. Then, a few days later, there will be a church wedding in most cases but some will just register their marriage, while some others again still think that the Romany wedding is sufficient. If the couple find out in time that they are not for each other, the marriage is broken off right at the start; otherwise, of course, they'll be rowing and fighting and half killing each other. That's the way most of them go on today.

There are two ceremonies used for marriage that I know of: jumping the broomstick and mingling of blood. The broomstick ceremony is the shorter of the two and it is used less than the blood-mingling ceremony. All that you do for this is for the couple to hold hands while they jump over a besom made of flowering thorn or gorse in front of members of their families. I have often heard of people having broomstick weddings but I don't know of any Romany today who actually used such a ceremony when he got married. But in the last century I know for a fact that some of the Welsh Gypsies did get married in that way. All the ones I know went in for the mingling of the blood.

From *In the life of a Romany Gypsy* by Manfri Frederick Wood, 1973

No celebration, however joyful, would be complete without an accompanying crisis. Merrymaking can lead to fights; family gatherings can stretch goodwill. Often the catastrophes remain vivid and, at a safe enough distance, have the power to make us laugh.

Dorothy:

I can remember when I was about sixteen or seventeen years old, John and May got married in the church down Rockwell Green. There were loads and loads of people there. We were living in Okehampton – we came right from Okehampton up here. We went to the wedding – there was so many they couldn't get in the church! We had the reception up Wellington here in a big hotel where Somerfield is now. We all went in there. When it come to, see, we expected all lovely food. But when it come to it, it was little tiny biscuits with a little bit of sprat on there! It was very, very fancy! We was all starving, wasn't us! Nearly everybody went out and got fish and chips! When it was music in the night – there wasn't any discos back then – it was people playing the guitars, 'Ooh! I don't know how to play this! I don't know how to play that!' Ding dong! It got on me nerves. So then we went down to the Barley Mow. Everybody was singing and dancing, ordered some sandwiches, we all enjoyed ourselves down there! It got to half past ten, eleven o'clock. Me father said, 'It's about time to go.' We had to go back to Okehampton. We went home – we said we'd never go to another wedding like that!

Christenings are not as big as they used to be. Years ago they'd invite all the people to a lovely party but today there's always dozens of children that come and they eats more food than the grown-ups! They spoil it for everybody – running round, bursting balloons. When me oldest daughter got married at the Beam Bridge Hotel, we had all the lovely balloons – all decorated. We invited about 150 – how many turned up? About 400. We had a buffet in the daytime – when me and me husband walked in the door, there was nothing left! We were the last to come in! We'd had a load of drink all paid for and when we went up for our drinks he asked for our money! People was going up and having doubles! In the evening time we had another buffet – it was a long table with sandwiches, potatoes, chickens' wings – you seen all the children running up! We went into the cookhouse and said we could do with some more sandwiches and they said, 'Do you want three hundred pounds worth?' It had already cost us a nice bit of money! The landlord said about paying for more drink and we said, 'Let them pay for themselves!' Half of them we didn't even know! They came for the food and to see what's going on. If I'm not invited, I wouldn't go.

I remember me sister's girl got married down Rockwell Green – she had six bridesmaids.

After, they said, 'All in the Village Hall!'

When we went in my sister said, 'There's nothing on the tables!' She went outside to the call box by the church and ringed up the caterers.

'Where's all the food to?'

He said, 'We're still cooking it!'

It was absolutely packed — you couldn't move — and when the people came carrying the trays of food they were just grabbing it! When they did put it down there wasn't much left on the tables! He said, 'I've got all the evening food — sandwiches, cheese, chicken legs, cakes.' We went in the kitchen, me and me dear sister, and put tea towels over it all. People was asking for cups of tea. We put the kettles on, put all the cups into rows, put the milk in, and went along with the big tea pot, just slap dashing it in! We had a bit of food — we was starving — our stomachs were quacking!

They said, 'More drink! More drink!'

Me sister said, 'I've already put a thousand pounds for the drink!' This chap's father came up.

'Come on,' he said. 'Let's have five hundred pounds to put over the counter!'

Me sister said, 'You can put five hundred pounds in — I ain't!'

When we went to wash up the cups we couldn't see the food! 'Whatever happened to that?' We never had the sense to look in the cupboards. Then when we were packing the cups away — they cupboards were ever so long back — 'What's that there in all they boxes?' It was all the sandwiches, the chickens' legs, the big blocks of cheese, the loaves of bread, the butter — all put back.

'Look at all this!' I said. 'We'll soon cut that up!'

We got it out, cut the cheese all up, got the chickens' legs on the tray and two or three people came in to take it out. People were so hungry they didn't know what they were grabbing! One man was going round with two chicken legs! Mostly everybody had some food. Then these two people came — me sister's daughter's mother- and father-in-law.

'What did you want to cut up all that food for?' they said.

I said, 'We didn't know it was there.'

'Oh, I did,' she said. 'We was going to have a party when we went back home.' They were saving it to have a big party in the Blackdown Hills!

Parties are certainly memorable (not always for the right reasons!) and Dorothy remembered one Christmas when a neighbour and her son came calling.

Dorothy:

She was one of the old-fashioned Travellers. She used to come up with her son every Christmas time. We had the big old fire going — big log fire. I got the drink out (Travellers eat on their laps), put out all the food: big ham — cut 'n up — pickles, you name it. It was Christmas time so more to eat and drink. The fire was going, the gang of us was in there — the more hot it seemed. All the food was gone. She was still drinking! Half past twelve she and her son said, 'Must get going now.' They only lived across the green. When she got outside the fresh air must have hit her. She was staggering from side to side. Where she was going from side to side she broke her high heels off! Next morning she come over.

'Cor, my dear,' she said, 'I enjoyed myself with the chunk on the fire.' (She called a log a chunk.) 'And the hock of bacon!' It was the best ham! She said, 'I never enjoyed myself so much. I never ate so much in all my life!'

Maggie's account of a special family Christmas is so warm and vivid that you can smell the goose cooking and hear the laughter.

Maggie:

Our own socks had an apple, a white mouse, an' nuts stuffed in the toes. The net one had sweets, tiny little scales, a ball, a paper hat, a tin whistle. All we ever wanted. We really was a happy band.

After our breakfast, me mam started to cook. Out come her big black pot, wiped out to make sure it was clean. Me mam had the goose on her lap, an' was shoving onions up its rear end, then just a smidgin of fat over it, plenty of salt an' pepper. Then she laid it gently in the pot, pushed the pot into the side of the *yog* to give it a slow start so the grease from the goose would melt an' not burn, then we washed an' peeled the taters an' swedes, onions an' cabbage. All was got ready.

Now was the turn of the spotted dick. A Christmas spotted dick. In a clean bowl she put flour, suet, salt, mixed dried fruit, currants, peel, an' a pinch of spices an' a small drop of brandy, mixed it all together with a drop of water till she got herself a dough. Then she got her big pudding basin, rinsed it out, shook the basin instead of wiping it, an' sprinkled sugar in it so that it stuck to the damp sides an' bottom, then in went the dough. The whole thing was then tied up in a pudding cloth, dropped in a pot of cold water to boil then simmer for a couple of hours. Me mam cooks according to what has been passed down through the past generations of our ancestors. I [the girl I was], in turn, will be taught to do the same, as will my daughter – if I ever haves one.

Everything was going well. Taters an' onions had been put in with the goose to roast. Smells from the pots was travelling for yards up an' down the road, then the farmer appeared, pulling a pram behind him, covered in brown paper tied up with string. We all stood and stared at him, me mam an' dad smiling. By the looks of they two this was no surprise visit. As the *mush* got close he took a bag off the pram, and pushed the pram to me mam.

'Oh, our dear Ellen, my dear sister!' Me mam's sister Ellen had sent the pram up to us on the train from Newton Abbot, Devon, packed with things she had begged for us while out selling flowers. In the pram was boots, shoes, coats, jumpers an' frocks, also clothes for the boys, sweets, oranges an' nuts. Me dad had gone to Midsomer Norton train station yesterday and picked it up, while fetching the coal, an' hid it in the farmer's barn to keep it dry, and from us *chavvies*, as a surprise for today.

In the bag the farmer *mush* had, was a bottle of beer for me dad, home-made mince pies for me mam and us. It was a grand Christmas we all had, there on the Mendips, tucked away on our own. We had a great time of it.

WORKING LIVES

The women would go around hawking and selling from the case and the men would do a bit of horse dealing or get a bit of scrap. There was one man used to go round selling carpets. He used to wear an old, smart suit. You know why he wore the old suit? For people to take pity on him! 'Look at the old suit he's got! I'll spend a bit of money on him!' There's a trick in every trade, my dear!

Dorothy

Gypsies call no man master. Their work ethic does not include jumping through hoops, climbing the greasy pole or joining the rat race. However much they might enjoy the trappings of wealth, they are not prepared to relinquish their need for independence, freedom and spontaneity. Their cheerful, easy-going approach to material possessions, a desire to travel light and the ingenuity to make something from practically nothing, all give a degree of immunity to the spectres of unemployment and poverty that drive the settled population.

Gypsies say they have survived, despite gloomy predictions to the contrary, because they are adaptable and resourceful, turning their capable hands to whatever needs doing.

Rodney:

Me and me brother Tommy worked on the motorway together for a while on the earth-moving gang – the M5 – we were there for two years. Before that, 1966, I was on the pig farm, then I went on to Monks – they did the culverts for the streams. Then McGregors – they did the concrete for the motorway and I worked laying kerbs with Dad, then I went on the earth-moving gang – which was on the big machines – the best money! It was hard work. Gerald Coward from over Ilton, Danny Kimber from North Curry, me, Tommy and me dad all pulled in on one field together. That was about '69 or '70. We done a seven-mile stretch – one of my best jobs!

So let's see if I can work it out – when I left school I went on the pig farm over Ilton. I was on there for a couple of years. Then I went to Monks, then Cementations – that's when we done the kerbs – then McGregors. I was only about eighteen and they wanted me to be in charge of six fellows, forty-eight to fifty years old. I said, 'I can't!' but they said, 'We don't mind! You know more than we ever will!' But I never did. I just stayed on the tractor.

Then I went on to the earth-moving gang. I started as tea boy and started jumping on the little D6 – the bulldozer – and having a go. I wasn't really supposed to have a go on it. It was a hired machine. I got caught red-handed one day.

The boss said to Gerald who was in charge of that section, 'Who's that on that D6, Gerry?'

He said, 'That's Rodney, the tea boy.'

The boss said, 'Well, you tell Rodney he's got himself a job.'

So they put me on the D6! Then I was on the compactor. I was number one compactor driver. You see them on tips – the machine with big steel wheels and all the spokes on, it pushes all the stuff down, makes it nice and solid and they can put the hard core and the concrete on. Well, it started to rain so we came out and we all went down the pub. The pub was packed. Out near Petherton way. It was dangerous for the big machines. The boss came back after a while. He wanted us to get back to work.

'We can't go back to work. We've been drinking,' we said.

He said, 'You get back to work or you're all up the road!'

He fired the lot of us. He got a load of students on the machines then, but after a few months they wanted us to go back. A lot of us didn't. So then I did a bit of scrap.

Scrap featured largely in the recollections of the contributors to this book. Gypsies have always understood the value of scrap and rubbish. Long before charity shops, e-bay and recycling centres, there was the clip-clop of the hooves of the rag-and-bone man's horse, or the cry of 'Any old iron!' Maggie and Robert's father, Leonard Smith, collected and sold scrap in Bristol.

Robert:

In the winter when he became motorised, and even in the horse-and-cart days, they done a bit of scrap. Other parts of the family would go tarmacing, tree topping, ragging – all the usual things.

Maggie:

I worked for me dad for eighteen years: on the scrap iron, driving his lorry, and he would put me in competitions, cutting the scrap metal, cutting the iron up.

Maggie's experience working with her father stood her in good stead as a young married woman. Her husband Terry received an object lesson in resourcefulness.

Maggie:

So we was stuck there this day and we didn't have anything and I thought, 'I'll get some money.'

I said to him, 'Where's the ash heaps in Bristol?... You know, the lorries that comes round every week and gets your ashes and your rubbish, where do they go? Where do they end up?'

He says, 'I don't know.'

I said, 'Then go and find out. Find out and come back and tell me.'

He couldn't understand what I'm talking about. Eventually he comes back and he knew where two of the tips was.

He said, 'What do you want with the tips when we've got no money?'

I said, 'Take some sack bags, take me to 'em, sit in the car with the baby and leave the rest to me.'

I bin and got through the barbed war and I've got brass, copper, aluminium – everything bar iron. I got all the metals, then I went to the next tip and got all the metals there. I knew where Manthorpe's was. Me dad had been there, down near Bedminster, so I said, 'Drive me to Manthorpe's.' I had the back of the car full and I had the boot full and we went down and we had a weigh-in. We had nearly a month's money and from that day on he wanted to be a Gypsy!

Linda's family always gave something in return for the scrap they collected.

Linda:

We went carrier bagging door to door – for wools, rags, metals. You'd go out with, say, 500 bags, drop them off, mostly council-houses, leave them a couple of hours then go back. For a bag of wool back then we'd give them a dozen pegs, a mini box of washing powder and colouring pencils. Then it progressed. In later years me and my brother would give three cups or two dinner plates or a bowl or a bucket. I started carrier bagging with my brother really when I was about eleven years old.

Anna also remembers carrier bagging – trading crayons, pencils and pegs for the rags thrown away by the householders.

Anna:

Me grandfather, John Gaskin, used to go out scrapping. 'E used to make the old jute mops and 'e'd make the pegs and flowers for me granny, Sally Gaskin, to sell.

Gypsies have long known the value of so-called rubbish. They might be forgiven a wry smile as the settled population finally begins to get to grips with recycling and accepts it has traditionally been profligate with the earth's resources. Maggie is sure that many Gypsies are returning to their roots, and re-connecting with their community.

Maggie:

I would like to get them all back scrap collecting, and it's coming back because we've had several scrap collectors call in here the last couple of months that I haven't seen for a very long time…dirt on their faces and on their hands.

They'm doing it, they're getting dirty. They'm earning their money, they've

Family group with the men
making pegs.

worked for it. It's their money and it's good to see, it really is good to see.

Rodney sounded a note of caution – the value of scrap can fluctuate so it is always useful to have a number of strings to your bow.

Rodney:

I was in Pearce's, the scrap yard in Taunton for a while. If you're down on your luck, scrap is something you know – something you can fall back on. You know the value of each bit of metal. Sometimes it's up, sometimes it's down. Years ago batteries were eighty pounds a ton, then today they're about thirty pounds a ton. They've really dropped. Car stuff – all of a sudden it's worth seven pounds a ton, then it's fifty pounds a ton. Up and down all the

RIGHT AND OPPOSITE:
Dealing scrap at Bedminster,
Bristol, in the 1950s.

time. You can't buy a load of stuff and say I'll just save it – you've got to get rid of it or you might lose out. Sometimes lead is worth a few pounds; other times it's been up to forty pounds before now.

I've always done repairs, from sixteen years old right up to now. I do me own repairs – car repairs, getting ready for MOT, welding. I'm self-taught. Some farmers, if they've got a problem they'll ring me up and come on over.

Like most Gypsy men, Rodney frequently worked with his close relatives. He turned his hands to so many lines of work that he nearly forgot to mention one important rural skill – one shared with his parents and brothers.

Rodney:

I missed out threshing! I did that for six years, off and on. For the thatch on roofs. I actually ran the threshing machine with the reed comber on top. The straw goes up, nice straight stuff, gets all combed out and used for thatching.

We were in the field with the binder; cut the corn in the field; go round and stitch it in sheaves. Mother used to come out – stitch the corn – and Father and me brothers. That was a family wossname. We all got together. We'd let the sun get at the corn, dry it out a bit, then pick it up on the trailer, take it back to the farm and pack it up. In the winter months you'd get the threshing machine nearby and chop it up on the threshing machine, put it through the reed comber, comb it all out and all the straw goes underneath in the baler. You'd bale that up and make your reed rick. Nice, straight thatch straw, all nice and slippery; comes out on the trusser at the end of the threshing machine. You pack it up and it's all ready then for the roofs. It was really hard work. Dusty. That was over Broadway, near Ilminster.

I used to check the machines – there's lots of moving parts. There's these big belts down to the tractor – if anyone got near to it they could get all tangled up in it. Common sense. You've either got it or you haven't.

Close-knit family groups have always sustained and strengthened Gypsies, not outside agencies, and working together as a family is a natural consequence. Men, women and children all play their part in providing for the family. We were told of a brotherhood – and sisterhood – of the road.

Anna:

If the men knew a man didn't 'ave much money, they'd say, 'Oh come on, we've got this stuff to pick up today.' They never 'ad nothing to pick up, but they'd never leave a person stranded, with nothing. If one of the women in the day didn't take any money out hawking, the other women would all just share.

Some of the people interviewed for this book spoke of a clear division between men's work and women's work.

Anna:

> The men would make the pegs at home and the elder flowers and the baskets and watch the children, while the women went out… Me dad would 'ave the wood gathered and the fire made and the kettle warming. They was called kettle-warmers in that day and age, the men was, and they'd put the kettle on for the women to come 'ome to.

Whatever the family produced to sell – pegs, wooden and paper flowers, posies and more – it was the women who went in search of customers, becoming expert at gauging their prospective customers.

Maggie:

> When we used to go round door to door, you could tell by the look on that person's face whether they was going to buy anything from you or not.

A trio of Gypsy flower sellers during the early 1940s.

Time for tea. No one has
been able to tell how the man
in this picture lost his hand.

Dorothy:

The women'd go hawking with the basket or the case. They'd say, 'You haven't got a bit of spare bread there?' That was monging. 'You haven't got a bit of bacon there, my dear, have you?' 'You haven't got a few eggs there?' Then they'd

Members of Jim Lee's family setting off with their hawking baskets. The picture shows Emily, Lucy, Rina and Beryl Lee.

go home, make a fire and have their supper! They'd do the best they could. The women would go around hawking and selling from the case and the men would do a bit of horse dealing or get a bit of scrap. There was one man used to go round selling carpets. He used to wear an old, smart suit. You know why he wore the old suit? For people to take pity on him! 'Look at the old suit he's got! I'll spend a bit of money on him!' There's a trick in every trade, my dear!

A lot of Travellers used to *chor* (a cauliflower) or a *canni* (a chicken). Years ago I know my father used to wait till the farmer'd locked the hens in. He'd go in the hen shed, catch hold his legs and wring his neck.

Chopping and changing is when you swap. Give me five shillings and you can have it! Dealing and wheeling. That's why Travellers go to the fairs! To see what they can get. Or they go in a pub and hope someone gets drunk so they can get it cheaper.

Me mother said years ago she used to go with her mother and down the bottom, on the corner, they had a little tip – a dump. They used to go and search there, pick up what they could, wash it out and go and sell it next day!

I used to go round with me mother selling from the case when I was about twenty-one. Me mum said, 'Oh, help me along.' She used to pack up this great big suitcase, packed with tea towels, brushes – you name it, it was in there! You'd have a hard job going along – you'd never go to one house on its own – it might not be very good there. You'd go to a row of houses.

I went with this big case, knocked on the door. 'Oo,' I said, 'My lover, you couldn't help me empty me case?' And they would look, see, and in about an hour I was sold out and me dear mother would be up the road working with her case and I would go and help her!

Some people might leave marks at the friendly houses, but if you told people where the friendly house was, that would be taking bread from your own mouth!

The work was always hard and sometimes outright dangerous.

Lisa:

> My mum used to hawk with a basket. She used to sell pegs and paper flowers.
> Made pegs and flowers by hand. She'd sell on the streets or door to door. My
> granny had five children, and my grandad died (I didn't know him) and she
> used to go out with a hawking basket, she told me this, to put bread on the
> table for the children. It was a hard life back then. Like she said, she could
> live on hardly nothing. These days it costs so much to live.

Dorothy:

> I was twenty-two when I married a Barnstaple man. His mother died when
> he was about four years old. She went out with a basket. His father was home
> looking after the two boys. She went out hawking from door to door and she
> got wet. She come back, and sitting around the fire she never took her wet
> clothes off. She cooked supper and in two days she caught pneumonia or
> pleurisy and she died. She was about twenty-nine.

Many Gypsy women remembered making beautiful artificial flowers. Wood turner
Stuart King gives lectures on Gypsy crafts. He learnt the craft from an old Romani
called 'Gypsy John' whose proud boast was that he was born in a traditional Gypsy
wagon at Stow-on-the-Wold's annual horse fair.

Whittle while you work!
Making wooden flowers.

Stuart King:

Pink and red roses were expertly moulded by hand from candle wax and fixed to twigs. Coloured crepe paper was cut with scissors, deftly folded, tweaked and wired onto a single twig stem. The most impressive blooms however, were created from wood, elder being the Romanies' preferred material. Elder produces extremely fine 'petals'. Flower heads in excess of six inches were common and resembled large chrysanthemums.

A short 'peg knife' is the only tool required. The elder should ideally be from two- or three-year-old shoots cut into manageable lengths about eighteen inches long. The knife is used to remove the bark, then with the back of the knife held firm against the knee the stem is pulled against the knife blade to produce a long curly shaving. This is the first of many petals that are subsequently created in turn; one next to the other as the wooden stem is slowly rotated and pulled against the blade. This continues until the flower head is released from the elder stem. The next step is to mount the flower head onto a suitable-looking stem. There is no need to drill a hole in the base of the flower, as the central pith of the elder is soft enough to allow the proposed stalk to be pushed in. Privet was the favourite choice with its straight growth and shiny dark green leaves.

The privet was usually 'harvested' after dark from the hedges of cottager's who would often unwittingly buy back their own privet, complete with flower heads the following day, as the Romani women went selling door to door. Some flowers were sold natural, others were softly coloured, either by using natural vegetable or fruit stains or the leached-out dyes from crepe paper put into a bucket of water.

Stuart King with the finished wooden flowers.

Maggie describes vividly how her father, Leonard, used to make his wooden flowers for her mother, Defiance, to sell.

Maggie:

The only tool used to make the flowers is me dad's peg knife. First he has to skin the sticks by slitting the skin from one end to the other, and peeling the skin off, then the stick is put back to one side to dry. When all his sticks is skinned he starts to make the big flower heads.

He has to judge how far from the end of the stick he will start to shave for the size of the flower head he wants to make. As he likes to make big ones he will bring his knife up the stick about seven to eight inches from the bottom end and will shave to within an inch from the bottom. This last inch is left clear. Each long sliver of shaved wood curls itself down to the last inch, then he starts all over again, shaving layer after layer. The skill is to make each layer shorter than the last one, so by the time he runs out of the wood part and gets to the pith in the centre of the stick, the flower is complete with a natural centre and finished, looking puffy, creamy white and it smells cushti too.

And that's magic, to see a thing so beautiful shaved out of a stick. To me they will always be known as me dad's magic flowers.

Nellie, who lives on the Blackdown Hills in Somerset, close to her son and his family, remembers making the wooden flowers she used to sell.

Nellie:

We did door-to-door selling, brushes, bootlaces, wooden flowers, pegs. The wooden flowers was beautiful. You'd put a cloth on your knee and shave the stick. You can't get the right knives these days and it makes your knees ache. I can make paper flowers, tulips and roses, and chrysanthemums. And I make wreaths.

Back at the wagon there was always plenty of work to be done for the family. When her mother and father were out working, Lisa was learning to cook and care for the younger children.

Lisa:

I was ten when I learned to cook over a fire. My mum was going doing the market, selling coats for a shilling, and she said to me one day, on a Sunday, 'Don't forget, Lisa, to cook a pot of broth.' She peeled the vegetables for me and I had to see to the broth to feed me and me sister. It went alright! My sister that's twenty-one now, I completely reared her up. Me mum and dad were doing the markets after the hawking baskets went.

Childbirth and the care of newborn babies was the province of the women.

Maggie:

> They had to have their babies with the help of whoever was there. They always made sure that they had women to take care of her, whatever happened. They always covered themselves by two or three families travelling together when the woman was expecting to go to bed. There'd always be women there – day and night. They'd try and pick women who'd already had children so they would know what they had to do.

The whole family joined in seasonal work.

Lisa:

> We done plum picking and potato picking – on a machine as well – and bagged up potatoes. That was lovely. We went to Evesham and done some plum picking and hop picking and we've done pea picking. None of that now. It's all gone.

Dorothy remembers that the women had a special part to play.

Dorothy:

> When picking plums, you let the men go up on the top of the tree with the women down the bottom. Picking plums, see, you ought to do gentle.

The gentle touch was also useful for picking flowers and ferns.

Linda:

> My grandfather used to pick fern from the woods over near Porlock, pack it in bunches, tie it up and send it to London and Manchester and they used to put it in flower arrangements and put it on the fish markets. Because it was bright green, when it was wet with the fish on the top, it looked nice. The gamekeeper lived in a little house and if he found the fern he'd rip it up. And my father used to say years after that, 'If we'd went and seen him and said we'd give him so much, he might have let us do it!' He said, 'Why didn't we have the sense?'
>
> My father used to pick snowdrops. He used to go with a galvanised bathtub. I've seen him come home with it full of snowdrops and me mother would sit and tie them in little tiny bunches and send them away.

Dorothy:

> Me father used to buy daffodils – we used to bunch them up, twelve to a bunch and sell them three bunches for a shilling.

Although everyone remembered the camaraderie of working together, there were occasional differences of opinion and tensions. Maggie's Aunt Polly, a pretty young widow, attracted the jealousy of other women workers.

Time to leave the warmth of the wagon and set off for a day of flower-selling. (By kind permission of the Museum of English Rural Life, University of Reading)

Robert and Maggie Smith's grandfather, Jimmy Small, with his second wife, Anne, twins Johnny and Henry, and Sophie. The family collected ferns to be used at the fish markets. It is joked that if you shake a tree in Devon, thirty Smalls will fall out! One relative has never set foot outside Newton Abbot.

Maggie:

In her younger days her father was a horse breeder and she was very horsey. Her first husband, Matty Broadway, was took into the [Second World] War and he come out, but he come out shell-shocked and he died shortly after and left her with four children. She used to come up to the pea fields. She used to travel with a baker's wagon from Newton Abbot up to Bridgwater to pick the peas, and she became a legend in the pea fields. She was very tall, very slim, and quite good looking. The women got jealous of her because it was a woman without a man. She used to pick with me mum and dad because they was cousins, but you could hear the skits [taunts], like, 'You're not to carry her bags of peas out.' When you went pea picking you could have twenty bags of peas to carry right across the field to the lorry to weigh them off. The women were jealous of her. She used to listen to all this, but she never said nothing at all. Went on for a few weeks. They all used to go into Bridgwater on a Saturday to do all the shopping and what not. She stood up in the pea field and she said, 'When I get into Bridgwater tomorrow, Vi, I'm going to make Bridgwater ring!'

Me mum said, 'Why's that, then, Polly?'

She said, 'I've stuck this for weeks and when I get in there tomorrow I'm going to make all these women pay for what they've been saying!'

None of the women went in – they was all frightened of her. They went to

Taunton instead of Bridgwater. They knew she meant it because me mum had warned 'em. She was fighting to feed her kids, and the women were jealous if the men helped her.

Feuds and jealousies notwithstanding, the hard work of Gypsy families was indispensable to agriculture in the UK. Few people nowadays give much thought to the major contribution to rural life and traditions that Gypsy families made in the recent past.

Robert:

Early mornings! Pea picking, hop picking, potato picking. We would always start early in the morning to get it done before the midday sun. Groups of our people would work on the farm all the year round – they may have planted the hops. The nomadic ones would go seasonally and in the months when that wasn't happening we would make pegs, flowers, go round doing umbrellas; making pots and pans. Machines do it now. It must be billions and billions of man-hours put in by men, women and children in agriculture to shape it how it is today. If you took that out the equation I don't know how it would be!

Some of the insults I've heard my people say when *gadjes* upset them – 'Before we came over they were still in the caves!' That was the extreme point of view but for sure we changed the face of agriculture on a massive scale. Fruit picking! Plums, cherries – Kent, the basket of England. Our people are still there. Right cross the country and no doubt all across Europe. We came to the recognition of the authorities at roughly the same time as progress in traditional ways of making a living broadcast all across Europe. We were ideally suited for farming – no need to worry about accommodation – make a bit of land available and a few pence for doing work they never got the locals to do. The locals weren't around – they had to make a living all the year round. We were like butterflies. We could flutter to pea picking or hop picking or cherry picking and be gone – a few pence and then move on. That suited us and it suited the farmer. No other group could do this – hence they're bringing them in from abroad. Didn't it suit our lifestyle! Didn't it marry the two together – right the way back from the Enclosure days.

Diana's Uncle Joe and Aunt Betsy pea picking in the 1950s.

Despite his love of the traditional forms of employment, Robert also found satisfaction in gaining qualifications to work outside the norm for many Gypsy men.

Robert:

You're never too old to learn. I went back to college quite late and passed the City and Guilds. I quite enjoyed it – ended up nuclear decommissioning! I had time on my hands – I'd started a course years ago on the City and Guilds with the coal board and all the pits closed down – and I wondered if I would have passed the City and Guilds. I went back and sat and took it. I only had credits – I never had distinctions – just passes and credits but I got it and that gave me the piece of paper that opened up doors to go into places like nuclear decommissioning and four years on the second Severn crossing. We done the bridge, put gas mains and water mains in the new MoD building at Filton. That little bit of paper can open up all kinds of doors.

Farm work was often a regular and reliable source of income for many Gypsy families.

Maggie regrets the losses that change has brought to the working lives of Gypsies.

Maggie:

They can go up tying the vines, picking the leaves out of the machines, but there's not that companionship, that gathering, that meeting any more. It's gone. I mean, in the days we did it, we had all the women and families that come from the big cities and they used to mix in with us and we used to feed their kids because they didn't know what hot meals was all the time they was away from home. And it was a social. Well, you would look forward to it from one year to the next; you couldn't wait till October come, once the peas was finished in August you was breaking your neck to get in that wagon and get up to Ledbury because you knew it was going to be a good time, it was going to be a really good time.

Not only have they got machinery to do everything, they don't want us. With our knowledge we've got about payment, if we went on the pea fields today, if we went pea picking, we'd want two pounds a box, but the immigrants will work for a pound a box, so it's cheaper to employ them than it is us. They don't want to know us any more. We've been brought up in it and we know the standard going rate. And who's going to stand in a field all day in the frost picking sprouts for what it works out for those immigrants – a quarter of what we would have earned? That was our work – sprouting, sweding. It was only the Gypsies that did it. They could rely on us, because we needed that work. We're phased out of a lot of traditional work.

Although many Gypsies, like Maggie, remember the past, even the hard times, with affection, some have reservations.

Nellie:

I was working all the time, really. We'd go down North Petherton every year

Large groups would work together in the fields, often singing to make the work seem less gruelling. They would relax together in the evenings with more songs and food around the fire.

then. I used to do land work; work in the fields on the machines, riddling potatoes and a bit of pea picking. I was round about nine or ten, probably younger than that. I used to get up in the mornings about six o'clock and go out in the pea fields working, then stop for a bit of tea, like – out on the fields. It was a lot of hours. It was a bit lonely – you made friends but you couldn't keep in contact.

Linda wishes she had been less restricted by tradition.

Linda:

Looking back, I would have loved the opportunities that my children have had. A lot of the girls got jobs in the nurseries and I was the only one left to help my father do the ferns, help with the horses, carrier bagging – whatever we done there was only him and me to do it. I wanted a job like the rest of them here. Me and me mother had a row.

She said, 'You can't get a job.'

I said, 'Can't I? We'll see.'

And I went and got a job [offer] down the nursery. The funny thing was thirty years on I went back to the same nursery and got another job. I never did go the first time – my mother wouldn't let me. I went thirty years after-wards. I suppose everybody can look back and say, 'I wish I'd done that.' This

Jim Smith, May, Sibby and the kids hop picking round Hereford way, 1948/50.

This Romani knife grinder looks as though he takes real pleasure in his work. (By kind permission of the Museum of English Rural Life, University of Reading)

is the longest I been in a job in one place.

Change was inevitable. Mechanisation and the move to towns and cities altered working practices for most of the population, and Gypsies were no exception. As the pace of life accelerates there is a danger of forgetting to celebrate the remarkable achievements of travelling families in the South West. For many years Pat, Katrina and their family, aware that the old ways were gone forever, ran Forgotten World, Somerset's Gypsy and Wheelwright Museum near Axbridge. Visitors could enjoy campfire cooking, stay overnight in beautifully restored vardos and see fascinating displays of costume and artefacts.

Pat:

When we set up the museum I didn't think, 'I'm a Gypsy celebrating my Gypsy origins.' It started with the workshops. Katrina did her wheelwright's course and she worked with her dad for a time and that's OK for a bit but it's hard work working with your dad! It's also very hard work working with wheels when you've got the felloes that thick and the thick steel and you're turning it over and over. She says, 'I'm not really strong enough for this job,' so she set up the museum to go with the workshops – we'd got all these wagons coming in to be repaired and restored.

Sadly, the museum is now closed, but the memories of times gone by remain fresh. As befits a group rich in the oral tradition, with a few vivid words, older Gypsies can bring the past to life. Younger family members enjoy the stories even as they come to terms with the need to adapt to the relentless present.

Rodney:

We're gardeners now. It's been five or six years. I still do all me bits and pieces of repairs as well, to keep the income up. We did a little tree job the other day – went there and the lady asked us to cut these trees down because they were over her neighbour's garden. We gave her a price, took them down. I cut the limbs on a piece of rope, made it nice and safe. They didn't get on too well with their neighbours so we had to be a little bit careful – I climbed up to make sure there was no mess! She was absolutely gobsmacked. I had a hug, Helen had a hug!

It's nice working for yourself, but paperwork's a nightmare. Helen does the paperwork. It's nice being self-employed. You can say, well, you'll start late and finish late, or start early and finish early. When you're in a regular job you have to be there at a certain time. I do some jobs for a local man – a Mr Turner. He's ninety-four years old. He says, 'I can't make people out who do a certain job they don't like. They just do it for the money. Enjoy your job!'

MUSIC

Gadzeske basavav andro kan, Romeske andro jilo.
(For the non-Roma play for the ear, for us play for the heart.)

Romani proverb

Happy memories of singing round the campfire or when working in the fields unite all the Gypsy families who helped make this book. Some songs record the old Traveller ways, or their love of the natural world. The universal themes of love, death and laughter are celebrated as the burden of day-to-day survival in a sometimes-unkind world is laid down or eased by music.

Diana:

We love step dancing, a few drinks and a good singsong – all the Romani songs and country and western. The old travelling men and women used to sing them around the fire. They'd always get a piece of board out and dance. They told a lot of stories. My mother used to tell we bedtime stories.

Linda:

The fairs were Barnstaple, Bampton, Holsworthy, Bridgwater. I only ever went once to the races at Epsom. They all used to go for a week at a time. When you'd go to the fair you'd have a new set of clothes, definitely. Everybody would meet up. There'd be singing and dancing. Even now, my cousin got married a couple of year ago and his relations – his father and his brother-in-law – plays the accordion. He brought his board up – no bigger than that – to do step dancing. Everybody would sing songs. On Marie's wedding video, after she went, they said, 'That's it.' I got everybody up singing. That's what they do – take turns singing. Country and western.

Robert:

Round the old campfire we were entertained. They would work hard, pea picking or hop picking, but in the evening it would be a fun time. Sometimes they'd get a few bottles of cider. My happy memories are of them all coming home from the pub and out would come the board and there'd be step dancing and singing. Home entertainment! I think it's gone now.

Tom, Ashley and Richard Orchard, summer 2002, when Ashley had just started learning to play the melodeon.

When work is difficult or repetitive, people often use music to lighten the load. Older readers may remember the radio programme, 'Music While You Work'. From chain gangs to sailors to Gypsies, a rhythm to work to and a tune to raise the spirits help the time pass more sweetly.

Maggie:

You've got to go in a hop garden. The rows are the length of the field. You get slow pickers, fast pickers, so you go away from each other, so half the time you can't see each other. You can hear but you can't see. Somebody'll start up a song and it'll get picked up all over the hop garden. No shouting, no hollering, but pure singing – no choir could out do what you heard. I suppose it's echoes. The singing in the hop garden. The *gadjes* would join in as well. It's something that you never forget. It shouldn't be forgotten.

The oral tradition ensured that stories and songs were passed from generation to generation, but there are concerns that as literacy levels and materialism increase among Gypsies, the old ways will disappear.

From left to right: Tom's dad singing; Tom with a melodeon; Mark Bazeley (Bob Cann's grandson – the man who started the Dartmoor Folk Festival) on another melodeon and Brian Byford sitting down (playing a banjo) on the Christening Day of Nathan's baby, Little Nathan in June 2002.

There are, alas, too few who appreciate the English Gypsies' contribution to the preservation of the nation's oral tradition, both in terms of its lyrics and of the grand old rural singing styles. Each year there are fewer Gypsy singers, for the younger generation have too many distractions and too many other priorities to want to dedicate time to learning songs about a life they can no longer relate to.

Musical Traditions Internet Magazine, June 2003

Among those working to maintain the Gypsy musical tradition in the South West, are Devon's Tom and Jean Orchard. This well-loved and accomplished family was devastated by the deaths in 2002 of their sons Anthony and Nathan. They talk freely about how talented the boys were, and how their brothers, Ashley and Richard, now continue the family tradition.

Tom:

They were very good singers. One played the boran – the Irish drum – and

Jean Orchard's grandmother, Dehlia (left) with her two sisters.

one played the bones, like spoons. When the boys died that's when Ashley picked up the melodeon [to play alongside his parents]. Me oldest son Richard plays the box – the accordion.

The melodeon's got buttons, the accordion's got piano keys one side and buttons on the other and the squeeze box is a concertina.

People come from miles to see the steps – people from America. I didn't think we'd ever play again when we lost the two middle sons, but Ashley's picking it up well. Give him another twelve months and I think he'll outplay me and I've been playing for years!

Nearly everyone in our family seems to be able to sing or play something, but that's not true of every Gypsy family. It goes back a long way. All my side and all Jean's side can sing and dance.

We are proud to be Romany Gypsies. Jean's mother was a good singer – her dad can play the piano accordion. Her dad just had a very bad stroke and lost his speech. It's all gone down one side. He's got a hard job to play his electric keyboard and the piano accordion. But he's coming around to play-ing the music. My dad could sing and play the box – all the family can do something. If they couldn't sing or dance years ago they used to fight.

I've been step dancing since I was six years old and playing the melodeon. We've played in all the local folk clubs, been invited to London, Glasgow, Manchester and Newcastle to play music and dance. Jean's got her own CD out – 'Holsworthy Fair' – and one of the songs on there ('A Wager, A Wager') is over seven hundred years old. Jean plays the penny whistle – our younger son Ashley plays the melodeon. He's very good – been playing ever since he was four.

ABOVE: Jean's granny, Dehlia, pictured at a wedding in Holsworthy Memorial Hall in 1982. It was the wedding of Tom's brother Paul.

RIGHT: Tom Orchard step dancing.

Music has been an important part of Tom and Jean's relationship from when they first met.

Jean:

> Tom had a tractor for work and he used to come and pick me up and he had an old eight track then, playing country and western – me singing along – so we both knew that we liked the music, and he always played the box when we were out. We were both interested in the music, but we didn't get together because of it.
>
> What happened was we went into the local pub at Holsworthy – he used to play the box and I used to sing along beside him, just enjoying ourselves, and we were approached and someone said you'd go down well at a folk festival. So we went and just joined in – the first few years we joined in with everybody else, then it became apparent that we stood out! As we had the kids and they grew up, they joined in and everybody liked it with them singing and playing besides us, all around our feet. They thought, 'Magnificent – we'll hire you to play here and there!'

When Anthony and Nathan died, it was hard for the family to carry on making music, but with loving support and encouragement from family and friends they began to perform again.

Tom:

We went to a big festival – the National Folk Festival at Leicester.

They said, 'Tom, You've got to go.'

I said, 'I don't know as I'll be able to play anything.' So we got on the stage – we cried. And everybody up there – there was about eight hundred there – they cried with us.

Then Ashley joined us, and within twelve months he was good enough to play with us, and the chap approached us about the CD. The CD sounds very well. And my oldest son's been busy bringing up his own children – he's got three under four – but now they're getting more spare time, and he said, 'Come on, Dad, it's about time I joined you now!' So the last folk thing we did, Otley in Yorkshire, a Gypsy thing a couple of months ago, he came up and joined us, playing his box and he danced on stage with his dad. We've got the whole family back in again now.

They asked us to make the CD for a long time and we've gradually done it. Everyone's pleased with it. It's gone into the colleges so they can study the traditional Romany way.

Jean:

It's a mixture of Tom playing on his own, Ashley playing on his own, me playing on the penny whistle, singing with them and singing on my own. It's a combination. It's Romany songs. I only know one Romany song with Romany words – 'I'm a Romany Rye, a fair diddikoi' – That's the only one I know! Inside the CD there's a little booklet I wrote all about our family.

'Holsworthy Fair' was favourably reviewed by Simon Evans in the winter 2005 edition of *English Dance and Song* magazine.

There are those who are prepared to raise their heads above the parapet and seek to build bridges and it is amongst these Romany ambassadors that we find the Orchard family. Through their family traditions of music, dance and song, Jean and Tom Orchard together with son Ashley are well known far beyond their native West Country and this album will undoubtedly carry their reputation even further afield. Jean's singing style is firmly in the Gypsy tradition, particularly noticeable on this album when singing 'Over Venders Hill' and 'Sixteen Come Sunday', two songs that she inherited from her grandmother Dehlia Crocker.

Tom's melodeon playing is fluid and expressive, qualities that he has passed on to son Ashley who plays alongside him on most of the instrumentals. Also of note is the cameo appearance that Tom's feet make on three tracks, reminding us that amongst his many talents Tom is also a champion step dancer.

Jean, Tom and family perform at festivals all over the country, and their exuberance ensures that everyone gets the chance to join in.

The CD cover to the Orchard family's 'Holsworthy Fair'.

Jean:

> When we went to Otley the other day it was typical of what we do. We did our little bit on the stage at dinnertime and they said, 'There's a session going on in the pub if you want to go on with your music.' When we went into the pub there was a group of six or seven people in the corner, playing to themselves – very nice – everybody else was just sitting amongst themselves nattering. When we left the pub they were all dancing, singing, jumping up and down!

Tom:

> It wanted a bit of a boost up! Sounds better, sweeter, after a few pints of beer! We said, 'Come over and see us on the stage this evening.' It was only a few tunes. We had a good time up there. We had Richard and Ashley and me, and me grandson, who's only four, in the middle. He stole the evening away! They were all cheering for the young one.

Tom has vivid memories of family gatherings round the campfire.

Tom:

> I was six years old when I started – I was by the fire, watching the men stepping and dancing – they used to get into a fight as well. There was one, Uncle Jim, he taught me and his brother, Uncle Norman. Uncle Norman would come in the trailer, go home paralytic drunk and fall asleep. Everybody's outside mouth tooting and playing, with a board dance on – all of a sudden the door'd come open, the music would waken up, and then he'd dance. And my

God, he could dance too! And these two taught me. We was away in Suffolk and there was two men up there stepping. They was called West.

They said, 'Do you know Uncle Jasper Richards?'

I said, 'Yes – he's a great-uncle to me.'

They said, 'Do you know Uncle Jim and Uncle Norman?'

'Yup,' I said.

Then he said his mother's brother was my mother's father – they were still stepping in their sixties. I was over the moon! They put one cousin there, and the other cousin there, and me in the middle, like I was still the baby stepping! They'd have the campfire, some mouth tooting and dancing, then one would tell an old story, then another two or three would sing, and they'd keep going all night until the beer's gone. I remember that just like yesterday.

Tom's uncles could be very competitive about their music and dancing.

Tom:

Uncle Jess and Uncle Jim, they went out calling for some work, they got down here to Launceston Hill, and the silly old sods, they got excited, and they got outside the car and they were mouth tuning to each other, saying who was the best dancer! They were all day long with this, and there were ructions when they got home. Me grannies got worried that they'd got lost or got hurt! All they were doing was mouth tuning on the side of the road!

Family life is paramount to Gypsies, and this applies to music as well. Like Jean and Tom, others spoke eloquently about the way the whole family shared their love of singing.

Maggie:

There's a song me mum used to sing a lot.

The cuckoo is a wise bird
He calls 'cuckoo' as he flies
He tells you good news
He don't tell you no lies.

It's all about the spring coming. It's a lovely old song. I never heard anybody else sing it, only her. I've got a disc of mum singing. Before my dad died, the doctor told me we was losing him. I thought he's such a fantastic singer I want his voice, so I borrowed a little recorder and took it down with a bottle of wine. We decided we'd all have a singsong together and I got both Mum and Dad singing together and talking to each other in between. Have you heard 'I'm the Man you Don't Meet Every Day'?

Tom Orchard's Uncle Jim, 1970.

Tom Orchard's Uncle Norman, 1970.

Drink up your glasses and call for some more
Whatever the damage I'll pay.
You can be easy and free
When you're boozin' with me –
I'm the man you don't meet every day!

It goes on and on! He only sang a bit of it 'cos he was getting confused but
Mum sings some lovely old songs – the Mother songs – 'You'll Never Miss
your Mother till she's Gone' and 'Mother, She Was Kind and True, she Loved
her Children too'. It was a big thing to have the mothers in the songs.

I sang 'Cold Blows the Blossom' over a grave a couple of year ago – I had
a cousin called Joe and he died penniless. The vicar come and give a sermon
and then I give mine and I sang over the grave about poor Little Joe, and
everybody joined in. It was a little Gypsy thing we did.

Cold blows the blossom, down falls the snow
Left in the wide world was poor little Joe.
No mother to guide him
In the grave she lay low.
A carriage came by with a lady inside
Look at poor Joe a-running behind.
She threw him a penny to buy him some bread
And as he was running he wished himself dead.
Cold blows the blossom and down falls the snow
Left to wander the wide world was poor little Joe.

From Cornwall, another branch of the Orchard family made a CD called 'Songs
from Cornish Travellers', recorded by Pete Coe in 1978. The singers, Betsy Renals,
Charlotte Renals and Sophie Legg, were 78, 77 and 60 years old respectively. These
three sisters and their family spent the early part of the last century travelling round
Cornwall in a horse-drawn wagon, hawking brushes, wicker baskets, drapery, rugs
and ornaments. Singing and making music were integral to their lives and the CD
includes the songs they learned from their friends and family. The album is packed
with marvellous music, from traditional songs such as 'The Dark-Eyed Sailor', 'The
Bonny Bunch of Roses' and 'Lord Lovell', to comic numbers like 'The Crab Fish'
and 'Just Beginning to Sprout', to broadside ballads like 'Young Billy Taylor'. There
is also some step-dance tuning or lilting. A few music-hall numbers and some
spoken reminiscences complete a fascinating glimpse into the past.

Jean Orchard:

Tom and I personally know Sophie Legg's son and daughter. They are only
half Gypsy, the Gypsy side being on their mum Sophie who was an Orchard
before she married Mr Legg. So were Betsy and Charlotte, of course, as they

Gypsies gathering round the campfire to share news, stories and songs.

were her two sisters. I think they were first cousins to Tom's grandad. They sang a lot of the songs that my granny used to sing so I would think that they probably moved around in the same circle.

Another highly regarded West Country performer was Wiggy Smith. The CD, 'Band of Gold', by Wiggy and other family members, is regarded as one of the best introductions to classic English Gypsy singing.

Wiggy (1926–2002) was born in a covered wagon parked on Filton Common near Bristol – the area now covered by Filton Aerodrome. As the oldest son, he was named after his father, Wisdom, but was nicknamed Wiggy to avoid confusion. In a similar manner, Wiggy's eldest son, also Wisdom, is nicknamed Figgy. In Wiggy's early years the family travelled in Gloucestershire, Oxfordshire and the West Midlands, sometimes living in tents, but mostly in horse-drawn barrel-top covered wagons.

Now I lived with my uncle for twelve months, him and his wife; that was Artie and Liza. That was when I came out of the Army, that was. And in them days there used to be nine of us as lived in a caravan – horse-drawn caravan. And when we got to bed at night, they used to sleep on the bed up at the top, the girls underneath 'em a bit and we boys on the floor. And [Artie] used to lay there and sing all the old songs and he used to say to his wife, 'Now I've had my song – now it's your turn, Liza. You sing.' And she used to lay there and sing all the old songs. I got a few that way.

One of Wiggy's uncles, Luke Smith, lived further south in Gloucestershire and used to sing regularly in the Nag's Head at Avening. He was a great singer, instantly recognisable with a long white beard down to his chest.

Like Maggie, Wiggy also remembered singing in the hop gardens.

> We used to have a great time on the last night of the hop picking, especially with the
> Dudleys [the people from Dudley]. That was all singing and dancing – everybody was
> into that, raring up! No fights or nothing.

Gwilym Davies, Gloucestershire-based folk singer and folk song collector, feels
privileged to bring Wiggy's music to a wider audience. Before Wiggy's death in
2002, Gwilym wrote:

> Wiggy now only allows Paul Burgess and me to record him. We are proud that he has
> put this trust in us, and he knows that we respect him as a person and as a performer.

There is no mistaking Wiggy's style as anything other than that of the travelling people. Compared with *gorgios* [non-Gypsies], the style is generally slower paced, of
greater volume, sung in a higher key and with the emphasis on the dramatic. A dec-
oration much used by Travellers and by Wiggy is that of sliding up or down to a note.
He uses this to great effect in his rendering of 'The Rich Farmer of Sheffield'.

To Wiggy, the story and the words mattered more than anything, and sometimes
he took a breath in the middle of a line or word for emphasis, something that non-
Travellers tend not to do. Wiggy, like many Traveller singers, was essentially a solo
performer, with the great talent of holding the listener's attention as the song
unfolded. One of Wiggy's recordings is of the well-known song 'Romani Rai'.

> I'm a Romani Rai, I'm a poor didikai
> I live in a mansion beneath the blue sky
> I live in a tent, and I don't pay no rent
> That's the reason they call me some Romani Rai.

> Now I'm roaming around the country
> And this is the life that just suits me
> I'm a Romani Rai, and a poor didikai
> And a Romani I'll remain.

> Now I live in an old Gypsy's wagon,
> With the rooftop all civvered in gold
> Now I'll soon think about getting married
> And having a wagon and tent of my own.

> Now I'm some Romani Rai, I'm some poor didikai
> I live in a mansion beneath the blue sky
> And I live in a tent, and I don't pay no rent
> That's the reason they call me a Romani Rai.

The word *rai* is not one that a Gypsy man would normally use of himself – *mush* would be more usual. *Rai* (sometimes written as 'rye') is derived from the same root as 'rajah', and was first used to describe those scholars who studied the Romani culture. George Borrow is probably the best-known example of such a figure and his first book uses this term as its title. The song, written for music halls by C. Bellamy and G. Weeks and performed at the turn of the twentieth century, has been adopted as a Gypsy anthem. All that remains of the original song is the chorus, used by Wiggy as the first and final stanza.

When Wiggy was a boy, an old Gypsy woman was well known on Exmoor for the songs she sang while wortleberry picking. West Somerset's collector of folklore, Ruth Tongue, had often heard a deep, resonant voice, singing long forgotten songs as she rode her pony near Worthy Wood. Then one day she chanced upon 'a very old gipsy woman seated comfortably on a springy cushion of worts, smoking her pipe… [with] her thin, hawk face under manifold plaits.' Ruth had been singing as she rode, and the Gypsy woman, Cordelia Cooper said, 'Yew do sing so tuneable as the dear God's small birds.' Thus began a friendship that resulted in the two women pooling old songs, and sharing the pleasures of singing together. Cordelia told Ruth of three songs written by Gypsies. Ruth writes that the songs 'show the grim humour, the careful turn of a good phrase and the single minded faith of the best of the gipsies.' The three songs are 'The Broom Squire's Bird Song', 'The Leaves They Do Fall', and 'The Worthy Wood Carol'. Ruth Tongue believed the first was probably composed by Duke Holland, who was at Over Stowey in 1870, and the latter by an Exmoor Gypsy, possibly a member of the Lock family, in the 1920s or earlier. Ruth believed that Cordelia's songs should be set down for others to enjoy. She cherished her memories of Cordelia 'altering time and melody as the mood took her' and bringing 'a memorable mixture of fire and mourning and a tenderness that whispered and faded into the silent watching woods'.

The Broom Squire's Bird Song
(A Broom Squire is a Quantock Hills Gypsy)

Of all the birds that ever I see,
The Colley-bird is the singer for me,
The Dove she croons for she would if she could,
The old cock Pheasant crows in the wood…

The Leaves They Do Fall
There's gold for to spend,
To be shared by all;
But when Death he do call,
As the leaves they do fall,
It will come to the last in the end, the end.

The Worthy Wood Carol
Sleep my darling, darling little son
Sleep my lovely, lovely little one,
You've a-come to die for we
All upon the Criss Cross Tree
Sleep then,
Sleep my darling, lovely little son.

FORTUNE TELLING

Whosoever uses the crystal ball must be prepared to eat ground glass.

Romani proverb (sometimes attribtued to economist Edgar R. Fiedler)

The nineteenth-century Gypsy scholar and writer Charles Godfrey Leland wrote:

Gypsies believe that there are women, and sometimes men, who possess supernatural power, partly inherited and partly acquired. The last of seven daughters born in succession, without a boy's coming into the series, is wonderfully gifted, for she can see hidden treasure or spirits, or enjoy second sight of many things invisible to men. And the same holds good for the ninth in a series of boys, who may become a seer of the same sort. Such a girl, i.e., a seventh daughter, being a fortune in herself, never lacks lovers.

Taken from *Gypsy Sorcery and Fortune Telling* by
Charles Godfrey Leland, 1891

In *Romany Magic* (published 1973), Charles Bowness is rather more sceptical as he writes that anyone can develop the ability for character reading: 'Playing on the credulity of gorgia women for centuries has bred a race of Romanies who know exactly when to pause for mysterious, dramatic effect.' He adds: 'There are two kinds of fortune telling, that which is merely a means of extracting money from the credulous… And the genuine kind of prophecy in which is displayed a true gift.'

The ability to tell fortunes may well be a true gift, but for many Romani women it is a mixed blessing. Some Gypsies consider second sight a curse, whereas others see it as beneficial. Anna, who goes to fairs all over the South West, suggested that no Romani would tell another Romani's fortune or look into their own future, and neither would they try to contact the dead. Nevertheless, she is clear that a talent that once seemed scary is now a means of reaching out to people.

Anna:

I first found out I had the gift when I was very little — about five. It's fearful for a child. Looking at people, I could see — I could see, really, their life. It was frightening to me, to be honest, but as I got older and I got to learn more, I'd ask the people, 'Did that happen to you?' and they'd say, 'Yes. How do you know?' Then I knowed. I think God's given me a lovely gift, to help people.

I started working with it when I was about twelve with me granny, knocking on the doors. She had the gift. My Aunt Violet, she still does fortune telling. There's not many, out of ten of us. At first I done the mind reading, now I do the crystal ball and your hand. Because all them lines, believe it or believe it not, has got your life written there. You look at Romanies' hands, they're very clear. You can see the lines very clear. We're not like other people. What's happened in them lines will never leave you. I like people who don't look down, who ain't got nothing to hide. They look straight into my eyes and that's how I can get into people. When people have got something to hide, they keep looking down.

I can hold your hand and read your palm, but to look into your face – the bestest thing I can get into is your brain and I can see in your eyes. If I see someone at a fair with anything bad, I let them go by. I'm not a person to tell them about death – I can tell them about what's already happened, which they already know, or I can prepare them for death. I like to tell the truth.

There was this young man. He was adopted – he didn't know his background.

He looked at me and said, 'Where am I going to search?'

I said, 'Start with your roots.'

'But I don't know anybody.'

'There will be somebody. Find them,' I said.

When I was talking to him like that he said, 'Oh, I do know somebody but I forgot them!'

I said, 'You tried to blank that out,' which he did.

Everybody wants to know their own roots. I can go back to my roots. It's nice to know I'm a true Romany.

Anna said that of her four sisters, one other had the ability to tell fortunes. She knew some men with the gift, and her youngest daughter has it, but is not using it at the moment. 'Some sells lace and pegs – they don't all tell fortunes. Everybody ain't got

Fortune teller Angelina Lee with her crystal ball.

the gift!' In the main, she spoke of the positive side of her work, but she did say a little about the downside.

Anna:

> Every person's different. Every person's interesting to me, rich or poor. A fortune's never, ever the same. But afterwards I get very bad headaches and I'm tired. I give all that I've got.

Anna is generous, and gives abundantly of herself, as the doctors and nurses who cared for her when she was very ill, discovered. 'When I had the operation in Torquay I had the head specialist come and have his fortune told. And the nurses. They helped me, and that was my gift to them.' Her attitude to payment is typically warm-hearted.

Anna:

> Sometimes they've been to these people who've tried to heal them – these people that turn the cards over – the Tarot cards. They've paid a lot of money – but for years I've only charged the same price as I charge now because the people's more important to me. I've seen the joy in their faces. Obviously I charge, I couldn't just do it for nothing, but if anyone's unhappy I won't take their money. To date there's not one that's been unhappy. I ain't no fake, and if I couldn't do it I wouldn't play with people's lives.

When they were little, Anna and Linda saw Gypsy women telling fortunes at the major racecourses. However much a race-goer studies form, there is still a huge element of luck in predicting the outcome of a race, so punters would want all the luck going and superstition is rife. Tim Sandles, who created the Dartmoor website www.legendarydartmoor.co.uk, referred to the Gypsy Stone at the old racecourse at Dean Prior, Buckfastleigh. People used to touch it for luck before placing their

Angelina Lee in her distinctive plaid skirt.

bets, but Anna, who lives close to Buckfastleigh, had never heard of it.

Anna:

> I've run the Derby many a day with some charms, me and me brother. Little black cats – or me granny would get coloured bottles, and she'd smash them up, make them smooth, and she'd rub the crystal ball over them and give wishes, like I do; little pixies in little boots; heather; pegs; elder flowers; paper flowers; smelling salts. They were terrible! When you smelled it, you'd get better!

Linda:

> I knew somebody who used to go to Epsom races for a week and tell fortunes – *dukkering*, we call it – to earn enough money to go to Ascot for a week. She earned enough money to buy an outfit for every day from Selfridges. She was the only one I knew who did it for a living. If my mother went hawking and found someone who wanted to know something she would do it. I think most Travellers are a bit psychic – me father used to say it's a man wants another woman or a woman wants another man or she's left him or he's left her [in other words, people's fortunes are dictated by their desires]...

Dorothy remembered times when telling a house dweller's fortune helped put food on the table for the family.

Dorothy:

> My mother used to do fortune telling. I used to go round with me mum. She could say what was going to happen. She had a crystal ball. When she used to go selling with the basket she had her crystal ball in a sock. Mum used to say,
>
>> 'Do you want your fortune told, my dear?'
>
> Some people used to say yes, some people used to say no.
>
>> 'How much do you want?'
>
> Me mother said, 'Just buy from the case and that will do.'
>
> Mostly my mum was true as anything. When she used to tell people's fortunes, she would never take money for it.
>
> The people would say, 'What have I got to give you?' Because they was poor the same as me mum she'd say, 'Give what you like.'
>
> They would always pack up food into a bag and give that.
>
> If it's born into the family some people can tell fortunes. Some can read your mind – another person can foresee things. Someone might read cards, or have a crystal ball, or sell the charms – lucky heather. I can foresee. Sometimes, not all the time, I can see what someone's thinking.
>
> It is a gift. I can see things happening as well. My son got the gift as well. Money, the Lottery – you don't see that! I know when people is going to die.
>
> The last one I did was over Bishops Lydeard. A man in the greengrocer's

shop wanted his fortune told. There was loads of people in the shop so I told him to come outside.

His wife said, 'After you've told my husband's fortune, could you tell mine?' I couldn't. I seen sorrow. She said, 'Why can't you tell mine?'

I said, 'I just can't. I'm very, very sorry.'

I said he was going to have a big house – and a load of money left him and he's going away. A couple of months later he left his wife for another woman and he got his big house. I seen sorrow.

If I saw someone was going to die I would say, 'Something's going to happen in the family.' You've got to ask that person, 'What's troubling you? What's wrong?' Sometimes you let that person tell you a little bit – they can carry on the sentence. They want to know if they're going to have money, or have another man, or have children or not. Sometimes it's nice if that person tells you their troubles and you can give them advice and tell them what to do. But you can't take on other people's troubles.

Despite some initial resistance, Pat found herself drawn to fortune telling, or *dukkering*.

Pat:

When Mark was still quite young he'd got a pony and he bought a Gypsy wagon and he parked it on the A38. Somebody in the village was having a garden party and came to us and said, 'Will you bring the Gypsy caravan? Will you dress up? Put all pretty lamps and cloths out and will you tell fortunes?'

'NO!'

'It'll be two shillings a go and they can only have two minutes. I'll be there at the door and I'll have a stopwatch. After two minutes I'll knock the door and say, "Time's up".'

I thought, 'OK. I'll accept that.' Goes to the library, got a book on palm reading. I thought. 'Right. Two minutes. I can tell them two lines. Life line. Heart line.' So I took sixteen pounds, one and nine pence and there was a whole queue of people all across the lawn and Mark was dressed up in his waistcoat and bowler hat.

He said, 'You'll get into trouble!'

However, people came in and sat down and when I held their hands it was, 'Here's your life line – you've got four children. This is your heart line – you've been very ill.'

Now, I can tell everybody something about themselves and I thought, 'Where is this coming from?' No idea. Just made everybody smile. So then I got all the books I could find on palmistry – and from then on I did palm reading – because I'd got something I could do.

I also did card reading. I started doing Tarot reading because a friend of mine had got cards and she'd written on all her cards what they meant and she said, 'Read my cards!'

I said, 'No, it's a load of rubbish.' She's shuffling the cards and I said, 'It's pathetic.'

And she said, 'Come on!' So I read the cards – she showed me how to lay them out – I'd never laid them out before. I'm reading all the things I could read.

Then I said, 'I just can't do this – I can hear a lot of arguments and rows and I can hear a baby crying,' and I said, 'I don't understand – take them all away.'

And she was expecting another man's baby – so there's the rows and the arguments!

There's something in it. Is it the cards? Or the concentration? Do you feel things from the person? They say some people can hold a piece of jewellery and tell a lot about a person. I had a lot of people coming to the museum year after year. They came and said, 'Everything you said last year has come true,' or 'There's one thing to go – I want you to tell me my next year.'

Pat realised that people's troubles could become overwhelming. Dorothy remarked, 'It can flock in and stay in.' It became too much for Pat to manage.

Pat:

People came because they wanted me to make them better, they wanted me to be able to say, 'You do this and you do that and it will all be alright.' You can't do that. I felt very hemmed in. They started to depend on me. One lady came – she'd just got married. When I looked at her hand there was a lot of black although her hand wasn't dirty. She'd just married a man she'd befriended who'd been in prison for so many years after murdering his wife. I didn't know until afterwards. Another lady came – her hand was very, very black. Her son-in-law killed her daughter and she'd got the children.

Pat's reservations about fortune telling could not be ignored, and she gave it up. There are others who share her concerns. The famous evangelist, Gypsy Rodney Smith MBE (1860–1947), was totally opposed to fortune telling

It is the fashion and the folly of the 'gorgios' that have to a large extent forced this disgraceful profession upon gipsy women. Soothsaying is an Eastern custom, a gift that westerners have attributed to Orientals. The gipsies are an Eastern race, and the idea has in course of generations grown up among outsiders, that they too can reveal the secrets of the hidden future. The gipsies do not themselves believe this; they know that fortune-telling is a mere cheat, but they are not averse to making profit out of the folly and superstition of the 'gorgios'. I know some of my people may be very angry with me for this statement, but the truth must be told.

Taken from *Gypsy Smith, His Life and Work, by Himself*, 1901

Many Romanies would take issue with Gypsy Smith, maintaining that the power is real – and sometimes dangerous.

Maggie:

> Don't under estimate the mystic of Gypsies, ever. People say to me, 'Can you tell fortunes?' No, I can't tell fortunes but one in about a thousand can. They're all mystic but there's only one in so many generations that can sit down and look at you and tell you from when you was a child to where you are today. You've got to leave it alone. I tell every person who wants to know their fortune, what will be will be. Leave it alone. What's going to happen to you is gonna happen, whether you know about it or not. So it's best not to know anyway. Who can prepare for death? Nobody can prepare for an accident or losing somebody or coming into money. It's just got to be left alone.

Anna is well aware that Gypsy Smith, and others, disapproved of fortune telling, and she has thought long and hard about the relationship between her work and her profound Christian faith. She believes she uses her gift only for good purposes.

Anna:

> It's lovely to go and help people. I don't look on it as work. I look as they're my friends to help. It's women and men come. When you get older you know you're helping people. It's lovely for me to go every year to the fairs, and see friends who've been coming since they were about fifteen and now they're matured and I've seen the successes – when I've told them who they're marrying and how many children they're having and what's going to happen. They're amazed. A fortune never happens straight away. When I go back every year there's little parts of what I've told them have come absolutely great.

In *Romany Magic* Charles Bowness describes the many tools of divination, including crystal balls, cards, dice, dominoes and tea leaves. A most unusual account of palm reading and more was published in *Country Life* on 6 September 1924:

> 'Now, my lady, let an old true gipsy hold your hand and tell your fortune.' I protested, but she held my hand in her bird-like claw. 'Ah, my lady, what you have read and studied. Never did I see such a mind to work. And you were not so happy when you were young.'
>
> This I consider the usual flattering guess for clients who imagine themselves brooding Byrons or romantic Disraelis. 'But never mind, my dear. Them as were so harsh when you made your run-away marriage,' and she looked at me shrewdly, 'they ye been thinking it over and one of them has died doing so; but there's still one left and saving money up for you, too. I see him. So don't fret. It'll all come to you, darlin'. And what is this, sailing over your hand, and there it is again? A ship! There is one you've loved just gone in a ship; but you're going to him soon. Don't be angry what old gipsy says – you have a funny temper, you have, and very queer and particular

about your friends. But not as strict as your own family was. You're not quite satisfied, are you? House nice but not quite what you wanted, and you are still unsettled.'

So she rambled on with hits and misses jumbled together. 'Get me a glass of water, my lady, and a white of egg, and I'll tell you what fortune waits.' She juggled it rapidly about and then called with excitement: 'Look, darling! Here it is; a ship, with silver beads on the masts and a name coming round it.'

Certainly something like a ship was arriving at the bottom of the water. 'Now, dee-ur, keep this till tomorrow, and remember what old gipsy said. You will see the ship plain after a night and the silver beads a-shining. Next time gipsy comes she will call and see if everything has happened as she said.' She hobbled off with many blessings, and in the window stands a tumbler where a ship as white as milk bobs upon the water.

RELIGION, BELIEF AND SUPERSTITION

I only believe in what I believe in and I wouldn't like a vicar to come here pushing religion down me throat. I would get quite upset about that, but if I had a problem I would go and ask him because I've gone to him…We believe in what we believe in just the same.

Maggie

Some authorities say that European Gypsies were once Goddess worshippers, but nowadays Gypsies tend to embrace the religious practices of the country in which they live, often mixing their understanding of God and Satan with a belief in good luck charms, amulets and talismans and the power of curses and healing rituals.

There are those who attribute the persecution of the Gypsies to beliefs widespread in the Middle Ages. Some Christians believed that a conspiracy of blacksmiths, wizards and women had been organized to attack the Church. Since many blacksmiths were Roma, the conspiracy theory expanded to involve them. Another belief was that Gypsies forged the nails used in Christ's crucifixion.

Today, Gypsies speak of the current surge of interest in Born Again Christianity. Amy's friend, Annie, converted after a very difficult time for her family.

Amy:

The last time I saw her she was looking great! She hooked up with my first cousin and they live on a site with the men over there and the women over there. Born Again Christians! Never known such a thing in our culture!

Dorothy and Maggie are somewhat sceptical of the Born Again movement.

Some of Jim Lee's relatives at the Born Again Christian baptism of Scoby Price, 1984.

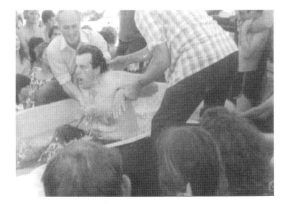

Family group with a man reading from the Bible.

Dorothy:

Most Travellers is very religious and believes in the Lord. We're not into that Born Again thing. My mother was very religious. She used to have a great big Bible. She used to read the Bible every week. Everywhere we'd go, me mum would have the Bible. She'd read it to herself. We wasn't allowed to touch it.

Maggie:

Yeah, we do believe. There's a lot of Gypsies and Travellers today that join this Born Again Christian lot, which I really don't believe in. That's my opinion, not theirs, because some of them are bigger sinners after than they were before... you see them drinking and fighting at fairs and stuff like that.

I don't quite understand it. I don't believe you can be reborn for a start, but if they can believe that that's what's happening and it gives them a new lease of life, I say good luck to them for what they believe in. I mean, I get Born Again Christians come here to do planning applications and to me it makes no difference, but if they believe, they believe. But I only believe in what I believe in and I wouldn't like a vicar to come here pushing religion down me throat. I would get quite upset about that, but if I had a problem I would go and ask him because I've gone to him. We've had Born Again Christians trying to get us to join their groups but we've never shown any interest in it at all. We believe in what we believe in just the same.

We do believe because when you're saying goodbye to someone, you want to sit right close to that box and you tell them, 'We will see you, we will meet again.' We always have that belief, that we'll all meet up again, and we have seen the spirits of several people. I mean I have; I've seen my dad here a couple of years ago walking across the yard. So yeah, we do believe it, they're there, they're waiting.

Numerous Gypsies have been very, very ill, practically died in hospital, and they've found their mum and dad stood at the bed telling them, 'We don't want you yet but we're here.' And they say, 'It was like a dream because me mum and dad were so real and the nurses couldn't see them talking to me.' When me mum was very, very ill a few years ago, me brother [Jesse, who died aged seven] went to her and she wanted us to go so that he could be there.

Gypsies famously hold a grudge, and some feuds are breathtaking in their intensity and duration, but the theme of forgiveness came up time and again, as in Maggie's account of her mother's final meeting with the man whose runaway horse killed Jesse.

Maggie:

He begged me mum's pardon just before he died. They two hadn't spoken for, it must have been forty years, because of me brother, and when he was on his deathbed, she said one day, 'We'd better go,' and she went down to Broadclyst. And he's in a caravan there and she was quite prepared to walk straight through and ignore him, but as she went to pass he said, 'Vi, I'm sorry for what happened all they years ago,' and they two then chatted as if they hadn't never stopped speaking. But just speaking breaks that elastic band that's keeping you apart, you know, at times like that. I mean, had they met at a fair and he'd tried to speak to her, it would have been different all together. She would have probably clocked him one. But because he hadn't got long to go she could forgive him. She was upset that it took a lot of years for him to do it because he couldn't admit he was at fault; it was his horse, not him.

I think when someone is dying – it's part of the old custom again now – if I was ill now and the doctor said I'd got three, six months to live, people that I'd fallen out with bitterly would turn up here and they wouldn't be turned around. They would come in and speak to me. I'm not saying they'd say they're sorry, but if they said, 'Hello, Maggie, how are you feeling?' and I said, 'Alright, thank you,' then it's gone. So if there was a bad feeling it's gone, and that does happen. If someone is on their deathbed you don't go begging their pardon, but...

Yeah, it's an old saying. 'I'll never forgive you; to the day I die I'll never forgive you.' And we all say it; we still use it a lot.

The need for forgiveness cropped up in conversation again and again.

Amy:

Eventually the biggest feud you could ever have dissolves. Eventually. I've never known any feud that has gone on until that person's died and they haven't asked forgiveness or given forgiveness.

The use of the word 'eventually' is telling! Before that, there could be some powerful feuding, often fuelled by cursing. Maggie, however, has had cause to reconsider her ability to curse; a gift left with her, she believes, by the old woman who healed her when she was scalded as a child.

Maggie:

When I was working in Boots, the women would come on the pavement selling heather and they'd get very violent with it sometimes and the girls would come and tell me and I said, 'Well, call the Police!'

They said, 'No! They'll put a curse on me!'

I said, 'You're being stupid. If someone's going to put a curse on you it would be me! I'm the one that can actually put curses on people!'

I can do it, but I promised my husband faithfully, no matter what state I gets in, I would never ever do it again. I would be beat rather than do it – I've done it and everything's come true. I had a house round here – I was accepted. Till I moved on this ground. Then I was the outcast. The council was being atrocious – everybody that knew us for thirty years went atrocious because we was going back to our Gypsy way of life. They got a petition up. Chappie came with £30,000 in cash in a bucket that he'd been round the village and collected to buy me out. That upset me. I got nasty.

Evangelist Gypsy Rodney Smith, who formed the Gipsy Gospel Waggon Mission in the 1890s with the help of a Scottish noblewoman, would have been heartened to hear Maggie say she was never going to put a curse on anyone again. He was deeply concerned about the spiritual wellbeing of his fellow Travellers.

Evangelistic work among the gipsies is slow and hard. My people have quick eyes, quick ears, and ready tongues. But for years – nay, for centuries – their hearts have been blinded to the things of God. There is hardly a race on the face of this globe to whom religion is so utterly foreign a thing. The gipsies are slow to comprehend the plan of salvation, and even when they have understood, they are slow to use it, because, for one thing, their trade is declining; they are depending more and more on the fortune-telling, and they know very well that if they become Christians that practice must cease.

Gypsy Smith wrote with a gentle humour about his conversion.

Then I began to practice preaching. One Sunday I entered a turnip-field and preached most eloquently to the turnips. I had a very large and most attentive congregation. Not one of them made an attempt to move away.

He travelled all over the country, and visited Torquay with his beloved father.

> My father is like a tree planted by the rivers of water, still bringing forth fruit. When
> I go to see him I kneel at his feet, as I used to do when I was a boy, and say, 'Daddy,
> give me your blessing. All that I am I owe, under God, to the beautiful life you lived
> in the old gipsy waggon.' And with a radiant heavenly smile on that noble old face,
> he answers, with tears of joy in his eyes, 'God bless you, my son! I have never had
> but one wish for you, and that is that you should be good.' Some time ago, when I
> was conducting a mission at Torquay, I talked to the people so much about my father
> that they invited him to conduct a mission among them. And then they wrote to me,
> 'We love the son, but we think we love the father more.' They had found that all that
> I had said about my father was true.

Gypsy Smith's grandson, Sonnie, and his wife, Rosemary, have carried on the dream
of converting Gypsies to Christianity. As a child, Rosemary used to love the verse.

> I wish I lived in a caravan
> With a horse to drive like a Gypsy man,
> Where he comes from nobody knows,
> Or where he goes to but on he goes.

Rosemary little knew that that one day her wish would come true; she married
Sonnie, a *techino Romani chail* (a Gypsy man).

Rosemary:

> I experienced with him the life I'd dreamed of, together with the hatred,
> rejection and false accusations that are so much part of his heritage. Today
> we live in a little house not far from the Gypsy stone in Epping Forest,
> which is the memorial to Rodney Smith MBE, the well-known evangelist,
> Sonnie's grandfather.
>
> We began to work with Gypsies For Christ, an interdenominational mission,
> about ten years ago and soon realised that we would need to have our own
> marquee and other equipment. So, our personal response to the Decade of
> Evangelism was to buy a caravan and put the Romani Gospel Wagon on the
> road. In October 1993 we were approached by GFC and asked to take over
> that organisation and now we have Gypsies For Christ travelling with the
> Romani Gospel Wagon, seeking to serve the Lord at home and abroad by going
> out to the highways and hedges to bring the people in as Jesus told us to do.
>
> In 1994 we joined forces with the Scripture Gift Mission to produce a book-
> let in Anglo-Romanese entitled *The Drom* (*The Way*) which is the story of the
> prodigal son. We have been able to distribute this booklet at a mission in East

London and at Priddy Fair in Somerset. It has been very popular and we hope it will create interest among the Gypsies in preserving their own language.

Kushti lavs
Good news
Mo-Duvvel kers us kushti. Mo-Duvvel koms to ker sor foki kushti. Mo Duvvel koms sor foki to av to jin the tatchipen.
Timothy 2:3–4 God our Saviour…wants all men to be saved and to come to a knowledge of the truth.
Mo-Duvvel kommed foki so much that he delled his kokkero yek chavvi. He delled lesti so that sor foci, that pen lesti's the tatchipen, shall never be mullered but jiv forever.
John 3:16 God so loved the world that he gave his one and only Son, that whoever believes in him shall not perish but have eternal life.

From *The Drom* (*The Way*),produced by Gypsies for Christ and
the Scripture Gift Mission, 1994

As a result of her work with Gypsies in this country and abroad, Rosemary is well placed to state that to make a friend of a Gypsy is to have a friend for life.

The Light and Life Mission sprang up in the Gypsy community twenty years ago. In July 2006 Emma John wrote in *Christianity* magazine:

French Travellers had brought the gospel over to their British counterparts and thought their message had fallen on deaf ears. But one man, Davy Jones, was inspired to preach to his own people. He took the word out to sites all over the British Isles.

Gypsy pastor Tom Wilson of Leatherhead has seen lives changed:

You know salvation is real when you see a woman who earns £5000 say she's not going to tell fortunes any more. [And] Gypsies and policemen are absolute enemies. My brother hated them. And the first person that God put beside him when he got saved in church was a policeman.

There are tensions between the Light and Life Mission and other churches – the mission is revival based, taking a strong literal line on the Bible, and this can fit very well with that part of the Gypsy community which remains rooted in traditional roles for men and women. Emma John writes: 'Needless to say, women may not preach in the Gypsy church, as they are not considered to have any authority over men.'

There is, however, a problem for those many Gypsies with a background in Catholicism as, 'The Gypsy church teaches a complete rejection of Catholicism and is uncompromising in its stance.'

These tensions are not present at The Church at Gun Hill, an Elim Pentecostal fellowship in Essex. The leadership team received a prophecy that they would minister to Travellers and Gypsies. Their first meeting was inauspicious as the Gypsy men, on seeing the outreach team approaching, jumped in their cars and drove off! Since then, relationships have flourished, as has understanding and integration between the two cultures.

Gypsy missions have visited the West Country several times in recent years – the most recent, in 2006 in Exeter, attracting many people.

Anna:

> There's a mission coming to Exeter and that will open your eyes! None of those people, lady, can read or write. Me daughter's got tapes there with the Gypsy men singing, and the women, and you wouldn't tell 'em from film stars. And they made the songs up themselves. Although yiz is like outsiders, I'll be honest with you, they'll open their hearts and they'll give you the best of welcomes. There's hundreds there and they'll take care of you. To see how many Gypsy people is there, and how calm they all are…

Although many positive comments were made about the missions, we also heard concerns that a competitive element was creeping in and the occasions are being used to flaunt wealth and possessions: 'Some of 'em just want to show off their Shoguns and new trailers.'

Many churches in the UK are alive to the needs of Travellers in their midst. Anna's local vicar visited her when she was ill.

Anna:

> Round here they call me the little Romany Girl and everyone knows me as that. The old parson come – I didn't know him. Come from up the village – he's heard about me. I wasn't very well. He said, 'I've heard about you, little Romany girl,' he said, 'and I had to come and see you immediately.' He prayed on me, God bless him. We had tea and we talked and when he sees me he says, 'We're proud in our little village of our little Romany Girl.'

Fear of the Devil is very real for some Gypsies. Maggie recounted a favourite tale told around the campfire, where there's plenty of warmth and reassuring company!

Maggie:

There was a woman up at Eatford Corner. I think she's dead now. All they had was a rod tent. They was leaving Newton Abbot to go up across the moors. She set the tent. Her man had gone to the pub after helping her put the tent up. She put the kids into the tent. It was in the gateway so they know'd they had to be up early the next morning because of blocking the farmer's gateway. But it was the safest place to be at that particular time. It come on and got to really late at night. She was sitting round the fire – kids asleep in the tent – waiting for the man to come from the pub. Anyway, up the road come the pig. She thought the pig would go on up the road. Well, he didn't. He wanted to go through the gate but to go through the gate he'd have to go through the tent and there was no way she was going to let him go through that tent with her kids sleeping in it. So she striped him with the kettle iron – solid steel with a crook on the end to hang your pots. She bin and striped the pig to drive him off. Well, the more she striped the pig, the more determined the pig was to go through, and he went through. Straight through the tent – ripped the back of the tent out – straight through the gate. The pig must be beat to death, bruised, half dead by what she done to him.

Because people had gone by and seen them in this gateway, she waited till the farmer came up before they shifted away, even though they'd packed up. She told the farmer, 'I'm ever so sorry, but I had to beat your pig last night. He ain't gonna be no good for bacon. He must be mortified – black and blue.'

'Well,' he said, 'It weren't my pig you beat, missus. That was the Devil.' And they reckoned she beat the Devil, but the Devil was in the form of a pig.

Religion may provide the backdrop for the lives of many of the contributors to this book, but certain superstitions are well in the forefront. Some creatures are viewed with such fear and distrust that their names are never mentioned.

Maggie:

We never ever say the word… It's bigger than a mouse, it's as big as a mole and it's got a long tail so we refer to it as the long-tail. And the things that climb the trees. If you'd mentioned that when you came in yer this morning I'd have said, 'It's no good! The day's gone! It's over!'

Me dad, when we had the wireless set, they'd come out with these words and he wouldn't go out all day. 'I ain't going out. It's worthless. Waste of time.' And he'd set home, making his pegs or sorting his rags. He wouldn't go.

The Crown Derby firm made a Crown Derby wagon and they were £475 each! But because it's Crown Derby and because it's a wagon we all wanted one. It wasn't until the first fifty of us bought these wagons and looked closely at them, we realised he'd put a long-tail on it! So the wagons are still in their boxes. I'll show it to you, but it will never go on display. So we went down to the shop to complain, down in Devon, and the man was there that done these wagons. I took me wagon back and he signed it for me with me name on it.

'I can't understand your people. I thought they'd go for them,' he said.

I said, 'Well, they would have done, but you made the biggest mistake you ever made when you painted them.' I showed him mine.

He said, 'Well, it could be a mouse!'

I said, 'It's not a mouse. The next one you make, come up to me.' He was making a barrel top. He spent two days here. I pulled me barrel top out and let him sketch and draw it and I said, 'You don't put this and you don't put that.' I gave him a list of what he couldn't do on this wagon because it wouldn't sell!

They won't even own it.

Diana, like many Gypsies, has a beautiful collection of Crown Derby. She also recalled some misbegotten wagons.

Diana:

They made wagons with bangtails on. Nobody'd buy them. That's one thing a Traveller hates – a bangtail. They won't say the word. They're bad luck. Remember the story of the Black Death in London. If the Travellers were getting ready in the morning to go out calling, years back, if anybody said that word, that's it. They wouldn't go out. They'd stay home.

Dorothy:

We don't say certain things…something in the grass. We says a rabbit, but not the other thing that goes into a hole. Long-tails. We don't say that – it's very unlucky. The children say it at school. But not at home. If we see a white rabbit in the dark, that's very unlucky. A black cat is lucky, or a white horse. Two magpies is very, very lucky. If you sees two magpies, you say, 'Lucky day!' Then you're bound to have a lucky day. If you was going down trying to look for work and you seen two magpies you're guaranteed to find a bit of work. If you sees one, you say, 'Aye, aye, Captain!' Some people would just go home if they seen just one magpie.

Robert:

One of the unlucky words we weren't allowed to say – we were told it was unlucky to say – was 'M O N K E Y'. We were told to say 'tatu'. I'm not superstitious but it was handed down – like long-tail. Travellers don't say 'R A T'. As children we weren't allowed to say that. It'd bring bad luck. They'd say, 'I'm not going out calling today!' One mention of it, 'I'm not going out doing anything today!' They're a superstitious lot!

Some Gypsies are uneasy about sharing their beliefs with outsiders, whilst acknowledging, perhaps reluctantly, that old secrets are being revealed, and access to information knows no boundaries. An anonymous review of Patrick Jasper Lee's 2000 book, *We Borrow the Earth – An Intimate Portrait of the Gypsy Shamanic Tradition and Culture*, makes this clear.

Robert:

I am a British-born Romany. It is incredibly rare to find a mainstream-published book about Romany life written by a Romany. I am not convinced of the wisdom of sharing such a large portion of a way of life that has been private for centuries with the *gauje* world. But that reservation aside, if anyone is going to write about us, it may as well be a real Rom rather than one from another race who will twist and misunderstand where we come from, our traditions and our way of life. For that reason, I recommend this book. If you want to know about us – ask US, don't listen to wannabes who think they know and know nothing. For this reason, this book is a good purchase… Romany on Romany.

The feelings about the birds and animals of ill omen are deeply felt. When teaching their Gypsy pupils to read, some teachers discover an apparently inexplicable resistance to certain stories featuring these creatures.

On the other hand, it is believed that some birds and animals bring good fortune. The wagtail is known as the Gypsy bird, and is the emblem of the Gypsy Lore Society. Their motto, in Welsh Romani is '*Oke Romano Chiriklo Dikasa E Kalen*', meaning 'Behold A Wagtail… And You Shall See The Gypsies'.

Diana:

> When they used to go out calling the old Gypsies would always like to see a yellowhammer – a little yellow bird. They'd spit on their palm and rub their hands together. They'd always have a good day. Always take a bit of money.

Welsh Gypsies believed that the yellowhammer might cure jaundice if caught and held in front of the face of the sufferer. Although some people, like Diana, regard the little bird, a member of the bunting family, as very lucky, and Scots believe you should never harm one or you will lose your voice, there was once a belief among non-Gypsies that it was the devil's bird. As a result of this, the yellowhammer, like the toad, was often subjected to great cruelty outside the Gypsy community.

Scottish writer John Bearcat Redmond tells of the superstitions he has encountered during his travels:

> Gypsies told me that if you wear a Badger's tooth around your neck you will be lucky in whatever you place wagers on… Some of the European Gypsies told me that if you have a chicken that lays an even number of eggs it's better to take one away so that the rest will all lay, if not there is an omen to stop the rest of the chickens laying. They also stated that if a cockerel is born from the eggs, that brings good fortune to the owner and their family… The Irish Gypsies believe if you kill a robin, a large lump will grow on your right hand and cause you lots of discomfort.
>
> From '*Superstitions of Nature*' at
> www.electricscotland.com/poetry/redmond6.htm

People generally have a wealth of superstitions regarding bad luck, and Travellers in the South West are no exception. It is considered unlucky to see someone cross-eyed or with a clubbed foot. Weasels crossing the road in front of you are unlucky. It is bad luck to see a crow alone in a field – best to go home! If you've forgotten something, carry on without it as it is unlucky to turn back, and looking back at a funeral procession means there will be another funeral soon. Because of the Crucifixion, Fridays are considered unlucky; no-one would move camp on a Friday. It is unlucky to wash blankets in May as you will wash someone out of the family.

Robert:

We had one relation, if he went out and seen a cross-eyed man or women when he was on the way to work, going calling, he'd go home. It's tribal – different sections of the tribe – there are variations in the superstitions and the way of life.

Dorothy:

If you go somewhere and your eye has an itch, you know something's wrong.
If your hand itches, spit on it and it's one to pay out and one to receive.

Portents of death and illness abound. Owls are messengers of death, and any bird pecking on the window means death will follow. Lilies are never taken indoors as they represent death. Putting a comb on a table means sickness will follow, and mixed-colour flowers in the home can mean someone is going to hospital.

On a less pessimistic note, if a bumblebee enters your home it means that a stranger will visit you, and if the soles of your feet itch this means that you are going to walk on strange ground.

Like a lot of people, Gypsies and non-Gypsies alike, Rodney doesn't really hold

Youngsters were taught to help with the chores from an early age; this girl is doing the washing.

with superstitions…oh, except for just one or two!

Rodney:

> Personally, I don't take any notice of superstitions. But if I see one magpie on its own I'll salute the magpie. I don't say nothing. Wherever I'm to, I've got to salute the magpie. There's black cats and white cats – but I always got mixed up! I thought black cats were lucky when they crossed the road, but a lot of people think it's bad luck. I saw a white cat cross the road not long ago – nothing really happened so I don't know what to think of that one!
>
> You don't wash your tea towels in with your ordinary washing. A lot of them put a pot on the stove and tea towels are separate from clothes. You don't wash with soap on a Good Friday – better have a good wash beforehand!
>
> My belief is if you harm animals on purpose, not accidentally, that is bad luck. To me, that is truly bad luck. That's my own belief – and a few others. I always used to think there's something about lucky heather – I bought some off a Traveller and she didn't even drop the price! Burning bread – that's bad luck. Burning food – what a waste. People starving in the world – burning food has got to be bad luck.

It is very tempting to look on any group of people as having more in common than is actually the case. To suggest that all Gypsies believe certain things is unrealistic. Human beings have long been rebels. Amy rebelled against the Gypsy practice of keeping to certain family names.

Amy:

> When it came to my time – times they are a-changing – we didn't choose the old-fashioned names. I wish we did now, but at the time, 'I'm going to call my child something out of a song!' Which I did. 'Carrie-Ann' by The Hollies. I was determined to change traditions.

When *gadjes* in schools or social services or other agencies first meet Gypsy families, they are often given daunting lists of taboos to help them understand Romani culture. Some Gypsies laugh out loud at some of these pronouncements; others keep their own counsel. The winds of change affect us all – Gypsy and non-Gypsy – but in the past, when tribal rules were stricter and secrets guarded more fiercely, the taboos were observed by many Gypsies and there is an understandable reluctance to discuss these matters with outsiders. Many older Gypsies, especially those born in Europe, would know of *Marimé* – a state of impurity brought on a person by the violation of a purity taboo. *Marimé* also means a sentence of expulsion imposed for violation of purity rules or any behaviour disruptive to the Roma community.

As in other cultures, there have been, and in some places, there still are, strict rules about what is considered clean and unclean. Menstruation, sex and childbirth are not easily discussed.

Maggie:

I know years ago when the woman was in that condition she was classed as unclean and if anything got on her clothes they was shunned by the rest of the family. Anything to do with sex was hidden so much then and today, yeah, it still is. Actually I think it's good. I really don't like our children having sex education in schools because I don't think we get as many unwanted pregnancies as many other ethnic groups get, and if they do they're made to marry as soon as that is found out.

Anything to do with the body – I don't think we ever learned anything. Even when I was fourteen I didn't know me mam was pregnant until she started showing. We weren't told. It was secret. But we didn't have girls getting pregnant like we have today. We didn't have all these unwanted kids. We thought kissing and touching you could have a baby. That saved you from getting into any trouble. You didn't know sex existed. I married my man when I was twenty-one and I was ignorant as pig shit. We didn't know anything about the body. Nobody told you. Even today the mothers and fathers won't allow the kids to have sex education in schools. I think it's brilliant. Otherwise the kids are made grown-ups before they've even been children. We used to play. You had your play years. Now you see them – ten and eleven years old – high heels and make-up, skirts up to their ass – running after the men. And the men running after them.

Anna:

We don't talk about private things in front of our men. That's dirty. I didn't know anything when I got married. I was just a girl of sixteen. I thought it would be like sleeping with my brothers. I was frit, lady.

Nowadays, although it is commonplace amongst non-Traveller families for fathers to have an active role in the delivery room, both Anna and Maggie were clear that no Gypsy man would want to be present during childbirth.

Maggie:

The women wouldn't allow it and the men wouldn't want it either because that is such a secret, hidden thing.

Most of the women when we was travelling had their children in wagons. I was born in a wagon, but the men would drive away when it was happening. When it was happening you wouldn't find a man on the pea field; they would just all disappear, but all the women would be congregating round the wagon.

The children would have somebody there to look after them. No matter what was happening, a death or a birth or whatever, there would always be someone there who would take care of the children. They would put a couple of girls, eighteen, nineteen, on to it. 'Look after them, don't let them come and interfere.' And we'd be took for walks to the other end of the field or whatever, but we knew nothing, absolutely nothing about the birth. We weren't allowed to know anything because that would corrupt us.

Anna was very concerned, out of respect for her parents, that anything relating to sexual activity was kept from them. The wagons of newlyweds were moved away from the main group partly for privacy, but partly to avoid embarrassing the older generation.

Anna:

> When I was 'avin' a baby, I'd used to try to 'old me breath, to make me belly look smaller, in front of me dad, or I'd always sit like this, or I'd turn me back to 'im, because me dad would know I'd been doing bad things... we're very private people like that.

Today, many Gypsy parents remain opposed to sex education in schools and several people said that they received little or no information at home.

Anna:

> Me granny would say to me mam, 'Little pigs's got big ears' – that meant we was chucked outside, then me dear old granny would probably have the midwife...
>
> There were only two years between each of us. Me granny would say, 'Oh look – you've got a new brother or a new sister. Look what the stork brought. Or we found this under the bush...'. Honestly, we looked everywhere for babies, and in ditches. We used to say, 'Well, whereabouts? Show us where.' And me granny would take us to the 'edge and say, 'Now there, can you see that mark? (Probably where she'd ripped a bit of bush out of the 'edge.) And I'd say, 'Yes, yes I can...'. You see, we never questioned that... we didn't know anyway from anywhere else: there weren't no TVs.
>
> When I was married...and when I went in the 'ospital, to have my first baby, I couldn't believe it. And that was the nurse that told me. And I said, 'You must be mad.' And they thought they 'ad a mad woman in the 'ospital.

Fortunately, Anna's other deliveries were less traumatic – after a protracted first labour she went to the hospital as late as she possibly could for her other babies.

Anna:

> I can remember when my Kathleen was about to be borned. It was the last minute: they couldn't believe I was smiling. I'd always know when me babies was going to be borned, because I'd be cleaning all the time. I cleant and I swupt, and I cleant and I swupt! I was cleaning the trailer roof, in the middle of the night, at 12 o'clock, and it was already clean, but I 'ad to occupy myself with summat.

Despite Anna's traditional upbringing, and reticence about sexual matters, she has made sure that her daughters are better prepared for childbirth than she was.

Anna:

> I told my girls and they will tell their girls. No one should go through what I did. When I had my first baby I thought I would be cut open. We don't put our girls on the pill, though. It might encourage them.

Anna, like so many people nowadays, can see that change is necessary, but progress is a double-edged sword and change is not always for the better.

Many of us, Gypsies and non-Gypsies alike, remember a time, not so long ago, when families, especially those in rural areas, lived their lives within a framework of religion, rules, superstition and duty. Sometimes the framework offered support; sometimes it was restrictive. There are gains and losses as that structure is examined and dismantled. Old beliefs continue to hold some people in thrall; new articles of faith arise to define societies. Whatever was said to us about organised religion, taboos and the power of superstition, most contributors to this book tended, like Rodney, to profess a quiet faith and treat belief as a private matter.

Rodney:

> I don't go to church – only christenings and stuff like that – but I am a believer that it all had to start somewhere. There's definitely something out there.
>
> I believe in that. If something goes wrong I say my own prayer underneath a tree out in the open. If you know you've done a lot of bad things you're not going to get your prayers answered, are you? There might be a chance if you're good enough – not pure down the line – but if you treat people halfway sensible, at the end of the day you'll feel better for it anyway. Treat people like you want to be treated yourself.

HERBS AND HEALING

Herbs and things did come into it. I probably drank from my granny something for colds. I can't remember being ill.

Robert

'Take 'un to the rider of a piebald horse for a cure.' Before the First World War, villagers in Somerset's Quantock Hills knew where to go for help with their child's 'Hoppy Cough'. Maybe they'd already tried putting a fried mouse in the patient's shoes, or passed the invalid over the back of a donkey and under its belly, before turning to the Gypsies, who sometimes used mandrake root to cure whooping cough.

Somerset folklorist Ruth Tongue (1898–1981) had a deep respect for the wisdom of Gypsy healers such as the Hawkridge Gypsy she met at Norton Fitzwarren, who told her to rub insect bites with the rough side of elder leaves to draw away the sting, then cover with the smooth side to encourage healing.

Sufferers of 'Brown Kitties' (bronchitis) were advised to drink elderberry syrup before going to bed, and many other illnesses were, and are, treated by the fruits of this wonderful tree, regarded as 'the healingest tree that on the earth do grow' by an unnamed old Gypsy woman (referred to here as Eliza) who shared her secrets with herbalist and writer Mary Thorne Quelch. 'They flowers and they leaves be terrible good for the scorbutics' (ailments related to scurvy). Her recipe for elderberry juice, mixed with equal parts of crab apples and blackberry juice, boiled up with sugar, makes an effective syrup for coughs and colds.

Elder flowers dried in the sun can be stored away until needed to stave off winter colds, then mixed with boiling water and a lump of sugar, making a soothing hot drink. The same mixture, left to cool, could be given to 'some poor soul as has got fever, and it will end their thirst'. The same infusion has also been recommended to soothe the nerves, induce sleep and reduce hysteria.

Many Gypsies believe that water from a spring rising under an elder bush has special healing powers.

When I was a young girl, I took a lady to one of them healing springs and us dipped it up in cans and bottles for her to carry away to send to her brother in London when that there awful eye complaint were running round the town. As we dipped it up I ses, 'God bless the water for his poor eyes.'

'Eliza', as quoted in *Herbs for Daily Use* by Mary Thorne Quelch

We were told that the elder is still very important to Gypsies.

Maggie:

Not only can the beautiful wooden flowers be made from it, but medicines as well. The flowers is picked and dried in the sun when in their prime, and used to hang round the necks of children with coughs and colds in winter. Some of the flowers is picked when in bud, put in a pot together with dry ginger, rosehips and sugar and simmered for an hour very slowly, then strained through a muslin cloth and put in bottles to be kept again fer the cold months. It's very good medicine for whooping cough or any persistent bad chest coughs. The berries is also used in cough mixture, and as a dye, to dye cloth, and we use it to dye flowers.

Maggie and Robert's granny played an important part in keeping the children healthy.

Robert:

Herbs and things did come into it. I probably drank from my granny something for colds. I can't remember being ill. The only broken arm I had was when we first got a car. We were pushing it and the wheel went over my arm and I had to go to hospital. I was too young to remember the pain.

Maggie also talks of her grandmother's final illness.

Maggie:

Me mam's mam used to lie in the rod tent because she was swelled up so much. The doctors couldn't do nothing for her. They didn't even know what it was. The women would bathe her in elder blossom and she'd be drinking herbs.

The medicinal use of the elderberry dates to the fifth century BC and was written about by Hippocrates, Dioscorides and Pliny. Country dwellers have long noticed that diseased sheep would eat freely of elder leaves and buds, and often were completely cured. The most interesting use of the fruit is in its application against influenza and recent research based in Israel has indicated that the herb has compelling antiviral properties. Elderberry juice was used to treat a flu epidemic in Panama in 1995.

Lisa remembers that her dad favoured old-fashioned, natural remedies for flu, bronchitis and asthma.

Lisa:

Dad always believed in getting a lemon, an orange, a little drop of cider, boil it in a saucepan, put it into a jug, let it cool down. It does work. If your chest is too bad, get a little bit of brown paper, warm it up, put a little bit of Vicks on and it helps you breathe.

Seventy years ago a Gypsy living on Exmoor told Ruth Tongue that another remedy for bronchitis was to smoke dried coltsfoot and bramble leaves. It may well have been the same healer who told her that a corn or a wart could be removed by applying juice from the greater celandine.

We were intrigued, if somewhat perturbed, to hear Dorothy's account of curing a wart!

Dorothy:

Rub the wart with a slug, then stick the slug on a thorn bush until a bird comes out and flies away with the slug. Then the wart will go away too.

Those Gypsies who lived on the Quantock Hills were known as Quantock Broom Squires, and one of them advised Ruth Tongue to lay the bruised leaves of marsh mallow on her sore, strained eyes. She wrote, 'I found that very satisfactory.' There were other uses for marsh mallow, famed for bringing good fortune and known as the 'mortification root' because of its capacity for cleansing and healing.

Perhaps you know as they're the best cure out for a woman's bad legs, or for any legs as is bad if you comes to that. You bathe they places with warm water in which you've soaked the leaves, or you poultice them with the crushed roots or leaves. And when they sores starts to heal you uses an ointment made out of the roots. And the leaves made hot in a drop of water and tied against your cheek with a handkerchief be good for a toothache.

'Eliza', as quoted in *Herbs for Daily Use* by Mary Thorne Quelch

A Gypsy from Langley Marsh, near Wiveliscombe, said that the juice of two juniper berries in hot water would cure 'interjections' [indigestion] and that, 'Gold rings on every finger will cure the falling sickness' [epilepsy] – which sounds better than a South Somerset cure from the nineteenth century which involved cutting the front paws off a live toad and hanging them on a red thread round the neck. Somerset country people in general had a wide range of gruesome remedies for 'information' [inflammation!] including a hot fomentation of stewed slugs, or wrapping the patient's feet in the warm corpse of a newly killed lamb. It was an Exmoor Gypsy who told Ruth Tongue that a decoction of sliced roots of heath milkwort would do just as well, if not better.

For those plagued with 'screwmatics' (rheumatism), Brendon Hills Gypsies prescribed a wineglass a day of an infusion of Traveller's Joy leaves. Another Romani remedy for rheumatism was wearing a small bag of burdock seeds round the neck, and the belief that a raw potato or two about the person was a preventative (perhaps because of the appreciably high levels of sulphur) led to petticoats with special potato pockets being worn in Georgian times.

Dorset Gypsies used to combine bramble tops and broom tops 'for all kinds of kidney complaints that ever be a-going. It will heal those what's pretty far gone, too.'

Broom was also recommended for sufferers from jaundice – a kinder remedy than the cattle-lice sandwich enthusiastically administered by a Triscombe quarryman sixty years ago. 'Afterwards, tell him what he ate. He may be sick, but he'll never have jaundice.' Perhaps, more accurately, he would never risk complaining about jaundice again! Going through life traumatised by bread must have proved inconvenient.

Many people know that linseed tea is invaluable when treating a cough. It is also a gentle laxative. Linseed, lemon and boiling water combine to make a cheap and effective remedy. Linseed can also be boiled with ginger and liquorice root, with blackcurrant jam, lemon and sugar added to taste. Eliza spoke of another use altogether, believed to have been of great benefit to Queen Caroline, the wife of George III.

> Them poor mothers what has a cruel bad time when their babies comes into the world needn't go through half nor yet a quarter what them does if only them 'ud drink linseed tea all through the nine months. It softens the bones and takes all stiffness away so that the baby can be born easy.
>
> 'Eliza', as quoted in *Herbs for Daily Use* by Mary Thorne Quelch

Modern-day sufferers from depression have been discovering the virtues of the plant known to Gypsies and other country dwellers as 'Blessed' or 'God's Wonder Herb'. The properties of St John's Wort seem little short of miraculous and Tutsan, a close relative of the herb, possesses the same qualities and is known to some as Heal-all.

> Do you see them clear dots on the leaves? And them there black dots on the underside of the flowers? Well, there be healing, soothing oil in them there spots and more in the leaves theyselves. And if you carry a leaf or two, an ill-wisher will have no power over you.
>
> 'Eliza', as quoted in *Herbs for Daily Use* by Mary Thorne Quelch

St John's Wort, which traditionally flowers on the day of the summer solstice, has been recommended for melancholy, mental delusions, bedwetting, chronic catarrh, wound healing (especially wounds made with a poisoned weapon), promoting thick, glossy hair, threadworms, strains, sprains, cuts and burns.

One old Romani remedy for severe headaches is to rub the head vigorously, then wash it with vinegar and warm water while repeating this charm:

> Pain in my head,
> Go to the Devil your father.
> You have hurt my head,
> Now go away from me,
> Home to the Devil.
> Go to the Evil One.
> Whoever treads on my shadow,
> Let him have the pain.

Legendary Gypsy resourcefulness and acute powers of observation ensure that max-
imum value is extracted from everyday things that others might take for granted.
According to a traditional Gypsy remedy for hay fever, fresh mint should be picked
everyday and placed in a muslin bag. The patient should sleep with the bag by their
pillow and in two to three weeks, their symptoms should disappear. Then there is
logic, as in prescribing beetroot juice as a blood-builder, for patients who were pale
and run down. However, it is a foolish man who follows the contraceptive advice
mentioned in Charles Elliot's *Rash Encounters*. The man is supposed to line his socks
with nettle leaves and wear them for twenty-four hours before engaging in sex.

The names of Gypsy healers are very rarely known to outsiders. The discovery
of digitalis is accredited to the Scottish doctor William Withering, but it was a
Shropshire Gypsy woman who gave him his knowledge. At the age of forty-six he
was the richest doctor outside of London, having bought Edgbaston Hall in
Birmingham. As evidence of his affluence, Dr Withering owned the first water
closet in Birmingham.

In 1775, one of his patients came to him with a very bad heart condition.
Withering had no effective treatment for him and feared that he was going to die.
The patient didn't much care for this prognosis and went instead to a local Gypsy
and, after taking her secret herbal remedy, he got much better. On hearing this good
news, Withering searched for the Gypsy throughout the lanes of Shropshire and
eventually found her, determined to know what was in the secret remedy. After
much bargaining, the Gypsy finally told her secret. The remedy was a concoction of
many herbs, but the active ingredient was the purple foxglove, *Digitalis purpurea*.
Digitalis extract had been used as a poison for the medieval 'trial by ordeal' (a judi-
cial practice by which the guilt or innocence of the accused was determined by
forcing them to undertake a painful task), and also used as an external application
to promote the healing of wounds.

Another unsung Romani healer enabled the world to enjoy the wonderful playing
of Gypsy guitarist Django Reinhardt. Django was born in a caravan in Belgium on
28 January 1910. His family travelled all over France, stopping on the outskirts of
Paris over the winter. At the age of twelve, he got his first banjo and two years later
he was playing professionally and was hugely popular. In November 1928, when he
was just eighteen, his caravan caught fire. Django and his wife were very poor, and
she made artificial flowers from a highly inflammable celluloid. The caravan was full
of the flowers. Django thought he heard a mouse, and investigated, using the light
of a candle. Hot wax fell onto the flowers. In the terrible fire that followed, one of
his legs and his left hand were badly burned. He was immediately sent to a hospital
with appalling injuries. The surgeon intended to amputate his leg, to prevent blood
poisoning, but his mother refused to give permission, trusting instead in the skills
of her own people. It took Django Reinhardt almost two years to recover, but a
Gypsy healer saved both limbs, except for the use of the two smaller fingers of his
left hand. In 1931, local bandleader Louis Vola took Reinhardt under his wing, and
two years later, they were both playing in the smartest clubs in Paris. The following

year, Django Reinhardt rose to international fame with the Hot Club of France String Quintet, revealed as a uniquely gifted guitarist.

Unlike Dr Withering's anonymous informant and Django Reinhardt's unsung saviour, Cornish Gypsy, Granny Boswell (1813–1906) was famous for her fortune telling and well respected around Helston for her wisdom and knowledge of charms. Ann Boswell came to England from Ireland in around 1846 and is buried in Tregerest Cemetery with her husband Ephraim Boswell, 'King of the Gypsies'. It is said she could cure scrofula (tuberculosis) by the aid of a small bag full of black spiders (quite how this worked is not clear), help young women find lovers, cure ringworm in cattle and break curses. She came from a long line of 'cunning folk' – professional or semi-professional folk-magic users.

Other names for cunning folk include wizards, wise men, wise women, doctors, conjurers and white witches. Cunning folk were frequently confused with witches. One commentator says:

> The key difference between the two is that cunning folk were real, whereas there is
> no evidence that witches existed outside the imagination of those who believed they
> had been afflicted by them. The magic of the cunning folk was preventative and cur-
> ative and so did not require visible magical phenomena to occur for people to believe
> in it, while that of the alleged witches was clearly absurd (such as turning into a hare
> or flying through the air) and so was presumed to occur while nobody was looking.
>
> Anonymous writer found on www.wikipedia.org, 30 May 2004

CAMPFIRE COOKING

We don't believe in junk food. We do like good food – taters, swede, bacon, sausages. Or do a nice pot of broth – you call it a stew. With a bit of crusty bread and butter, that's a nice meal… It was a better, healthier life. You do a piece of toast on the fire; it tastes a lot better than what it do in a toaster. It's cooked proper. Now it's all frozen food. I was ten when I learned to cook over a fire.

Lisa

All over the world, Gypsy cooks show a characteristic resourcefulness, using fresh, local produce, and adopting local dishes in a way that has led some people to question whether there is a Gypsy cuisine. An Internet search yields many Gypsy-style recipes, including a passionate love song to a cup of Chai! Chai is a spicy blend of Indian aromatics, Chinese tonic herbs and fine teas, designed to warm the body from the inside out.

Waiting for the kettle to boil. The kettle is hanging from a kharvisaster *(kettle-iron).*

The first taste of you washes my heart with gold,

waxes my moon,

brings me to the depths of primordial bliss.

The second sip binds my eternal soul slave to your divine kiss.

With the third I am set free,

climbing toward heaven as a morning glory embracing a tree.

A fourth sip brings me to the brink,

my heart full of joy into your eyes I sink.

Used by kind permission of Calico of Mr Spot's Chai House, Seattle

Older Gypsies in the south west of England are almost as passionate when they remember the delicious meals their mothers and grandmothers cooked over the open fire.

Diana:

My mother was a brilliant cook. She used to make old-fashioned puddings – meat puddings and currant puddings. They used to be brilliant. She'd make the bestest pot of soup you could ever taste. All sorts went in it – mutton, bits of steak, stuff like that. She'd roll her own pastry for the meat puddings. All done outside. You know like they do a jacket potato now in an oven? She'd always do hers underneath the ashes – build the ashes up and push them under the ashes. They were brilliant. Used to always fry rabbit – it tastes better. Not let them bide too long. Tastes like chicken – the white part on a chicken. That's what they taste like. I still cook eggs and bacon on an open fire. Tastes better.

The men are making pegs while the women prepare a meal.

Anna agrees that food cooked over an open fire tastes extra good. Her granny always made her own jam and bread, and custard cakes on an open fire and taught Anna that ash is the best wood for cooking over as it doesn't smoke.

Anna:

> Don't 'ave the green wood. Just 'ave the dead wood. Me granny could go in an 'edge, and I could go in an 'edge, and you wouldn't know we'd been there, so we ain't killin' the good 'edge… Really we're cleaning the 'edge, like you clean a tree, 'cos you never damage what's going to feed yer or what's going to warm yer.

As a child, Anna's favourite foods included breast of mutton, cooked on a stick over the fire, freshly caught trout, sausages, lamb kidneys, black pudding, flat chips (called Gypsy chips) and stew. Her mother's hare broth with dumplings made from the finest suet and plenty of salt and pepper, was mouthwatering.

Anna's mother, Harriet Price, was very resourceful when it came to feeding her family, and her father, Fred Smith, was renowned for curing bacon.

Anna:

> Me mam would beg – scraps from the butcher, that 'e'd throw away. 'Do you 'ave this and that?' A bit of stew, boilin' chicken – she always got good food. Before we 'ad fridges, me dad would cure bacon – put muslin around it to preserve it.

Girls were expected to cook for their (often) large families from an early age, and were taught to make nutritious meals, often with ingredients brought back by the men.

One man and his dog cooking on an open fire.

Maggie:

When I was nine I could cook for nine. That was how they trained us up.

Lisa:

We don't believe in junk food. We do like good food – taters, swede, bacon, sausages. Or do a nice pot of broth – you call it a stew. With a bit of crusty bread and butter, that's a nice meal. Years ago, with the rod tent, they'd cook outside – which was better. More tastier.

It was a better, healthier life. You do a piece of toast on the fire; it tastes a lot better than what it do in a toaster. It's cooked proper. Now it's all frozen food. I was ten when I learned to cook over a fire.

Anna:

Supermarket food 'as no taste. What they call organic is only what we always 'ad years ago…

When a Somerset Gypsy pupil was preparing for her food technology GCSE exam recently, her family were vastly amused by the thirty pages she was expected to produce on the subject of macaroni cheese. Nella, who could cook dinner for her whole family while still in Primary School, was characteristically succinct: 'My dad won't eat that slop, Miss.'

Nella's brother also found the demands of secondary education a trial. He much preferred to be out in the open air with his dog, rabbiting. Traditionally, rabbit was enjoyed by many families, but myxomatosis has all but put paid to that.

Nella:

I liked cooking outdoors, 'specially bacon puddings. And Christmas puddings, with stout and sherry. Bacon puddings? Pastry, bacon, onion, doughboys – all

The hedgerows were a source of income for travelling families as they would carve flowers and pegs from the elder that grew there.

*Jukkles (dogs) are
important to the Gypsy
life for* shussyin', *but are
usually not allowed inside
the wagons.*

kinds of filling. It tasted better outdoors. People coming down the road would smell the bacon pudding – mmmm! And we 'ad rabbit stew – roast or in a casserole. My uncle used to go out with his ferrets and Jack Russell. Came back with a lovely lot of the rabbits. There was a little oven in the caravan. Wouldn't eat it now.

During the Second World War it wasn't just Gypsies who cooked rabbit; house dwellers appreciated the hunting skills of Gypsy men and boys, relying on them for a supply of much-needed protein. The men and boys trained their dogs to catch rabbits – the dogs were highly skilled and valued accordingly. Small dogs were faster – better for bending and turning.

Anna:

We 'ad an old dog called Spring. We never 'ad a dog that was called Useless. We 'ad a dog that would always fill our bellies. That dog was looked after good.

Anna always knew when her brother was going out rabbiting – he would put on his big coat with large pockets to hold the rabbits.

The other meat historically associated with Gypsies is that of the hedgehog. The most common method for cooking hedgehog is to roll it in clay, bake it in a fire and then remove the hardened clay; the spines come away with the clay.

At one time, it was believed that eating hedgehogs would cure all sorts of illnesses, including leprosy, colic, boils, stones and poor vision. In the mid-fourteenth century, scholar and writer Konrad of Megenberg wrote:

> …the flesh of the hedgehog is wholesome for the stomach and strengthens the same. Likewise it hath a power of drying and relieving the stomach. It deals with the water of dropsy and is of great help to such as are inclined to the sickness called elephantiasis.

Some European Gypsies still eat hedgehogs as a cure for poisoning and for removing evil spells, but to Diana and Dorothy, it was just a delicious meal, usually eaten cold.

Diana:

I've had hedgehog! They'm nice. That's a red meat. That's a really dark meat. They'd always put them on a spleeder. That's a piece of wood – like a long stick. They'd do the hedgehog, stick him through the spleeder – push him up, and stick him in by the fire, so all the fat drained off. Different people do different things to get the bristles off. We used to put a stick on his back, backwards and forwards and his head'd come up. Hit him on top the head and shave him off. Lovely. Better than a bit of steak. If anybody was having one now, I'd have a go!

Dorothy:

They'd put the hedgehog in the clay and throw it in the fire. They'd always kill the hedgehog first. And they'd kill the chicken or the rabbit today, but it would still be warm so they wouldn't eat it until the next day. They'd gut 'n, pick the fur off or pluck it – hang it from a tree for three or four hours, cut 'n off, wash 'n and leave him for next day. If Travellers had chickens and that chicken died, they wouldn't eat that chicken. Throw it away or bury it. Never eat tame rabbits. I was about eight years old when me mum cooked the last rabbit but I wouldn't think about eating rabbit now because of myxomatosis.

Dorothy's family would never eat their own livestock, and perhaps unusually, their fresh eggs and milk benefited other people!

Dorothy:

We used to have a smallholding down Okehampton. Cows, calves, dogs, sheep. If a chicken got broody, we'd buy the eggs from the farm with the cockerel running with them, then put the thirteen eggs under the chickens. Always thirteen. One might die. We'd keep the little chickens in until they was two or three weeks old.

They had the mash, and if we had stale bread we'd mix it up with hot water for the old chickens on a cold morning – cluck, cluck, cluck! The farmer used to come and buy our chickens and hens off us, and we'd go into

Okehampton and buy a chicken! All cleaned and done! Never eat our own. Another thing – the chickens used to lay all the eggs – what did we used to do? Pack up the eggs – go and sell all the fresh eggs, then go in the supermarket and buy a dozen! Wouldn't eat our own eggs! All free range! We never kept no cockerels. We used to think, 'Why keep a cockerel if he don't lay eggs!' It would have been better if we did.

Me father would get a bucket, milk the old cow and let the dogs drink the milk! We used to have two pints a day delivered from a woman who had a dairy farm just over the bridge to us!

A favourite dish, referred to by almost all those involved with this book, is the speciality known as 'Joe Grey'. The origins of the name are long lost.

Anna:

The old food is coming back again. Meat pudding. Joe Grey was a bit of cheese, a bit of onion and a bit of bread in the pan and fry a bit of bacon. It was proper dinner.

Maggie:

Me mum cooked Joe Grey. Joe Grey is bacon, taters and onions cooked in gravy over the open fire. I always hated onions. You could smell that when you was down the road fetching wood or water, whatever. Half a mile away, you knew what she was cooking. You could smell the onions of her Joe Grey. Whether it was a medicine or not, we had onions nearly every meal. It was something that you had to have. None of us'll touch garlic. I'll eat raw onion but I won't eat cooked onion. I'll eat bread and cheese and onion until I look

Many older Gypsies have very happy memories of meals being cooked on an open fire, with most agreeing that the food tasted better than if it was cooked indoors.

like it. That was one of our meals — bread, cheese and onion. I won't eat cooked onion or cooked currants. Not sultanas. But onions — when I'm doing Terry's liver and onions, I'm there. I'm in a lane somewhere and the snow's coming down. I can lose myself just cooking Terry a meal. Smells meant a lot to us.

There is one traditional dish that Maggie remembers with distaste — in fact the very name of it has become an insult in her family!

Maggie:

The horses was in the middle of the field and at night our fire was always the liveliest, singing, dancing, and the cooking of the panche. God! The smell of it would drive you round the twist. The sheep's stomach. They would scrub it for hours; they would be scrubbing this thing with scrubbing brushes and then they would be put in pots and boiled but the stink that come out of that! I used to say, 'Mum, don't you even think about getting any of they panches!'

And when me dad used to be upset with anybody he used to call them 'panche mouth'. It was a way of saying that, you know, you're like a sheep's guts. 'Go and sit down, panche mouth.' He'd always come out with that phrase. 'If I was you, I'd shut up, panche mouth.' Instead of swearing at a man he could call him a sheep's guts, just using panche, because they're very cute, Gypsies, very sensitive, very good at making up nicknames and sayings. They had their own way of doing it. It was good. You don't hear it today. I sometimes say it now for a joke, and I said, 'Oh, go and sit down, panche mouth,' to me son the other day and Terry said, 'You sounded just like your dad then.' But I just like to use it because otherwise it's lost. I'd like him to take it up. I don't know that he would know what it meant, and it's not swearing, it's not dirty; it's just a funny little phrase that should be kept up.

In days gone by, no Romani woman would rely on a cookbook — in this, as so much else, the oral tradition prevailed. However, there is now a book that could be enjoyed by Gypsies and non-Gypsies alike. Carol Wilson's *Gypsy Feast: Recipes and Culinary Traditions of the Romany People* was published by Hippocrene Books in 2004. Carol remembers how the Gypsies came to her Yorkshire village when she was a child in the 1960s.

Romany women, bedecked with gleaming gold jewellery, went from door to door selling their wares. They would offer lucky heather and freshly picked flowers, as well as the tantalising prospect of reading our mothers' palms and foretelling the future.

Her fascination with the people she met then led her to celebrate their culinary skills in *Gypsy Feast*, which evokes a memorable picture of the old ways, recipes, feast days, marriage customs, and funeral feasts, reflecting a unique way of life that has almost disappeared forever. Carol's chicken stew recipe has a timeless quality.

Chicken and Vegetable Stew

This was made with an old hen or cockerel. You can of course use chicken instead, but cook the stew for less time.
Makes 3 to 4 servings

2 tablespoons butter
2 carrots, chopped
4 to 6 slices bacon, chopped
2 large leeks, chopped
^{1}/4 cup flour
1^1/4 cups water or stock
1 boiling fowl
1 small cabbage, chopped
A few stems mixed fresh herbs
Salt and pepper

Preheat the oven to 350°F. Heat the butter in a large pan or flameproof casserole until melted. Add the carrots, bacon, and leeks and cover the pan. Cook for a few minutes over a low heat to soften but not brown the vegetables. Stir in the flour until lightly coloured then add the water or stock. Add the chicken, cabbage, and herbs and season to taste with salt and pepper. Cover the pan and cook for 2 to 3 hours (depending on the toughness of the bird).

Used with the kind permission of Carol Wilson

Carol does not go so far as writing a love song on the delights of a nice cup of Chai, or char, but her Tea Punch sounds tempting.

This reviving drink combines the scented bergamot flavour of Earl Grey tea and the cool refreshing taste of mint. Bergamot is related to mint and has a wonderful aroma of bergamot oranges, after which it is named. The liver and digestive system as a whole benefit from mint which eases colic, cramps and indigestion as well as nausea. Mint also has a mild effect on the nervous system and increases vitality.

Makes about 6 cups
3 Earl Grey tea bags
Sugar to taste
Juice of 6 oranges
1 lemon, sliced thinly
6 sprigs fresh mint
Ice cubes

Pour the boiling water over the tea bags and leave to infuse for 5 minutes. Remove the tea bags, and stir in sugar to taste. Add the orange juice, lemon slices and mint sprigs and chill for several hours. Serve in tall glasses, poured over ice cubes.

Used with the kind permission of Carol Wilson

If anyone reading this would like a recipe for Hedgehog Spaghetti Carbonara, Cornwall's Arthur Boyt, a retired non-Gypsy civil servant, is writing a book on roadkill cookery. His argument is that people don't turn up their noses at an apple which falls out of a tree – so why should they recoil at the idea of meat which they chance upon? Arthur's ideas would not find favour with many modern Gypsies, but their ancestors might well have nodded in agreement, provided that historic taboos, known as Marimé, were observed. Gypsy law prohibits cruelty to animals and they may only be killed for food. Anna was at pains to tell us that Gypsies do not kill animals for pleasure or sport – only for food. The eating of horse meat is a serious offence. According to customs of certain tribes, any Gypsy eating horse meat may be severely punished or banished from the tribe. The relationship of the horse to the Gypsy has historically been such a close one that it is unthinkable to eat this animal. For a different reason, cats and dogs are also forbidden as foods. They are considered polluted because of their unclean living habits; cats are considered particularly unclean because they lick their paws after burying their waste. Many Gypsy women talked to us about strict hygiene rules when handling food.

Dorothy:

Before I touch food, I always wash. And I always wash my meat. Other people's touched that stuff. What I always do with my chicken – I take it in the bath-room – pours the water right through it, then puts it into a saucepan, then boil it for five minutes, bubbling with an onion, take it out after five or six minutes, put it in to roast, with bacon. I always rolls up the bacon and dips that in hot water.

Our animals don't come in. Our dogs don't come in. They could stand at the door but not come in. We wouldn't have a cat in. We'd have a bird, and fish – a canary or goldfish, but we don't let dogs and cats in. We know someone with two big slobbery dogs – we'd have a cup of tea, but we won't eat there! Would you?

FISTICUFFS, FAIRS, A BIT OF COURTING…AND A FEW MORE FISTICUFFS

I remember Harry One Dog. You know at the fairs there was a tradition there'd be a fight between Gypsies. He used to say, 'Fair play — one dog, one bone!' That was his saying to make sure it was a fair fight so he got the name Harry One Dog.

Robert

In Tipton St John Church there is a small plaque to a little-known fighter, Young John Small.

Maggie:

Young John Small was a big lad. He actually fought Freddie Mills, the boxer, and won. He was me mum's first cousin. Freddie Mills had heard about Young John Small. Freddie Mills was a professional — Young John Small was a fist fighter, and they fist fought and he lost. They got drunk and ended up on one hoss. They put a plaque up and it was mentioned at his funeral.

Young John Small was part of a Romani tradition; fighters who grew up in a harsh environment, and learned to look after themselves from an early age. It is hard to find agreed rules for bare-knuckle fighting, and those that do exist seem somewhat

Harry 'One Dog' Isaacs, Robert Smith's niece, Cherry, and Leonard Smith at Priddy Fair during the 1990s.

basic: a round is not timed, but ends when a fighter is knocked down; once floored, a fighter has thirty seconds to come up to the 'scratch', which is a marker in the centre of the ring; fighters are not allowed to rest and are instantly disqualified if they fall from exhaustion. The culture of this world, at its extreme limits, has been well evoked by Bartley Gorman, described by some of those who contributed to this book, as 'a gentle giant' and 'a true gentleman'. Gorman became the bare-knuckle champion of England and Ireland in the early 1970s, and also fought at horse fairs, on campsites, in bars and clubs, in the street, down a mineshaft and in a quarry.

'Have you come to fight me?' I asked.

'I haven't come for a picnic,' said Fletcher. 'We're going to fight for Burton's vacant crown.'

To be honest, I didn't really feel up for it; I was stiff from moving all that tarmac. But I was showered, shaved and sober and had no excuses. There's no putting a fight off for a day with Travellers: when you're challenged, you fight. With Will and Bob leading the way, we all set off to walk the few hundred yards down a gravel track that cut through fields into Hollington quarry. The moonlight was so bright you could pick up a pin. The quarry was a levelled area a few hundred yards across, enclosed by cut walls of stone: a natural amphitheatre. In the middle was a building with a large spotlight on the side. Someone switched it on and the yard was bathed in a yellow glow. You could make out the big saws and lumps of stone lying all around, spindles and broken church crosses and puddles of water in the reddish mud where lorries had driven through.

The men formed a loose circle around us and Fletcher took off his shirt, his braces still dangling from his waist. He was butty and solid and even in the half-light I could see his skin had a sheen; he wasn't some drinking man just pretending to be fit. He was in prime condition...

I stripped off, ready to go in jeans and American shoes, though I would have liked my handkerchief to tie around my waist, like the old pugilists used to.

Bob Braddock stepped forward, his bowler hat held high in his hand. 'This fight is for the championship of the gypsies of England, Ireland, Scotland and Wales,' he declared. 'Whoever witnesses it here tonight must go forth and tell it how it was, and if they do not, then they will answer to me...'. There were to be no rounds, no kicking and no hitting a man on the deck.

'He's going to test you out, owd lad,' whispered Will Braddock into my ear. 'You had better win this one because I've got an acre of land on you.' And so, heel-deep in red clay mud under the glare of the quarry spotlight, we fought to be King of the Gypsies.

With a sharp jab flush on my nose, Fletcher drew first blood. I was too confident, with my hands too low. They haven't fetched a mug here, I thought. I unleashed some power on him and he fell back against the door of a corrugated shed. He let go a right and it missed but as he came back he hit me with an elbow below the eye and put pins and needles in my head.

The boundaries of a prizefight are fluid; there are no fixed ropes to keep you in.

You can cover a lot of ground, moving, jumping, tripping over things, banging up against buildings, with the crowd all the time melting and reassembling around you in a swarm. We scuffled around, the mud up to our ankles, the Kidds shouted, 'Muller him,' which means 'kill him' in Romany, and our Sam shouted, 'Carib,' which means the same in Irish Cant.

Fletcher pulled me in. He had the grip of a wrestler and nearly threw me with a cross-buttock. I ripped myself free and after that there was no need for Nelson Boswell or anyone else. I unloaded with both hands and demolished Fletcher. He floundered, ducking down to avoid my blows and I knew he was finished. He caught me with a desperate body shot but I smacked an almighty left hook into his jaw and he fell in the clay.

'Count,' I ordered Nelson. I was always a man for the count – it means there can be no argument afterwards. Nelson tolled off the seconds up to ten, but there was no way Fletcher was getting up.

Fletcher's friends helped him up. He and I had nothing more to say: I rarely talk to my opponents afterwards and anyway, he didn't seem too friendly. We went back in the pub and the celebrations began. By 5am I had drunk twenty-eight bottles of Newcastle Brown, and the party went on nonstop for three nights and days. The Nunns disappeared back to the flatlands of Norfolk but other travellers arrived at the Raddle from Ireland, Wales and Cornwall, pulling their trailers onto the car park and the surrounding fields: Prices, Lees, Hearns, Finneys, Calladines, Rileys and many others. We sang all the old songs: 'The Wild Rover', 'The Black Velvet Band', 'The Shade of the Old Apple Tree' and Will's favourite, 'The Man You Don't Meet Every Day'. Though thousands of pounds had changed hands in wagers, I never got two shillings out of it. All I wanted was the title – I had considered myself the best man for years, and now it was 'official'.

Extract from *King of the Gypsies: Memoirs of the Undefeated Bareknuckle Champion of Great Britain and Ireland*, by Bartley Gorman and Peter Walsh, published by Milo Books Ltd, 2003

Gypsy pugilists have always been well represented in the milieu of underground, or shall we say, unofficial fighting. At fairs, one practice was to put a stick in the ground, challenging people to a fight. In days gone by a few were known as 'gentleman's fighters', as aristocratic patrons would seek out fights for them, and place wagers on them. Hundreds of guineas would be won and lost in such bouts. Fighting booths were erected on commons as well as fairs. Sometimes, several hundred people would watch unknown fighters take on established boxers.

Boxing booths were still to be found on many fairgrounds in the mid-twentieth century. There were, of course, the mainstream attractions: dodgems, waltzers, big wheels, ghost rides, houses of mirrors, walls of death, coconut shies, penny slot machines. In addition, there were the sideshows that caused slight disapproval: freak shows, 'marvels of nature' in the form of the fat lady, the bearded lady, the five-legged sheep, Siamese twins, 'Teeny Tiny Tony, the World's Smallest Pony', 'Great Omi, the tattooed zebra-man'. Finally, there was the downright dangerous, to which the Gypsy boys gravitated.

Traditionally, the boxing booth was a large tent with a false front, on which there were painted lurid depictions of boxing scenes. Inside the booth, fighters would await challenges from the audience. There would be heavy betting, and sums such as twenty or thirty shillings, and in latter times, five pounds, would be paid to those foolhardy all-comers who lasted up to three rounds with the champ. Wiggy (real name, Wisdom) Smith, born in 1926 in a covered wagon parked on the fields of Filton Common near Bristol, who subsequently became well known as a musician, was one such young man who could be encountered at fairs around the West Country, challenging the boxing-booth champions. Boxing was in the family blood.

> I had an uncle – my father's brother – he never swore in his life. He'd never say 'Dammit!' My God, he was up here [over six foot] and he could fight. And all that he'd say was, 'God bless you my son. I hope you'll live long.'

Sometimes, Gypsy boys would be taken around to more distant fairs, and planted in the crowd. Of course, the winnings were welcome, but all this was still more about honour.

Dorothy:
> Then me father would tell another tale – years ago, when he was about six-teen. If they went to a fair and there were young men there, they would fight to see who was the best fighter. They would fight till they knocked one out. The tale would go around – Plymouth, Exeter, all around – to see if he was the best fighter and they'd come for miles and miles to watch them fight. The Travellers would have a good time. The young people and the women didn't go to the pub, but the older men did.

Within Gypsy society, fighting has been viewed, traditionally, as the mechanism by which differences are resolved. There is nothing underhand, no scheming, no back-stabbing, no lawyers. Quite simply, people refer to it as 'the Gypsy way'.

Robert:
> In my childhood days fights was a common thing, and what would happen if there was a disagreement one with the other was rules. They couldn't just meet and fight – you'd have to fight fair. I told you about Harry One Dog – lovely man – one of the patriarchs – there to be sure that fair play was taking place. Once you'd gone down, that was it. They'd jump in and say, 'That's it!' When you got up, if you wanted to fight, it could carry on, but in general, it was stopped and you'd have to shake hands. I can remember a few instances where if there was a falling out between brothers or another member of the family or another Gypsy group, the tradition was they would fight at six o'clock in the morning. This isn't the fairs. They'd come from the other site or wherever they was stopping, bringing two or three with them to make sure there was fair play.

The fight would take place then. They were bare-chested, bare knuckles. The fight was controlled. They'd fight as soon as [until] one went down or was bested; the others would step in and that was it. They'd shake hands and it was all over. The psychology was that if both sides were serious and they turned up at that time of the morning, then it was a genuine fight – a genuine grievance and they'd sort it out with fisticuffs. But no more – nothing else was allowed. No-one could hit anyone else or bring a weapon in. It would solve the grievance. I've never known when they haven't walked away friends. It's been finished.

Rodney is a gentle, courteous man in his middle years, mildly spoken, a man who chooses his words with care, who believes that almost all differences can be settled in a civilised manner, and whose eyes light up at the memory of a good fight.

Rodney:

People used to tell the other lads, 'Go with Rodney. He'll keep you out of trouble.' I'm not running scared or anything, but I was never really picked on; I didn't ever get into arguments. I remember this bloke, Bob Cuthbert, in Chard – when it was a bad place. There was this argument and he threatened to cut this Traveller's privates off. There were about eight Travellers. We all used to drink together. We were sat by the door, me and my cousin, Reg. Well this Cuthbert came up to one of the Travellers and knocked him through the pane of glass. The next thing everyone was scuffling around, having a go. I was just standing there, wanting to know what it was all about. Reg threw me his jumper and said, 'Rodney, hold this.' Then all the Traveller boys were chucking jumpers and shirts in my direction. At that moment I saw Cuthbert and another fellow with a knife, and another with a block of wood. I just had this rush of blood to my head. Just as I got stuck in, the police arrived. I'll

Diana's grandad Horace (left) squares up to her Uncle Andrew.

always remember because two of the Traveller lads, Nathan and Jake, had the same shirts. Nathan was a really big bloke and Jake was tiny. What do they do but collect their shirts from me, and put on each other's. The police let me go, but Reg got six months, you know what for? He'd been so wound up, that in the furore 'e'd gone and knocked the light off the top of this Panda car.

It should be remembered that fighting seeks out Gypsies as often as they look for fights.

Maggie:

There was a lot of violence. We grew up with violence one way or another. Me dad and the policeman would very often end up fighting and they were always ready to have a go. It was like a medal if they could beat one of the men. We've got one here now, retired now, quite an old man. Very often he says, 'Yes Maggie, I can remember fighting with your dad and his brothers.' He used to go out to do it, see who could beat who; it was a violent world.

Lisa:

Some of the women would fight better than men. Over children – that would cause rows if the kids went out fighting. At the end of the day, five minutes after, the kids would be playing again after causing that big riot! Travellers won't give in! I had a fighting do at school with the *gadjes* – they'd wind you up. They'd look up and say, 'Here come the stinking Gypsies.' I'd say, 'Hang on a minute. Whoa! We're not stinking, dirty Gypsies!'

One of the sources of excitement at fairs is the volatility of the atmosphere. People look forward to them for months. They are places for 'chopping' (making deals), getting together with the extended family, meeting up with old friends, making new friends, and settling a few old scores along the way. When Gypsies talk of the fairs, there is a tendency to become misty-eyed with nostalgia.

Lisa:

I can't wait for when the fairs comes along. It's lovely to meet other people. The fairs is lovely – lovely stalls. You meet loads and loads of people. I may not see a person for five or six years – you go to a fair and you bump into them. It makes your day! People you haven't seen for a helluva long time. It's a nice day out – Glastonbury Fair, Priddy Fair, Stow, Epsom Fair, Derby Day in June. Stow Fair is my favourite. There's lovely gold stores there – jewellery – and nice china. It is a good day out. I don't send the kids to school. I lets the school know.

Diana:

A lot of courting couples met up at the fairs. And there were fights for money. I don't like boxing. I don't like to think of young men being there, punching one another's heads. But it's nice when they can take care of themselves.

Lisa Packman with her
father and horses at
Bridgwater Fair.

The first thing a Traveller would do when they go in a fair is go and look round the animals – then afterwards they'd go and see what pretty ware there is – have a walk round the stalls. The first thing they'd go to is the crockery stalls: Crown Derby ware; the big punchbowls and plates. They make lots of animals; they made wagons with bangtails on. Nobody'd buy them.

Linda:

It's not like it used to be. Nothing's like it used to be. There's no such thing as Barnstaple Fair. There's no such thing as Holsworthy Fair. What stopped all of it really and truly was drinking and driving. I'd know my father drive home from Barnstaple Fair drunk as a lord. Fights? These days it's the Irish. Never get

Leonard Smith at
Bridgwater Fair, late 1970s.
(Used by kind permission of
Mick Garland)

a Traveller mixed up with the Irish. We don't like it. What I can remember when I was a child at the fairs – usually the men would get jealous of the women. Usually it was the drink. Very rarely that it would go on after. If they had a row at this fair, then they went to another fair, they might have a go, but usually, no. Nine times out of ten it was the drink.

Jim recalls travelling the whole country, going to fairs: Cheddar Gorge, Bridgwater, Appleby, Yarm, Newcastle... He still visits as many as possible, selling charms. His favourite event, however, was always Epsom Races, which he describes as a 'beautiful fair'. His childhood memories are of rows of tents and campfires, with Gypsies cooking outside.

Defiance Smith (right) with a friend at Bridgwater Fair, 1980s. (Used by kind permission of Mick Garland)

Defiance Smith (right) with a friend at Bridgwater Fair, 1980s. (Used by kind permission of Mick Garland)

Jim:

> You couldn't just walk past, when you were small. You'd always have something shoved in your hands, a bit of bread, whatever people was cooking. In those days, everyone looked after anyone else's children. They'd know where every child was.

These recollections are of the late 1950s and early 1960s. It seems to have been a period in which Gypsy existence was straddling eras, as exemplified in the tale below.

Jim:

> When you got there, everything would be mixed in: there would be wagons and horses and trailers and motors. Me uncle, Uncle Saley, bought this motor, a perfectly good motor, and when it conked out, ran out of petrol, 'e thought it were finished, it were broke, and he went back to 'is 'orse. So everyone asks, 'Where's the motor?' And 'e says, 'Well it was finished; it were broke down. It was all conked out.' He didn't understand it. So he just left it at the side of the road, abandoned, and went back to 'is 'orses.

As a reminder of past times, fairs are symbols of inter-generational coherence, communal warmth, and general high spirits. Furthermore, they have been eagerly anticipated as places where the unusual may occur, as Wiggy describes:

> Once at Stow Fair, for a bet — we had a brown-and-white horse called Spot — and they had a bet up there that nobody couldn't pick him up. And he was fourteen hands high. Me dad got in underneath him, arching his back... and his two legs apart and

*Leonard and Maggie Smith
at Bridgwater Fair, 1992.
(Used by kind permission of
Mick Garland)*

he picked him up a couple of inches off the floor. That horse – me dad could call him
– 'Come on Spot' – and he'd come, and me dad could give him a pint of beer and
he'd drink it just like a man. I'd never seen such a thing in all my life.

One of the most exciting aspects of the fairs has been the opportunities for courting, though young couples often had to do this outside the vigilant gaze of family
members acting as chaperones.

Linda:

My mum and dad met down Barnstaple at Barnstaple Fair years ago. That's
where Travellers met, still do sometimes but it isn't like it used to be years ago.
The older generation would get someone to play the accordion and everyone
got paralytic drunk. Fairs was where young people met. They'd pick up their
partners there. Years later you'd go to a dance – you'd drive miles for a dance
– even I've been to Birmingham for a dance – a gang of you'd go together.

Jean:

Tom and I met at a wedding, and Holsworthy Fair was the first place we went
courting. It was the wedding of Lorna and Danny Gregory. Lorna's mum was
my mum's first cousin...their dads were brothers...Sanders. Danny was a
very good friend of Tom's 'cos his brother was killed in an accident where a
gas cylinder exploded and Danny witnessed it and he went a bit on edge! So
Tom's dad took him under his wing to help him get better and my Tom and
Danny worked side by side for a while. Tom had been invited to the wedding
'cos of being his friend.

Tom:

Jean's Granny got married on Holsworthy Fair day – where they were so clever – instead of inviting everybody to a party, everybody came to the Fair and that was where they had their party!

However, a fair would not be a fair without a good fight.

Tom:

If they couldn't sing or dance years ago, they used to fight.

Due to fierce family loyalties, disputes have extended, invariably, beyond the central protagonists.

Robert:

If you talk about fights – our people can get a few drinks in them and they do fight at fairs over a horse and who's done what in the family...

I can remember at Peasedown St John, near Bath, the fair came and this show boy was mouthy, and I said something to him and he wanted a fight, so the elder ones of the show-people put us where they used to throw the darts – the other ones was made to keep out. It was just me and him. Anyway, I won. But the next day I went to the fair and his father come up and he said, 'I hear you had a fight with my boy and you didn't beat him fairly. So what's going to happen is: we're moving up to Timsbury – I want you and your father to come up there at six o'clock on the morning and you'll fight this out again. You've got to fight my boy again.'

I didn't tell my father. This is something I've never told my family! I knew what would happen. A lot of his brothers were living in the area. My father at that time was the only Gypsy I knew who'd 'ad a bare-fist fight with a policeman. The policeman upset him – he was an aggressive man – he took his tunic off and they was going to get in a fight. My father was like that. He was in his forties. Short-tempered. Nice man, my father, but he had that temper. I knew if I'd have gone home and told him what the man said, the first thing he'd have done was go up the fair then, and he'd have been up and sorted it, and it would cause a more serious thing. More importantly for me, I'd have had to fight this boy again I'd already beat! So I just kept me mouth shut. I ignored what the father said to me because if I'd told my father it would have just flared up, and I would have been a troublemaker in my mother's mind – she hated violence. She was a very bad-tempered person but she hated violence! I couldn't have won either way! It wasn't worth it. I'd have had to fight that boy again and my heart wouldn't have been in it. I would have stirred up a hornet's nest.

Maggie:

With me mum and dad – we travelled a lot on our own – because you'd get families, you'd meet up. Some of the kids would be bullies and give us a hiding. That would end up with the fathers having a fight. This is how some of the feuds are today, how the feuds started, because of the fathers fighting over the children. They would protect us.

If they got fighting – if an argument broke up – they would meet five o'clock the next morning as sport and they would fist fight...bare to the waist...and they would fist fight, five minutes a round. Whoever won, they would shake hands at the end of that fight and they'd go off, but if a family member done something like stole anything or hit a child – something nasty – that feud would go down through the generations. But an argument that cropped up at a fair – 'I'll meet you next year this time and we'll have another go!' The women wasn't allowed to watch. The men would all go – all the boys and men would go. The only time you saw a good fight was at a fair. Me dad was always ready for a fight. He'd fight at the drop of a hat. I was the same. Years ago it was the thing that if the men fought, the women had to fight whether they knew anything about it or not. We've progressed a bit now.

I was always very quick-tempered. I took two men on three years ago – big men – because they blasphemed me dad – me dad was dead and couldn't answer back. They made a ring for me; the other Gypsies made a ring. One of them I was having a go at tried to rip his shirt off. One of the Gypsy men said, 'I'll tell you what, son, if you takes yours off to Maggie, I'll have to take mine off to you.' I'm protected anyway. We've got this policy: we do not speak ill of the dead. If you don't like them, keep your opinions to yourself.

Lisa:

You do try to get on. You try to help each other. But if they get rowing, that fight goes on and goes on and goes on right through the years and don't get forgot. These days it don't happen a lot. It did years ago with older generations. You just try to get on with everybody.

I can remember my dad fighting years ago. Over kids. 'Don't do that to my son, mate. Let's see you do it to me.' Then it would cause a great big row, a great big fight. It would go on and go on. And you don't insult people's parents. It's bad.

To this day, most Romani people will argue that fighting remains the best way to resolve grudges, whether such disputes arise through a wayward glance at someone else's wife or through someone else's great-grandfather having sold your great-grandfather a dud horse. There is a custom, too, that when a fight occurs at night, there should be a re-fight the next morning, because it might have been the drink talking, and that jeopardises any resolution. Ritually, fights end with a handshake, even if those involved fully intend to bash each other's brains out once again at the next opportunity.

Horses – Chopping, Nashing, and Pouffing the Grais

When the little chavvies gets up, they take the grais down the pani…then we all have bread and kel and a piece of stinger… Some of the old raklis dodikins to the gorgios. They go out with the juckals shushing and a lot of muskros are in the pov.

The little children are asleep in the wagons. When they get up, they water the horses, then everyone has bread and cheese and a little bit of onion. Some of the old ladies tell people's fortunes. They go rabbiting with the dogs, and a lot of policemen are in the field.

Zilla Roberts, describing Appleby Fair, quoted by John Ezard, 1976

For some Gypsies, the likelihood of a *gadje* understanding their affinity with horses is about as likely as a tortoise imagining the majesty of flight.

So it came to pass that I stood upon this hill, observing a fair of horses… There was shouting and whooping, neighing and braying; there was galloping and trotting; fellows with highlows and white stockings, and with many a string dangling from the knees of their tight breeches, were running desperately, holding horses by the halter, and in some cases dragging them along; there were long-tailed steeds and dock-tailed steeds of every degree and breed; there were droves of wild ponies, and long rows of sober cart horses; there were donkeys, and even mules…

Members of Nellie Danes' family.

An old man draws nigh, he is mounted on a lean pony, and he leads by the bridle one of these animals; nothing very remarkable about that creature, unless in being smaller than the rest and gentle, which they are not; he is not of the sightliest look; he is almost dun, and over one eye a thick film has gathered. But stay! There IS something remarkable about that horse, there is something in his action in which he differs from all the rest: as he advances, the clamour is hushed! All eyes are turned upon him – what looks of interest – of respect – and, what is this? People are taking off their hats – surely not to that steed! Yes, verily! Men, especially old men, are taking off their hats to that one-eyed steed, and I hear more than one deep-drawn ah!

'What horse is that?' said I to a very old fellow…

'The best in mother England,' said the very old man, taking a knobbed stick from his mouth, and looking me in the face, at first carelessly, but presently with something like interest; 'he is old like myself, but can still trot his twenty miles an hour. You won't live long, my swain; tall and over-grown ones like thee never does; yet, if you should chance to reach my years, you may boast to thy great-grand-boys thou hast seen Marshland Shales.'

…and now there was a change in the scene, the wondrous old horse departed with his aged guardian; other objects of interest are at hand; two or three men on horseback are hurrying through the crowd, they are widely different in their appearance from the other people of the fair; not so much in dress, for they are clad something after the fashion of rustic jockeys, but in their look – no light-brown hair have they, no ruddy cheeks, no blue quiet glances belong to them; their features are dark, their locks long, black, and shining, and their eyes are wild; they are admirable horsemen, but they do not sit the saddle in the manner of common jockeys, they seem to float or hover upon it, like gulls upon the waves; two of them are mere striplings, but the third is a very tall man with a countenance heroically beautiful, but wild, wild, wild. As they rush along, the crowd give way on all sides, and now a kind of ring or circus is formed, within which the strange men exhibit their horsemanship, rushing past each other, in and out, after the manner of a reel, the tall man occasionally balancing himself upon the saddle, and standing erect on one foot. He had just regained his seat after the latter feat, and was about to push his horse to a gallop, when a figure started forward close from beside me, and laying his hand on his neck, and pulling him gently downward, appeared to whisper something into his ear…

From George Borrow's *Lavengro*, 1851

There is a subtle difference between skills passed down through generations and those acquired in a single lifetime, and the bond between the horse and the Rom is often conceived as something almost mystical.

According to Pat, the link connecting her youngest son, Mark to his Romani ancestors had been almost broken.

Pat:

We lived in the West Midlands – Dudley. There was Mother – just me, only me. No brothers and sisters. My mother had a brother that lived in Kent – I never saw much of him – and my father was the only survivor out of his family. My father was a businessman – the son of a businessman. My mother's family were Romani but I was never brought up with any of that. I'm really on the fence – neither one of them or one of them. That's actually how all my family feel as well. Is that good? I don't know. Katrina's always been an observer and so is Sacha – he's accepted by Gypsies. They both are. Mark, the youngest, can talk the lingo. Everybody knows them but they can always go into the other world. They are two different worlds…

My dad, because of being a businessman, perhaps, he didn't like to associate. She (my mum) wasn't able to do anything involving them (her Romani family). She wouldn't lose face… She must have taken me to see her family sometimes and that's why the old men remembered me but I can only remember the big black kettle – and this big black kettle sticks in my mind. As I grew older and couldn't find the kettle I can remember being quite upset – my mother had probably thrown it out. We'd moved into a nice house in a nice area. We weren't living at the back of the shop. I can remember going in the old wash house with the bathtub and the old fireplace and the kettle. The kettle was the main thing – round the fire with the kettle going.

Nevertheless, there was something that gradually drew both Pat and Mark back towards their roots.

Pat:

Mark was already out on the road. He'd gone at an early stage. As a youngster he was constantly in need of horses. He'd got to have horses. He used to sit on the arm of the couch with a cloak and he was Richard the Lionheart. He had a dog on wheels and he used to go and get my washing line and harness it up – and he'd sit there – clip-clop, clip-clop. He'd bring in some grass and you'd got to feed and water this horse – there was no inclination of horses around at all. I actually always wanted a horse – my mother bought me a china Beswick and she put it on the piano and she said, 'That's the only horse you're going to get, my girl.' It makes you wonder. As I say, Mark, he was horses, horses. He led them to believe at school he'd got a horse in the field and it had vanished one day. The teacher rang me up and was worried. I said, 'Little girls have imaginary friends – he's got an imaginary horse.'

There was a doctor in the village had got Shetlands – they are the world's worst horses for children. He would come back bruised and battered and covered in mud and he was going to do it and he'd bring one up to show me and I thought, 'He's a little boy! He's going to come back in pieces,' but he didn't. He was never deterred. There was a point up in Gloucester there he had over forty horses.

Before the Horse Whisperer was heard of there was this horse at Stow, and

Mark saw a bloke get him off the lorry. That bloke tied the horse's rope to the tree and drove the lorry away so the horse walked down the ramp as he drove bit by bit because he was such a wild horse. He hauled him in and he stayed by the tree. He knew nobody was going to touch his horse. Mark watched him all day. This stallion stood there and nobody went near him. At the end of the day he couldn't load that horse and Mark knew it and offered him some silly price. The bloke was really stumped and that was it – but within a week that horse was driving a wedding carriage. Mark did have him castrated some months later and he sat on his side and he cried! He cried for him. To actually get that wild horse driving a wedding carriage was wonderful. I'd see Mark coming down the A38 riding the wildest thing – but he's not a rider really – he likes driving.

Robert Smith, whose brother had been killed by a runaway horse, never lost his love for the animals.

Robert:

My father's people were associated with Priddy Fair for generations back – he always had horses. His first job was looking after horses – when the adults were gone out in the daytime calling or making a living he would be home with the horses. People used to come to him for miles around for anything to do with the horses. He knew them inside out – he's learned that by being with them every day of the week for years when he was growing up. He loved them. I do. It's inherited. I've still got that affinity with them.

The fairs were important – like Priddy – our people would take horses down to sell to the farmers for the horse-drawn implements on the farm. There was a market there. They'd also chop amongst themselves. It was two shillings for a horse – half a crown for a horse! If a horse was winded they could tell. They didn't go too much on looks: they got to know the animals. They'd sell it to another Traveller, 'Look, I bred this horse – he'll pull a wagon, pull carts – children.'

One of my beautiful memories is up near Chippenham on one of the downs. It was a beautiful summer's day. Once me and my brothers and sisters was down the woods and we found our horse tied up feeding along the lane. My father came down to get him and he gave us a lift back on the horse – all of us kids on the back of the horse up through. A beautiful summer's day. They'd know the horses inside out – all the ailments and how to cure them – like us. Herbs and things did come into it.

However, the love of horses is not universal.

Nellie:

I used to keep horses: Spider and Ramsay. Riding horses? I tried it once. I felled off.

Lisa:

I don't like horses! I'm petrified of them. I wouldn't hurt 'em. My dad would put them on carts, driving them, or get in a race. Some horses they do like thirty miles an hour. I wouldn't get on! Too fast for me. Touch wood, Dad have never had no accidents with a horse. I think it's the way you break them in. You don't put a horse into a cart if it's a wild horse. You gotta make sure that horse is broke in. You could cause a big accident – cars back or front – or you could kill yourself. You have got to be careful. Touch wood, all the horses Dad bought – they've always been nice, quiet horses.

Breaking in horses is seen as something of a gift.

Lisa:

You put the bit in his mouth and put something heavy on the back of 'e to break him in. If he takes to the bit then he's alright. You put the harness on and if he wants to go to the left, you pull 'im to the right. If he wants to go to the right, it's back to the left. That's the way you've got to learn 'em. I've seen my dad put these great big weights on the back of the horse, taming him down and letting him drag until he gets broken. Dad could break a horse in in one day.

Anna recalls helping her uncle to break in horses from the age of eight.

Anna:

Me uncle used to come down here, load up horses off the moors. They were worth breaking in because then there were plenty of carts around with you people, and you'd always buy a little horse for a child. They'd rub the ear and talk to them.

The only way to proper break a horse in – you could break them in easily –

get an old motor tyre, a big lorry tyre or one from a tractor – get the harness on it – don't break your 'arness, 'cos the 'arness is precious. The horse would be going mad, 'cos 'e 'ad to get used to the harness first. You'd play about with 'im, take 'im all around.

Then you 'ooked on the chains to the tyre, but away from the 'orse…and it was the person what 'ad to sit on the tyre would've been guiding the 'orse. And it would try to kick out at yer, but it was too far away from yer, so the weight of the tyre would wear the 'orse out, and when it was really weared out, then you could make it turn left or right. Then after that, you'd put it in a cart first, 'cos you couldn't afford to smash the wagons up – you couldn't really afford to smash the cart up.

Well, gradually, you'd wear it out and wear it out and wear it out, till it 'ad no more go in it. By then it was calm. It would take weeks… What some of the men does is get by a big canal or river – take him in and he'll wear himself out getting back. Jump on his back and a horse won't kick you in water you know – but when he's coming out, then he'll kick you! You'd better be fast enough jumping off!

Us children, we knowed 'ow to calm 'orses straight away: 'old onto the mane, make sure your legs is tight into the guts, and then 'old on for your life!

Me uncle used to break in 'orses and he'd chuck us on the back – bareback; we always ride bareback. When we was little, they used to look very big, the big black and white mares. He'd say to you, 'No saddles, just the old bridle.' He'd say, 'Hang on, child, put your two arms round the mane and hold on tight.' You'd tighten your legs right in and wrap yourself around – the back's that big your legs would only be halfway. You'd hold on tight, and when it reared up, it was like you was going up a mountain, but when you come off, you couldn't cry in front of him! You'd feel the pain but he'd get you again and chuck you back on again. 'Oooh, there's a *gadje* child,' he'd say. 'Get back on child, get back on, and hang on.' It was the men making the 'orses get broke in, like me uncle; we thought we were breaking the 'orses in fer 'im, and we was proud just because we hung on for dear life.

I like riding bareback. I like seeing a horse broke in proper. Years ago they'd use an old tree trunk to hold him down – you'd kept him going in that field; keep him up and down, up and down, don't let him breathe. You can hear a horse – he snorts when he's winded – he snorts when you've got the best of him. It'll wear you but you've got the best of him. And then afterwards, he's your best friend and he'll pull your wagon anywhere. You've got to have an old Irish horse, or a Welsh Cob, or a Suffolk Punch (though they're dying out; not many about now). You've got to get a good thick 'orse to carry the weight of the wagon.

Some Gypsies talk not of 'breaking in' horses, but of 'gentling' them, and for most the idea of harming horses is anathema. However, in his description of those he recalled from his childhood, the Devon farmer, Richard Matthews, suggested that some Gypsies were not averse to cruelty.

> They roamed on common land at Roncombe. A tent or caravan. The children some-
> times wore no shoes on their feet. The women did the work, selling clothes pegs. The
> men looked after the horses and let them in our fields by night. They drank a lot of
> cider. At Honiton Fair they would sell their horses in the street and fight one another.
> A gypsy on our land had a lame horse, so he drove a nail on the other foot to make
> it walk evenly. The police were called and I believe he went to prison.
>
> Taken from Richard Matthews' self-published pamphlet
> *A Farmer's Story: My Life at Roncombe Farm*, 1995

However, such behaviour does not seem consistent with most accounts, and the fact is that most Gypsies speak about horses with an affection, and at times, reverence. Indeed, in terms of everyday life and Romani identity, the existences of horses and their owners are entwined.

Rodney:

I enjoy horses – especially the ones we've got now – Shires – lovely gentle horses. I've had all sorts – Shetlands, miniatures. I bought a miniature in Taunton. Helen thought I went looking for a big horse. Tommy Wells, this travelling person in Taunton, said, 'I've got a miniature stallion for sale.' I bought it off him. He had a transit van, so I put it in the transit van, and it stood between the seats looking out through. I had to stay in Taunton so I said, 'Drop it along back home.' So he popped up here, and said, 'I've got a delivery for you.' And Helen's expecting a big horse and this horse got out – not more than three foot high!

Helen rides them – I've broke horses in by having them on the chain, doing the gentle touch, sitting on their backs. I go that far so the horse is fairly safe and then someone else finishes them off. I just touch it, talk to it, smooth it all down, lean over it so it doesn't mind you at all. It gets used to the weight then I get the saddle on. Then see what the horse does. Common sense at the end of the day. You go through. You take notice. Not too close – get back a little bit. There's nothing worse than someone breathing down the back of you. You can feel it within yourself. I was in my twenties, I suppose, when I started with the horses and dogs. I had that gift to calm them down – get them used to you, get their trust. Never force them. After I thought I'd finished a fellow came from Honiton, a good horse rider. I'd tell him what I'd done; he'd jump on the horse's back, rode it around. No problem at all.

We did it with Helen's horse now. We call her Lucky Touch. Used to go down the stable – try to get near her but she was so jumpy. I got this glove, filled it with straw, put it on the end of a stick – you didn't want to get too close to her back then. Then I'd reach out, smooth her with the back of the glove. 'That's enough today,' I said to Helen. 'Come home.' Back home we'd come. Go back the next day; same thing again. She started to get used to it. Used to put a bit of feed on top of the stable door. She'd eat the food off the stable door. About three or four days later, when I put my hand there with the feed, she's feeding out of my hand without knowing it. She jumped a little bit. I kept on, slowly touched her face – slow all the way. By the time we finished we had her in the field with Helen sat on her back. Then we took her down to Hemyock to have her finished off. Most of the work was done. Someone said, 'Just jump on her back!' If something goes wrong, that's it then. She could bolt right up, get put down, do a lot of damage to yourself.

Maggie:

The new foal, Storm, will have to ride on the back of the trolley with her head sticking out of a sack-bag, so the mare can see her at all times, as her feet is still too soft to walk very far. This is the way Gypsy foals travel for the first few weeks of their lives. The reason for the sack-bag is so the foals won't struggle and hurt themselves.

As she gets older she will be allowed to run free for awhile, but at four or five months old she will be tied to her mother's head harness, where she will stay until she is two years old. Then she will be fitted with a set of harness of her own, but not to pull anything, just to get used to the feel of it, although she may be used as a tracer after the age of two. Our men states that to pull the wagons before the age of three do's more harm than good. All the while the foals are being broken to harness without realising it. Gypsies won't break a hoss's spirit. There is no need to treat them bad in any way. Our lives depend too much on them – they are part of our family group. Of course, she will be free to run loose each time we pull in, while the mares are kept on a long chain to stop them running off.

In fact, the grown-ups worked out a job for us young *chavvies* generations ago. It's known as *Turning the Grais Sherrule* (Romani for turning the horse's head back the way it come). It's a nice job in the summer or late spring, for we chavvies had to spend hours up the road with the hosses between us and the wagons so they could be free and eat the grass off the verges, and we had to watch them and turn them back if they started to wander. Our hosses is crafty and would try an' sneak by us, so we are always turning them back towards the wagons, where they would be turned back towards us again.

Indeed, Maggie is one of those individuals who possesses that rare talent of conjuring up such scenes from childhood, as if she is still there.

Maggie:

Dad and his family used to pick the wagons by which horse was in the front. They all knew each other's horses. 'There's Old Jack! I know who's coming up that road! I can see who's pulling that wagon!'

Smells meant a lot. The smell of the rain, the smell of the rotting vegetation on the Common – smells played a big part in our lives. You can smell a horse sweating as well as see it when he's pulling – you remember our horses used to do ten, fifteen miles a day pulling a load. And it was a load – everything we owned was in that wagon and when it come to the brows – you get a little nap in the road – the horse would start sweating up and you could sit on that foreboard with your legs dangling over and smell their feet – smell their sweat. Every horse's got like a rotteny smell in their feet 'cos of their hoofs. You could smell every smell that went along.

Maggie also had vivid recollections of *pouffing the grais*, sneaking horses into farmers' fields in the dead of night, and then removing them before first light to avoid detection.

Horses were also kept for *chopping* (dealing) and for *nashing* (racing). A term often used, *gryengro*, means horse dealer. At times, racing has taken place in somewhat informal ways.

Diana:

We had horses, wagons and carts. I liked the horses. We had about three. We didn't use to ride bareback. I remember there was a race on the A303 – between Podimore Roundabout and Ilchester. They had a horse race. The police were quite good – they never stopped the race. It was early in the

Members of Nellie Danes' family with a coloured (piebald) horse.

morning – about six o'clock. Everybody heard about it. A lot of people had
a few bets on it!

We do a fair bit of horse trading. I go to all the horse fairs. Appleby – I've
been to Priddy. We go to Stow twice a year. The horse fair has come back to
Bampton two years ago. Sherborne Pack Monday – I can remember when
that was a horse fair. All the Travellers with the horses and wagons would
gather up the lane just before you get to Sherborne – where the traffic lights
are – there's a lane up on the left and we used to call that Dog Kennel Lane.
That's the Traveller nickname. There'd be fifty lots.

He [Diana's husband, Arthur] had a few horses to sell – and dogs. He had
the horses on chains then, up and down the lane, getting used to the traffic.

Traditionally, fairs were the highlight of the year, and for a number of families travelling to places such as Honiton, Priddy, Stow, or as far afield as Appleby, the greatest
excitement was to be found in horse dealing. From the 1970s, in particular, there
was a move from real to metaphorical horsepower, and yet the fairs have remained
central to group cohesion, enabling people to renew relationships. Meanwhile,
chopping, making deals on horses, has continued, involving Shetland ponies, donkeys,
and of course, the sturdy piebald cobs, also called coloured or painted horses, traditionally favoured by Gypsies. There is a prejudice against certain 'wall-eyed'
horses, and different shades of eye colour are considered to denote 'evil' in a horse.
It is said that such horses can never be trained.

Making deals can involve protracted negotiations, and there is a ritual surrounding
negotiations. Nowadays, horses are more likely to arrive towed in horseboxes,
rather than pulling wagons, but their symbolic importance remains, and they are
still considered to constitute capital and provide useful investments, with thousands
of pounds changing hands in some cases.

There are old tricks to ensure the best deal. For instance, it is difficult to know
the difference between, say, a seven- and twelve-year-old horse because they have
almost identical teeth. Dealers have to be cunning in their assessment, and they will
be seen to look inside the mouth, as well as pull the feet up and look underneath.
If, while the feet are off the ground, something sharp, say a thorn, happens to get
embedded there, that is all part of the contest of wits. After purchase, the horse
mysteriously loses its limp.

In general, there is a reluctance to take a good horse to a fair. To ensure the sale
of an ungovernable horse, stories are told of herbal potions to calm them.
Backcombing the hair on a horse's leg, and then adding baby powder, gives an appearance of general wellbeing. However, within the Romani world, a bad reputation is
likely to have repercussions for the future, so such strategies are usually reserved for
the gullible *gadje*.

GYPSIES AND GADJES

A BATTLE OF WITS

Cakka rokke chivvy, gadjes jellin the kai.
(Keep quiet child, there's non-Gypsies coming.)

                  The first words learned by Robert as a child

There is a tale recounted by a number of Gypsies, almost acquiring the status of myth, in which each teller swears that the person involved was a family member. This is the story of a family who had been tricked by a *gadje*. Basically, they had bought a horse from this *gadje* and, as they were illiterate, this had all been done in the traditional manner, through verbal agreement and a handshake. However, no sooner had the transaction been completed, than the seller had informed the police that his horse had been stolen, and the animal had been confiscated. Some time passed, then one day, the same *gadje* man reappeared, trying to buy a horse from a member of the same Gypsy family. After a short deliberation, the grandfather of the family informed the man that, indeed, he had a horse to sell, but it was not there with him at the time, and he should return the next day. Later that day, he removed the shoe from a horse's foot and placed a pebble inside it. On the following morning, the *gadje* returned to purchase the horse, but was back within a few days, claiming that the horse was lame. The grandfather shrugged, replying that the horse was sold as seen, but after some negotiating, agreed to buy the animal back, at a fraction of the original price. When the man had left, he removed the pebble from the horse's shoe, and within a short time, it was fully recovered.

In general, however, it is clever not to be too clever. In rural communities, farmers have traditionally depended on Gypsy labour to collect crops; this was a relationship based upon mutual convenience, balanced on a fragile edge.

Poisoning the Porker

To mande shoon ye Romany chals,	Listen to me ye Roman lads,
Who besh in the pus about the yag,	Who are seated in the straw about the fire,
I'll pen how we drab the baulo,	And I will tell you how we poison the porker,
I'll pen how we drab the baulo.	I will tell you how we poison the porker.
We jaws to the drab-engro ker,	We go to the house of the poison-monger (apothecary),
Trin horsworth there of drabs we lels,	Where we buy three pennies' worth of bane,

And when to the swety back we wells	And when we return to our people we say,
We pens we'll drab the baulo,	We will poison the porker;
We'll have a drab at a baulo.	We will try and poison the porker.
And then we kairs the drab opre,	We then make up the poison,
And then we jaws to the farming ker,	And then we take our way to the house of the farmer,
To mang a beti habben,	As if to beg a bit of victuals,
A betti pogado habben.	A little broken victuals.
A rinkeno baulo there we dick,	We see a jolly porker,
And then we pens in Romano jib;	And then we say in Roman language;
Wust lis odoi opre ye chick,	'Fling the bane yonder amongst the dirt,
And the baulo he will lel lis,	And the porker soon will find it,
The baulo he will lel lis.	The porker soon will find it.'
Coliko, coliko saulo we	Early on the morrow
Apopli to the farming ker	We will return to the farmhouse
Will wel and mang him mullo,	And beg the dead porker,
Will wel and mang his truppo.	The body of the dead porker.
And so we kairs, and so we kairs;	And so we do, even so we do;
The baulo in the rarde mers;	The porker dieth during the night;
We mang him on the saulo,	On the morrow we beg the porker,
And rig to the tan the baulo.	And carry to the tent the porker.
And then we toves the wendror well	And then we wash the inside well
Till sor the wendror iuziou se,	'till all the inside is perfectly clean,
Till kekkeno drab's adrey lis,	'till there's no bane within it,
Till drab there's kek adrey lis.	Not a poison grain within it.
And then his truppo well we hatch,	And then we roast the body well,
Kin levinor at the kitchema,	Send for ale to the alehouse,
And have a kosko habben,	And have a merry banquet,
A kosko Romano habben.	A merry Roman banquet.
The boshom engro kils, he kils,	The fellow with the fiddle plays,
The tawnie juva gils, she gils	He plays; the little lassie sings,
A puro Romano gillie,	She sings an ancient Roman ditty;
Now shoon the Romano gillie.	Now hear the Roman ditty.

As sung by Mrs Chikno, and recounted and translated by George Borrow in *The Romany Rye*, 1857

One and a half centuries after the recording of the above song the battle of wits still goes on between Gypsies and the settled population. Over the years, many farmers have turned a blind eye to a certain amount of pilfering, and overall, their responses to Gypsies have alternated between ill treatment and acts of charity. Gypsies have responded likewise, sometimes with friendship, sometimes with tricks.

Anna:

The old farmer'd let us stop in a field over Christmas time. We'd do a bit of work in return… We'd never go to the ends of fields to get potatoes. We'd go to the middle, and the farmer would never see us. We'd 'ave a few potatoes or swedes, but we'd never be greedy, as we knew we'd 'ave to go back next year.

Maggie:

Me Grandad used to tell us a true story – it happened down at Bristol – one of the lanes at Bristol, years and years ago. They pulled on the side of the road and they had to out wait the farmer and the farmer was never early to go to bed, he was always the last one to go to bed. They wanted to *pouff the grais*. Because the horses worked hard pulling wagons all day, they would find, during daylight, his best seed field for his mowing grass and when he went to bed the hosses would be put through his gate and they would have to be got out, because the farmer was an early riser, at first light before he even knew they'd been in and out! That was called *pouffing the grais*.

The practice of sneaking horses into the farmers' fields at night has been corroborated by farmers, such as Richard Matthews, in his account of life at Roncombe Farm at Sidbury in Devon during the first half of the twentieth century:

Mr Northcott, brother Sam and I went to see the Gypsies, they had been troubling us by putting their horses in our fields by night. This boy of about eight years old was cheeky to me so I wanted to fight him, but he ran into his tent with his mother. The next day I met him on his own on Roncombe Hill. I asked him his name, and he said Goodwin. I said, 'You won't have much wind left in you when I finish with you!' Then I hit him in the ditch and left him there. He wasn't cheeky any more.

Taken from Richard Matthews' self-published pamphlet,
A Farmer's Story: My Life at Roncombe Farm, 1995

In many cases, however, Gypsy children who overstepped the mark had far more to fear from their own parents.

Dorothy:

I remember my mother giving me a bloody good hiding for something stupid. Me sister and brother was playing in the farmer's cornfield. Because they wouldn't let me play with them, I went and told me father, and me father called me brother and sister up, made me sister get in the bed and he tied her leg to the bed because she was spoiling the farmer's corn. In the middle of the night me sister said, 'I wants to go to toilet!' Me father used to dig a hole in the ground and we used to go in there then cover it with earth. I untied her leg so she could go – when she come back I tied her up again – seven o'clock at night till seven o'clock in the morning.

Such sternness is often rationalized on the grounds of reliance on the settled population for small acts of kindness that, in times of hardship, could be the difference between starvation and survival.

Dorothy:

I can remember me granny years ago – they used to live in wagons and tents. The women used to go out hawking, door to door, selling pegs, lace – anything they could get their hands on. They used to take the kids with them and the kids always used to stand at the gate. The mothers used to go to the doors selling and they used to ask, 'You haven't got a bit of bread for the children?' Certain of the people used to give them bread – give them all sorts. They never used to earn much money – like five shillings a week. They never had enough money to feed all the children that they had.

Linda:

When me father was a boy – he was only about seven – he used to look after the horse and cart when his sisters and his father were picking the ferns. He'd walk up and down the lanes and he'd wait for them. Sometimes he'd be there all day. On the way back through they'd go in the bakery and knock on the door and say, 'Can I have a glass of water? I got a couple of pennies – can you let me have a couple of stale cakes?'

Many people recall childhood memories, of arriving somewhere, pulling up on grass verges at the side of lanes, whenever possible close to a spring, pitching tents, perhaps going to knock on doors to ask for a kettle of water, and then seeing farmhands appearing to drive them away.

It was not just the violence with which Gypsy children had to contend. There was the muttering, the suspicious looks, and the name-calling. At the same time, there are memories of farmhands and other villagers, including local bobbies, coming to sit round campfires, sharing food and stories. Before people had landlines, not to mention mobile phones, people recollect policemen cycling to sites to pass on news to families. Still more common was the way in which the children of the settled population seemed to be drawn to the encampments: many would visit them despite their parents' disapproval. For their part, Gypsy parents were also apprehensive about these friendships.

Lisa:

> We always had friends that weren't Gypsies, but not very many. Dad didn't believe in it. 'They're no different than you, Lisa, but just be careful who you're getting about with.' We was never allowed to go to their houses. Me mum and dad wouldn't allow it. 'We don't know who that is. Could be paedophiles or anybody.' I wouldn't care – I didn't mind. I'd say to the girls, 'Come back to our trailer!' Well, you couldn't say trailer to the *gadje* girl – she didn't know what trailer meant. We had to say a caravan. She'd know what that meant then. We always made people welcome.

Robert:

> To keep us close to home our parents would tell us horror stories: one of the lanes we'd come up at night we'd hear of people down there with chains clanking, purely to keep us away from that area.

In the interactions between Gypsies and *gadjes*, there is a certain odd symmetry: Gypsy parents have suspicions about designs upon their children; at the same time, Gypsy groups have always acquired new members, runaways, people in trouble.

Diana:

> When the last war finished, a lot of Travellers took on children that runned away from home and took care of them. They grew up as Travellers. Loads of them.

Maggie:

> Every few years we would end up with children belonging to some of these

Three gadjes *pea picking with Defiance Smith, Maggie and Robert on the right.*

girls who had got into trouble. We've got one now called Joey, who lives in
Chippenham. Wonderful lad… They didn't 'ave any children of their own.
Took 'im and reared 'im. He asked me seven years ago, 'Can you remember
who my mum and dad were?'… It was either comin' with us or dyin', I told
'im. 'E's as much of a Gypsy as I am…

In tales of unwanted babies being handed to them lie the origins, perhaps, of the
wider myth about stolen babies. There is an irony here, as evidenced in the first
words learned by Robert, '*Cakka rokke chavvy, gadjes jellin the kai*', for Gypsies lived
in dread fear of their own children being seized by the authorities and taken away. It
would appear that no official records were kept of threats to remove children from
families that did not go to encampments designated for Gypsies. However, several
people were able to recall tales of children being taken into care around the middle
of the last century, and subsequently sent on ships to Canada. Some remembered
having to hide.

Diana:

No one ever chased us up to go to school. It was after the last war and the
mothers were scared somebody would take us so a lot of the travelling people
would hide their children up. Different kinds of people came over when the
last war was on and they got worried. A lot of children got killed and taken
and sent away, and the Romani families thought it was going to happen to
them. They kept them up the lane out the way. I remember being hidden. Me
father always used to have a wagon, and he always had a big stick pushed in
between the shafts with a green sheet over it, and he'd always say to us children,
'If you hear anybody coming – underneath. Nobody'll know you're there.'
That's what he used to say to us. We'd hide for whatever time it took them
talking. We could hear what they were saying, but they never heard us. We
never used to make a sound. They'd sell Romani children abroad. That's why
we didn't get an education. Our mothers wouldn't let us go – especially the
girls. They'd dress the girls in a pair of jeans and wellington boots, and keep
something on their hair to make them look like boys.

Among the mainstream population, there were tales of children who vanished, taken
by the Gypsies. There was actually some substance to such stories, but the basis of this
was often in a service that hidden and shifting people could provide for the mainstream population: collecting waifs and strays, helping to hide those in trouble.

Such children disappeared from official records, a phenomenon mirrored by
another event, no trace of which is to be found in records. Maggie recalls the sudden
panic when some men came looking for Gypsy children, when she and the other
youngsters were hastily hidden by the adults. This took place around 1950, when she
was about ten years old. She remembers an occasion when a black car arrived at the
Common where they were camped, a man in a suit getting out, waving official papers

that stated that they had to stop travelling and move to a site. If they refused, he said, the children would be put in care and taught how to read and write. That night, after the men had returned, they fled. Maggie could remember her father subsequently tying sacking around the horses' hooves, so that they could pass through villages before sunrise in silence, so that nobody would know of their passing or destination.

Nevertheless, she says, some children were taken.

Maggie:

What they did was to count them. They told us that they would start building encampments... If you didn't go to the encampments, your children would be taken into care... What they did with these children was take them into care, take them to ships to take them out to Canada...like adoptions... The paper-work would not come to light... We had no-one to stand up and speak for us.

All of which needs to be understood in an historical context. From the Middle Ages there had been specific legislation passed by Parliament, aimed at Gypsies and wandering mendicants, designed to expel all who chose not to become sedentary, on pain of forfeiture of life and property. Wandering Romanies were hanged for nomadism until the 1650s in England, and 1714 in Scotland. Lesser penalties remained and were handed out to those apprehended as Gypsies, including whipping, hard labour or perpetual banishment. Children between the ages of five and fourteen could be taken into unpaid bonded service until the age of eighteen for girls and twenty-four for boys. Laws attacking vagabondage continued to name 'Gypsies' specifically as late as the Vagrant Act of 1824.

That Gypsies felt an affinity with social outcasts is hardly surprising, and it is reflected in their account of a well-documented Dartmoor tale. This is the story of 'Jay's Grave'. On a narrow lane below Hound Tor there is a small burial mound. It belongs to an orphan girl known as Jay, or alternatively as Kitty Jay, or Mary Jay. Her story is as follows.

Towards the end of the eighteenth century an orphaned baby was taken into the Poor House at Newton Abbot. In those days the practice was for children of the Poor House to be named in alphabetical order. When this baby arrived, they were up to the letter 'J'. She was given the name Jay but, as in those days the name was also a slang term for a prostitute, the Christian name of Mary was added.

The girl remained at the Wolborough Poor House until her teens, where she supervised the younger children. Then she was sent to Canna Farm, outside Manaton, as an 'apprentice', which basically meant that she could be set to any work, either in the house or in the fields. It is thought that it was, perhaps, here that she received the name Kitty.

Here accounts diverge. Although some versions tell of Kitty Jay having been raped, allegedly by a young farmhand, others state that she had a relationship with the son of the owner of the farm. Whichever the case, she seems to have been driven away from the household, branded as a slut. Subsequently, she was found hanged in a barn, presumed to have committed suicide.

None of the three local parishes – Manaton, North Bovey or Widecombe-in-the-Moor – would bury her on consecrated ground, so she was buried at a crossroads, where road and moorland track converge, the point at which the three parishes met. This was a common custom at the time, to ward off evil spirits. A stake was driven through her heart, to stop the Devil claiming her soul, and to prevent her from returning to haunt decent, God-fearing inhabitants of the locality.

Nevertheless, the place did acquire the reputation of being haunted, and in 1860, her grave was opened by a local farmer, James Bryant of Hedge Barton. Though some locals had argued that there were only animal bones in the grave, a skull and bones of a young woman were found. They were re-interred, either in a coffin, a box, or a basket, depending on which account you believe.

Throughout the year, fresh flowers are to be found by her grave, but rather mysteriously, no-one has ever seen them being placed there. Local legend attributes the act to pixies. A number of motorists, passing at night, claim to have glimpsed spectral figures in their headlights; others report seeing a dark, hooded figure kneeling by the mound. This spirit has been identified either as one of those who drove the girl from the farm, or more specifically, as the man who got her pregnant, condemned to watch over the girl and the unborn child throughout eternity.

However, Gypsies have their own take on this forlorn tale, a slightly different version of the official account. Their story tells of a girl named Jane, a young girl taken from the workhouse to be a skivvy. She was sexually abused – either by the farmer, his son, or both – and on the discovery of her pregnancy, the girl was thrown out of the home. She went round the village from door to door, but each door remained closed to her. Subsequently, she was discovered hanged, and her body was taken to this desolate spot on the moor. Jane was fourteen years old at the time.

According to them, the farmer himself subsequently went mad, and killed himself on the same spot. The Travellers who passed by named her Kitty Jay, and took heather to the grave in her memory. Often, they would go out of their way with their ponies and traps to do so, and to this day, it is the Gypsies who tend the grave, bringing flowers.

MEMORIES OF WARTIME

In they wagon days we never cost this country one halfpenny. In fact, we done more for this country than people have ever reco'nised us for doin'. During the war our men was took, all our fathers was in the forces. We've got photographs of 'em in uniform.

Maggie

Over the decades, relationships with the non-Gypsy community fluctuated, never more so than during the Second World War. Some people recall being given ration books, then being made to queue for longer by shopkeepers, and sometimes treated with disdain. To some extent, this may have derived from the perception held by some people that Gypsies were not contributing to the war effort, and it is true that many Gypsy men were reluctant to serve in the army.

Dorothy:

A lot of Travellers used to go fighting in the First War, but when the second one come, some of the Travellers said, when they was eighteen or nineteen, that there was something wrong with them, so as not to go in the war. My dad had ulcers. They wouldn't take him. As soon as the war came, they had to go in the army or work on land – go on a farm or into the forestry. Some men who were strong and healthy, when they went to the medical, they would be examined and say there was something wrong with them. They didn't want to go and fight. The ones who went in the First War all got killed.

Jim:

During the war, some of the Traveller men pretended to be diabetic. They would eat lots of sugar when they came round recruiting. Quite a lot ran away, and hid in Scotland or Wales. Then a lot of them got tired of the hiding, and said, 'It's our country, let's go home.' So, in the end, a lot of them ended up going off to fight.

Diana:

Me dad didn't get called up, but all his brothers did. Only two come back out of the six. Some of the men done a runner. Me mum had four small boys, and me sister, and she was expecting me. Me father was in hiding, but he wasn't very far away. He used to tell us a story that back in the war – they used to call them the redcaps – they come up to me mother once and said, 'Have you got a man here?'

She said, 'No, I haven't go no man.'

'You have,' he said.

She said, 'I haven't. Nothing to do with me.'

They used to have bayonets on the top of the guns, and they goes all up and down the ditch with their bayonets, and they cut my father. He wouldn't whimper. He couldn't go nowhere to get stitched. They'd have took him.

The Gypsies used to help with the food in the war. I heard me mum and dad talk about it. Me dad saw a parachute on fire – he run and reported it, then he ran off himself – he had to.

According to most accounts, a fair proportion of Travellers did end up serving their country. John Gaskin was one of thirteen brothers, and most of them were called up. The youngest brother was too young to sign up, just sixteen years of age, but he was desperate to accompany them. In the absence of official papers, they were able to smuggle him in with them. He was the only brother not to return, bombed in action. John Gaskin himself returned shell shocked, lapsing into dreams in which he was confronting phantom enemies with a bayonet.

Many of those men who remained during the war years helped in other ways, willingly or not, according to the individuals concerned. Ethal Lee was one of those who was recruited early on during the war and put in a factory assembling tank parts. Although it was assumed that he had no appropriate skills for the task, the foreman was astonished to note how quickly he picked them up, merely by observing others on a single occasion. His wife, Thorney Lee, became a land girl.

Although they would avoid the towns, on account of the bombing, many men were often tracked down by soldiers. Leonard Smith was picked up around the back lanes of Wedmore. He served in the Home Guard, in Bristol, as a fireman. His daughter recalls her memories of those days.

Maggie:

In they wagon days we never cost this country one halfpenny. In fact, we done more for this country than people have ever reco'nised us for doin'. During the war our men was took, all our fathers was in the forces. We've got photographs of 'em in uniform.

We wouldn't see me dad, so me mum said, for months on end. He'd get away and come back and find one wagon and say, 'Have you seen so-and-so?' And they'd have to find where you were stopping by word of mouth.

The women never had no men. There wasn't a man left. They wasn't satisfied with that. You get a family with a boy of fifteen that looked seventeen or eighteen – they were took. We couldn't prove their ages – they weren't registered. They got used to people saying, 'That boy's only fifteen,' but they'd say, 'He don't look fifteen to me,' and he was took!

Defiance Smith, Maggie, her brother and cousin Alice in the early 1940s. There were always other people on hand to help with the children.

They didn't just take the men. They took everything else that went with them. The boys, the horses, even the harness. The lot. They'd take it. They took the horses out of the shafts of the wagons to send abroad to pull the guns. Commandeered, that's what they said, 'We are commandeering your horses to use in the war. They will be sent out to the front to pull the big guns.' We was left with one horse an' a few foals to pull three wagons. I often wonders if any of our horses got killed over there, but one thing I do know is, they would have gived their best as best they could. I cried me yocks out when they took um. Part of the family they was, just like our Patchie an' Ticker is now.

The women had to make the best of their road. And we'd have old knackers that could hardly pull and young foals that weren't broke in to move so they could get food.

Of course, there are always exceptions, and reminiscing on the subject, one woman (who preferred to remain anonymous) recalled her grandmother being less than devastated when her husband was enlisted to fight.

I remember my gran saying, years afterwards, that when they took me grandad, though she pretended to cry at the time, secretly she were well pleased. They were welcome to the old so-and-so, that's what she told me, and that taking the horses was far worser than taking the men. Mind you, you never met me grandad!

Lunch break in the 1940s at Fordgate near Moorland, Bridgwater. In wartime meals had to be eaten by day because of the blackout. The picture includes members of Nellie and Diana's families, with adults from left to right: Aunt Trainett, Uncle Henry, Aunt Anna (with Nellie), Uncle Arthur, Aunt Emmy, Uncle Henry, Uncle Andrew, Aunt Diney.

More common, however, were feelings of loss and dislocation.

Anna:

When the war came, my dear old grandad, he went in the war. He had one brother get his hand blowed off. My dear old Uncle Johnny he went in the war. They took all the Gypsy men. The Gypsy women were left on farms to be land girls and work in the fields – not to get a wage but so they could leave the wagons. The biggest girls would go in the fields and the women'd go out selling as they'd always gone.

Me mam and me aunties, they worked as land girls on the farm, in the fields, but me granny couldn't work in the fields, so she used to walk out around the doors selling lace and pegs and elder flowers.

During the war…my granny 'ad these tickets, coupons, but tickets were no good to 'er. My granny would change them for a couple of eggs or something.

Maggie:

I was four year old when the war ended. I can't remember much about it [a conversation she overheard between her mother and her aunt after the war], an' it's only three years ago, so things is still tight for us. Now me mam is telling me Aunt Mae how frightening it was when the bombs was being dropped, as we never had shelters to run to – just the hedges or woods to hide in. We was left to get on as best we could, an' look after our *chavvies* on our own. Nobody had time to worry about we lot; the *gadjes* had their own problems. I lost track of me family back down in Devon. Me brother Bobby an' our Ellen's man, Bob, was took in the army, so up an' down the country we was all in the same boat.

Maggie's family stayed in Bristol during its blitz in order to be near their father, who kept running away and then getting caught. Although at the start of the war, Bristol was generally regarded as relatively safe, during the course of 1942 the Luftwaffe regularly targeted the city with explosives and incendiary bombs on top of which it dumped barrels of oil to fuel the flames. It was during this period that the medieval city centre was destroyed and it wasn't until the spring of 1944 that the final 'all clear' was sounded in the city. Children were evacuated from Bristol, but obviously not those such as Maggie and her brothers and sisters. Times were hard after the war ended too.

Maggie:

During and after the war our life was *shussyin'* — because we would keep and feed every village we went to. We could pull up into a village (it went on a few years after the war when everything was rationed) and the baker would be selling rabbits, the butcher would be selling rabbits and the coalman would sell rabbits and when we pulled near a village they'd all come up and give us their orders! Our men would be rabbiting day and night!

They never knew about ration books until they went calling, and the people in the houses said about it one day and the woman helped me mum get her ration books. It was only people that could read and write that helped them get ration books. We had our ration books. I used to boil mine out with Parazone to get the stamps out so I could use them again. In fact, everybody did. We had to or starve.

And when Family Allowance come out, a lot of our people wouldn't have it because they thought they were selling their children to the government. If they took the money, their children wouldn't belong to them any more. Because of lack of education, and fear.

In the view of many Gypsies, their skills were crucial to the survival of the wider population, a factor that is barely acknowledged.

Maggie:

Lucky fer us we had our *jukkles* (dogs) to ketch *shussies* (rabbits). We sent the bits of boys out *shussying* to help keep us. We've never gone hungry. There's too much meat and wildlife out there in the countryside — we've never as children gone hungry. The only thing we had to buy was bread and milk. All the rest we could provide for ourselves. And in the war we'd provide for the villages we went through. They relied on us. I know they'd say, 'Oh, the Gypsies are coming again,' and they'd ring up the old *gavver mush* and say, 'The Gypsies are here,' but you wouldn't even have your fire lit before the baker, the milkman — everybody would want rabbits or ducks, or pheasants for their customers.

That would feed all the people that would slam the door in our faces the next day when we was trying to sell them a few flowers. There's a lot more

to the Gypsy than meets the eye. We did play our part in the war. We lost
loads of our men. In some cases, the men's names are up on the war
memorials. They were rounded up and took.

As Gypsy women were accustomed to physical work, working in the fields was no
particular hardship. In the disruption to family and community life, it might be said
that their privations were not all that different to those encountered by members of
the settled population. With limited access to radio or newspapers, however, the
sense of disorientation and uncertainty was magnified. Often isolated from the rest
of society, with only fragments of news coming their way, it was easy for those
remaining to be prey to rumour and heightened anxiety.

Pat:

A lot of Romani blokes went into the army. There's the tales that they
escaped…they broke their arms, their legs…but they did go. A lot of them
went into the army, into the war – and the woman has got the horse and the
wagon and she can travel around and look after herself and the kids – and
she's got five or six left – 'cos the older ones had to go as well – and she fears
that Hitler's going to land in this country. People are saying he's going to take
over. It's quite a scary thing – you don't get a dark night now, a black night.
There's always streetlights. In those days the night was black dark, and you
could go round a corner and you could bump straight into a German soldier,
and he's going to take you away for all you knew – he could have landed out
of his parachute. So if she's in the village shopping, the village people are saying,
'What you gonna do, dear? You ain't gonna be able to be travelling long.
Hitler's gonna come, and he's exterminated all you Gypsies.'

Old Age

My granny sang a lot. We took 'er to the pub once. She sang from morning till night.
The landlord said, 'You'll 'ave to take 'er 'ome now.'

Nellie

Growing old can be a bleak and lonely business for far too many of the settled population, but among Gypsy families, it is the norm to care for family members in old age with devotion and tenderness. The insularity of the nuclear family when compared with extended families, the importance the settled community place on privacy and autonomy, the dictates of career patterns and consumerism, all mitigate against caring for older relatives. Gypsies have little truck with this way of life and the resultant treatment of the elderly.

Amy:

Our old people hardly ever go into homes. The grandchildren will look after them if their parents are gone. No matter what it takes they are kept as near as possible because we treasure them. They are the head of the family. They might not be able to do anything, but they are the head of the family. You wouldn't do anything with their property or belongings. There's always somebody taking care of their family, wherever you go.

Maggie:

Part of our culture is that when our parents get old we don't put them into care. They're took back into the family. I haven't got any daughters –I've got two sons – but I haven't got a worry in the world. I'm not saying my daughters-in-law wouldn't have me, but the boys would say so.

Rodney:

Old people are well looked after. You don't hear of them going into homes unless someone goes completely off their head and they've got to be in somewhere for their own safety and they get the best care. I can't think of anyone offhand that's been put away because of old age. We always used to say that about me dad when he was alive – that's something that will never happen. You're used to your surroundings, and if you can get someone to look after you... It's the right way, of course it is.

Rodney's granny, Anna Isaacs, and his cousin Sophie.

Jim pointed out how important it was for many older family members to keep working – Gypsies and non-Gypsies alike can be so identified with their occupation that retirement does not come as a blessing.

Jim:

> When me old grandad sold 'is 'orses…and when he come out of 'is wagon, he just died. And with the other old people, like me granny, she was out with a basket all 'er life; me grandad passed away first, and me Aunt 'elen, that was 'er daughter, said to 'er mum, 'Don't go out any more, mam; we'll stop 'ome, no problem.' But she said 'I can't; I can't stop at 'ome.' And when she stopped at 'ome, she died. It was only the getting up every morning and doing it, that kept them going. I've seen the same thing time and again: when they're made to stop home, they don't last long.

Fortunately, there are those who can't be made to stop home! Anna's aunt, Violet Gaskin, is still on the road in her eighties, still dealing in horses, and still going selling out of her basket, while her husband, Ernie Gaskin, goes out scrapping.

Sometimes, however, retirement cannot be avoided. Then the family support network comes into its own. Maggie looked after her mother, Defiance, for four years, making sure her last days were as happy and comfortable as possible.

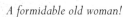

A formidable old woman!

Maggie:

> She had her tiny little bed over there in that corner; in fact she died there in that corner. And she was in hospital twenty-one days, then she was home twelve days and thirteen nights, and she sang all the songs that we'd grown up with. When she'd been singing them previously she'd forgotten some of the words and some of the verses, but when she was over there dying she knew the song word for word and never missed a verse or a word. It seems like it all came back; even the tunes was better than what she was singing, you know, before she was ill. And she mentioned everybody right through the generations. But she was so happy, the carers used to come through the door and she would start singing to them, and she would be singing until they went and then she'd be away again.

Like so many people featured in this book, Maggie approached her mother's old age

Maggie's grandparents Dannal and Emma Butler (centre), early 1950s.

with practicality, humour, respect and love. There was no suggestion that her mother's
needs were a burden.

Maggie:

> Well, when mum was very old I had her intercom and she never knew it was
> there. If she was distressed in the night I could come over. And after mum
> had died my friend was telling me her mum was getting like it and I said to
> her, 'Well, when I come down I'll bring you that intercom but don't let your
> mum know it's there. And don't be upset by what your mother says when
> she's on her own. I used to lay in bed and I used to hear my mum cuss me,
> call me all the names under the sun, and when I come over there in the
> morning she was sweet as pie, but because she was on her own, she could
> have her say.'
>
> And she said, 'My mum won't do that.'
>
> Anyway, a few weeks later she phoned me up and she said, 'That bloody
> intercom! I knows all me mum's business and all her feelings about all of us!'
> So you do get to hear a lot of things you don't want to hear.
>
> She'd have all the food that she wanted and it was usually packets of crisps
> and you could hear it crunching in your ears on the intercom and you'd turn
> it down and then when she'd finished eating you'd turn the volume back up
> in case she fell down or anything. And then she'd sit and talk to herself. 'This
> is nice.' And then she'd ramble. 'If my Maggie was here now, I'd tell her a
> thing or two. Wait till tomorrow!' And by tomorrow morning she'd passed it
> and gone on, but you do hear a lot of things.

Maggie's father, Leonard, like many other Gypsies, had a deep desire to revisit
certain places before he died, and Maggie made sure that, wherever possible, his
wishes were fulfilled.

Maggie:

> When we've got someone very ill and dyin', they have to go back. When my
> dad was very ill, I took him to every conceivable place he mentioned in that
> few months he had left. It's our custom. We take 'em. They go happy. Or if
> they ask for someone, it might take a few weeks to track them.

This tender concern towards Leonard Smith was also demonstrated by an old family
friend – aided and abetted by a loving daughter.

Maggie:

> He *chopped*; me dad would have dealt on his deathbed… In fact…the week
> leading up to him going to bed a lovely old man called Georgie Smith
> brought up a harness or two to give to me dad…with the blinkers. And I said
> to him, I said, 'Instead of giving it to him, have a deal with him first.'

And he said, 'Oh, it's a present.'

And I said, 'I know, but deal for it instead.'

And they dealt, and me dad said, 'Pay him, Maggie.'

I said, 'I will.'

And outside, he said, 'I don't want that fiver, Maggie.'

And I said, 'You've got to because he's dealt, you've got to have the fiver even if you go and spend it on drink. You've got to have that fiver.'

And in the end he said, 'Well, you're right really. Looking at it like that, your dad owes me, doesn't he, 'cause we dealt?'

Maggie's dad was delighted with his bargain. He talked about it all that day.

Maggie:

'I done a deal this morning, Maggie; did you see me have a deal this morning, Maggie?' It was brilliant because it give him something other than not being able to get back out of the chair to think about.

While Leonard Smith went on his final journey, and revisited all the places he had known, Anna recalled her grandmother embarking on something slightly different prior to her death – an imagined odyssey through her memories.

Anna:

When me granny was dying, she was saying, 'Now come on John, we're not stopping there. Look who's 'ere.' And it was like, you know, it was really there. They could really see the people…

Inevitably, some old people are less lovable than others, and as a child, Maggie was unenthusiastic about visiting her granny. Her mother was well aware that the visits were difficult for the children, and did what she could do minimise the pain.

Maggie:

We used to go to the Prince Lane, but because granny used to bully us kids, me mum would try not to take us there. She used to warn me dad, 'You'd better have a word with the old woman to leave these kids alone.'

Anyway, we went to see the old granny. An' she'll be only too glad to have us: fetch me this, fetch me that. She never stops. Anybody else would run out of breath, but not her. Our grandad is kind an' gentle and happy. The old granny is just like a crab apple – proper sour. She's tall, dressed from head to toe in deep black, smokes a clay pipe, wears a big black hat, an' drinks like a fish. That's me granny, an' we *chavvies* is warned not to upset her, or else. Like me mam would say, 'What a life, eh.'

It was never ending. You couldn't sit, you couldn't eat, you couldn't play. The old woman would have you running for wood, fetching water, picking

flowers, getting blackberries. She was such a demanding, bossy old woman.
We used to feel sorry for Grandad. She put him through it. She wasn't a
little person. She'd sit and eat sweets in front of you and she wouldn't
dream of sharing! And it was my sweets she was eating! She'd be getting the
sweet coupons! I can see her coming now. She'd get in the Jug and Bottle,
because the women couldn't go in the bars. She'd have her Guinness and
stay there until she'd spent every penny she'd got going out calling. There
was nothing to bring back for the old feller. She'd come down, singing and
going on – we used to run and hide. There was smoke coming out of her
pipe! Her pipe was only that long – we used to say, 'Please God, let him set

Maggie's granny (on the right), probably early 1950s.

fire and burn Granny's nose,' and it did! On her deathbed it was. When she wanted the last puff the day before she died she was mooching, and they thought she was looking for her purse but it wasn't – it was her pipe. Anyway they gave him to her and lit him up and he flared right up and burned her! And me dad said, 'That's you two children! You've been wishing that on the old woman for years!' And it happened! It did burn her. She was a character all to herself. But not a nice character. I was talking about her to my cousin. He said, 'Work! She wouldn't let you stop working!' You couldn't be children. You was work horses.

Almost all those in this book spoke of their older relatives with affection and love.

Nellie:

My granny sang a lot. We took 'er to the pub once. She sang from morning till night. The landlord said, 'You'll 'ave to take 'er 'ome now.'

Anna:

It's a joy to look after our old: every minute's precious to them.

Caring for parents seems to be the norm in Romani families, where a lot of family responsibility falls on the oldest daughter and the oldest son.

Diana:

My older sister looked after Mother and Father. She didn't get married. I've never asked if she wanted to. It's been on the tip of me tongue – it's not an easy question to ask. She looked after me father till the end – she looked after me mother till the end. You generally find that in the old Romany families. It would not be me – I was the second one. No matter what they had to discuss they'd always tell the oldest girl – it would all be discussed with she, and the oldest son. The ones in the middle would have to listen and keep it shut! Me sister – when me mother died – she was a woman about fifteen stone, and she went down to about nine. It really broke her heart, Mother passing. She had her for all that time. They did everything together.

When Linda's grandparents were getting on, their children made sure they were comfortable in their old age – though not without some resistance.

Linda:

I can remember my granny and grandad on the riverside. The earliest memory of them; he had his own ground near Barnstaple and they made their place themselves – I was thinking about this the other day. It was all made out of galvanised. It was two rooms – you had to go down two or three little steps. It was very dark in there and all they had – it was like a bus window – you

Old woman in a bonnet, out in a hop field.

couldn't open it. Then they had a curtain pulled across halfway and that was the bedroom and there was no windows at all. On to the side of this, they used to call it the linhay and that was made of galvanised and they had an open fire in there with the iron – the hook.

[Grandad's] children said, 'You can't go on living there no more – it isn't warm enough for Mother.' He give at the time £2,000 and they bought this two-roomed shed with all windows and they had a Queen Anne stove – black leaded – and a chimney going up. Me granny wouldn't move in for nearly twelve months. Me mother got them this big armchair and me grandad used to go in there every day and have himself a sleep in this big armchair. Before that they were on a farm with their children between Bideford and Barnstaple – he was a horse dealer. Why ever did they leave a farm to move to this place they made theirselves – I could never understand it! No toilets – running water, yes, but no toilets. They both lived there till they died.

Maggie also shared the responsibility for caring for her aunt with the other women in the family. When her uncle organised hospice care against her aunt's wishes, there was a falling out that was never healed.

Maggie:

My aunt down in Devon, she was seriously ill and I said to Terry one day, 'Would you come down and tell me if you think I'm needed because I'm thinking about going for three days and then coming back for three days and

Leonard Smith's first cousin from Bristol. (Used by kind permission of Mick Garland)

then going back again.' And he went down and he just sort of watched all what was going on and he said, 'Yeah, you're needed.' So instead of going down permanently I was down every three days, but on the other days that I wasn't there it was her sisters and nieces that were.

She actually died in a hospice because her husband put her in there, but all she did was beg to go home and it was so cruel, so heartbreaking, that we were in tears for the last two days of her life because she knew what was happening to her. And she wanted to go home so desperate. In fact, when I went down on the funeral morning I went to her box and I said, 'You know you're home; you've got home. You're home.' And it's what she wanted, it's what we wanted, but we couldn't go against her husband.

He didn't want the trouble of looking after her, that's the truth, you know. He's dead now and I wouldn't follow him because of what he done. Lots of us didn't. Because we never forgave him. I never went in hospital to see him and I didn't follow his funeral because of what he done to my aunt so I didn't forgive him either. A lot of us didn't forgive him because sitting with her so many hours we knew how she was feeling, we knew she was desperate to get home to her own bed, but he would say, 'No.' And then when his turn came nobody bothered with him, so it's a way of punishment. He was punished for what he done.

Maggie's brother, Robert, spoke eloquently of the high regard for old people in his community as well as shedding light on the sometimes bewilderingly frequent references to Gypsy Kings and Queens. The title would be given to an older person who was accorded great respect.

Robert:

My Aunt Helen was a gorgeous woman, beautiful – in my mind she's become a Queen. It's that placidness and loveliness that generates that – and wisdom. The older you get, you learn more, so you hand it down to the younger generation.

The same tender care and high regard can be heard when Rodney talks about his older relatives.

Rodney:

Uncle Bill and Aunt Tilly used to pull around me granny because she was on her own. They'd be around together. We used to visit her regularly and me great-granny Nella. Her daughter stayed with her till she was an old woman, taking care of her, all her life. That woman lived till around ninety years old – smoked a pipe – outside around the fire. You'd go there and you'd have the best bread and butter and whatever they used to put on it – always new bread. Whenever you'd pull up there it was out with a cup of tea. I used to look forward to it. A lot of the older women smoked pipes.

Gypsy woman with her pipe.

Mutual suspicion and prejudice damage relationships between Gypsy and non-Gypsy to everyone's detriment. In reality, both communities have much to offer the other. In their fierce protection of the family and care for older people, Gypsies demonstrate age-old values that benefit all communities.

No doubt Maggie's children, like so many others, will willingly play their part when the time comes. She has a very clear idea of where she wants to end her days.

Maggie:

I've always said the only way I'll leave this place is carried out – feet first – I've got me dad's old mare buried down the bottom – I've got the wagons out there in the shed – I've got all me Gypsy life here around me.

Overgrown Tracks
and
Burning Wagons

Years ago when they used to have the funerals — people used to travel miles and miles. And every-body would be dressed in black — no other colour... They'd come home then to the place where they died. They'd have a big fire going. The women would be doing the food all the time. No drink — just cups of tea...

Dorothy

Near Haldon Hill in Devon, hidden away yet within earshot of the traffic on the nearby A38 and A380, there is a path leading through the woods, to a place where Gypsies came to bury the babies who had died at birth. The place now is untended, its precise location forgotten by all but near relatives. The babies here were buried in bloater boxes. Across the country there are many such places.

Out on the road, for mother, as for child, birth was a time of danger, particularly during the winter months. When a woman 'went to bed', there was no medical infrastructure. Exposed to the elements, in her tent or wagon, there were only the other women to tend her. There are tales of pregnant women who have predicted their own deaths. Maggie, for instance, recounts how her Aunt Emmy, when still only two months pregnant, predicted that she would die, but her child would live. Despite her mother's entreaties — 'Look at the size of me, an' I got five, an' me less than five foot tall' — her daughter just repeated, 'I knows what I knows. The child will live an' I will die.' When the time came, her prediction, indeed, turned out to be correct.

It was always rare for Gypsy women to allow non-Gypsies to assist during childbirth, and when they did end up in maternity wards, it was usually due to past tragedies or difficulties. Pat described her mother's experiences.

Pat:

She had a terrible time having a baby, so she didn't have any more. She thought I shouldn't have had any babies. I was twins, but the other one didn't survive. She was four days in labour. You think that's horrendous, but Katrina [Pat's daughter], she was three days. She actually lost one and so did Mark's first partner — she was probably riding horses and had a miscarriage. A couple of weeks later she said, 'There's something going on.' Saw the doctor, and she was still pregnant. There's twins all around the family. That's quite strange, I think. So my mum wasn't going to have any more. In four days they only gave

her the tiniest drop of water. It was this horrible labour ward and there was
a little window up there, and she could hear a plane and thought, 'Oh, if I
could just see something different – see that plane cross the window!'

Romani existence was ever hard, the fragility of life being evident from the first
moment; most families can tell you of infants and young children who died of sickness or through accident. Maggie's own brother, Jesse, died at the age of seven,
killed by a bolting horse, and she and her brother, Robert, each recalled the trauma.
In Robert Smith's view, the event was a turning point in the family's life.

Robert:

I was born on the side of the road in a horse-drawn wagon and travelled the
nomadic way of life until my brother was killed in 1950 when he was seven.
From that moment on my mother lost the heart for travelling.

According to Robert, death was a recurrent feature of his childhood, and it was
expected that the whole family would attend funerals of distant relatives or friends,
even when it entailed a long journey.

Robert:

Always the fairs – fairs and funerals. As a child, that's all I remember. I've
been to funerals and I don't know whose funeral I've gone to.

Jesse Smith's walking funeral,
1950.

Some of these funerals would involve hundreds of mourners. Robert recalls there

The funeral of Jesse Smith,
aged seven, at Box in 1950.
The mourners walked for
four miles.

being around three hundred at his mother's funeral, the town of Glastonbury and the surrounding roads being jammed up by the procession. Such occasions are carefully organised after a death; in the past, publicising such large-scale events relied on traditional communication networks.

Robert:

> Now we've got telephones to keep in touch but it used to be word of mouth. If someone died up in Hampshire, within a few hours it would travel down by word of mouth. Different groups would pass it on to different groups.

Jesse Smith's funeral after
he was killed by a runaway
horse.

The hearse departs from the Smith family's home.

That's how we ended going up to all these countless funerals but who they were I didn't know!

Nellie recalled there being thirteen limousines at the funeral of John Isaacs, a man, who by all accounts, had always concealed evidence of his wealth, living with extreme frugality. John, whose home was 'basic', and whose preferred vehicle was a battered old Cortina, had made a fortune collecting materials such as copper, bronze and aluminium, and was reputed to carry thousands of pounds in his coat pocket. According to one acquaintance.

Some of his stuff was really hot when it went in, but cold by the time it came out. He would turn in his grave if he saw the price of copper now!

Nowadays, the authorities are informed by undertakers of funerals that are likely to involve huge groups of mourners, and police are called in to try to ensure that processions take place as smoothly as possible. Even so, some funerals can still the heartbeat of whole towns.

Tom:

Our sons got killed in a car accident just gone four years ago. We had over a thousand of the family turned up for the funeral. And everybody (all the *gadjes*) closed their shops in support for the family. There were three and a half thousand people in the street – everyone knows our family. The local police were brilliant. The local council wouldn't let anybody pay for the car parks.

We've got a show we do every Christmas here – because the town was so good to our family. We do the Engine Rally in the town – without charge because the people were so good to us in the town and locally. It's the only way I can think to thank them – to play for charity, for the boys.

In the past, the sheer scale of processions at funerals frequently led to chaotic scenes and tensions between Gypsy mourners, local communities and the police. When following a dead body, it is viewed as bad luck to allow any break in the cortège, and traffic signs are simply ignored. One hears of particularly anarchic road scenes in cities such as London, with traffic lights changing countless times to absolutely no effect.

In rural communities, funerals can entail a final pilgrimage by the mourners, passing through a series of towns and villages. Lisa recalls there being well over five hundred mourners and lorry loads of flowers at her grandmother's funeral, which travelled from her Aunt Brit's (Britannia) near Tewkesbury back to Congresbury Huish, near Weston-super-Mare. Flowers are of special significance on such occasions, as is evident from Maggie's account of the funeral of the famous bare-knuckle fighter, Young John Small, who had once won a fight against former world light heavyweight champion (and subsequently, friend of the Krays), Freddie Mills.

Maggie:

There was a big crowd and he left money for the Village Hall to put on every conceivable food and drink because he wanted everybody to celebrate his life, not his death. They all got drunk and had an absolutely fantastic time. His daughter Mary made his wreath – she made a cross. When we lose someone, we go crazy over flowers. Mary said she was going to make her father's family cross. She said, 'I'm going to use the flowers out of the hedges. Whatever's growing at the time. No boughten flowers. No cultivated flowers. Flowers from the countryside.'

Funeral morning she come up and fetched me. She had it in her van. She said, 'Come and help me get this wreath out.' We opened the back of the van up and the wreath is as long as what this van is. As she bin and passed it out to me, I got to the foot of the cross and she had the two arms of the cross. She went to swing it round – turn it – and bin and caught it in the hedge and ripped some of the flowers out. Well, I laughed, but you could never laugh at Mary – she'd stretch you out in a second. She said, 'If you laughs, I'm gonna kill you!' I had me fist in me mouth. She said, 'Go and scratch some more out.' It was the time of the year when all the banks is covered in this tiny white flower – when it dries, it goes like a bead and you can pop it. We had to get that and rescue some of the flowers to redo the arm of this cross. That's what 'e wanted. That must 'ave been the flowers we used before people was cultivatin'. I know they begged flowers out of people's gardens and made their own wreaths as well as had boughten wreaths. They'd make their own. It goes back many generations. Whatever that person meant to you – it could have been a horse; it could have been a pint; it could have been a walking stick or a whip – whatever, this is what we have made now. It's cropped up in recent years. It never used to be. Now every funeral 'as the Gates of

*Members of Jim Lee's family
at the funeral of Paddy Lee's
mother.*

Heaven, with the gates open. But we don't have to explain to each other because we all know if you only take one flower, that one flower would mean something. Or if you took a big wreath, it's because that meant something. It's all to do with meaning and feeling. It might have been that, years ago, they picked flowery herbs to put on the graves. They might have picked flowers off the elder because it might have kept that person going for an extra number of years. Today the funeral is the flowers.

It is traditional to make floral tributes personal.

Rodney:

If someone loved playing darts – the flowers would be shaped like a dartboard and some darts. If they liked their horses, it would generally be the shape of a horse, or horse and wagons, all these shapes – cushions or whatever. There was a place in North Curry used to do the flowers. They go to people they trust. We've made one or two – get a base of Oasis, and a plastic edge and you can put water in to keep it a bit longer. I made a heart once. A young feller bought it for his granny's grave. That got me going. There's a call for it.

It is customary for Gypsies to hold a wake after a death, and the period between midnight and one o'clock is sometimes referred to as the 'bewitching hour', when family members and close friends sit up with the dead person, and talk or sing to them.

One of Maggie's vivid childhood recollections is of the death of her Aunt Emmy: the collection of lorry loads of wood to keep the *yogs* burning, over which the kettle was heated to make successive cups of tea; the *chavvies* put to bed in their square tents, while their elders stayed up through the night with the lit candles in Aunt Emmy's wagon; the open coffin; the respect given to the private farewell at midnight from her husband, Blacksmith Joe.

There are other Romani customs concerning death, such as filing past the coffin, touching the hands or face of the dead person, and following the coffin into the church in pairs – those not in pairs have to wait outside the church. For twelve months after a death, it is viewed as a mark of respect to wear black.

Dorothy:

Years ago when they used to have the funerals – people used to travel miles and miles. And everybody would be dressed in black – no other colour. White blouses, white shirts. They'd come home then to the place where they died. They'd have a big fire going. The women would be doing the food all the time. No drink – just cups of tea. That was the old-fashioned thing they used to do. Never believed in drink at a funeral.

In the past, it was often hard to find burial places.

Robert:

It's only quite recently that we was allowed to be buried in the churchyard – simply because we wasn't in a settled place and didn't attend that church in that parish. Even now you can't get buried in another parish unless you've bought a plot there. Up to quite recently, we couldn't be buried anywhere, so what used to happen, the men at night, not the women, would go off and bury those people. You could have run over some of my ancestors coming up here today – they were taken to all the loneliest spots and buried in the dead of night and only the men would know. There was no other way. It's like when they burnt the wagons and the tents. It started off they burnt all the goods in the tents; when they had wagons, they burnt the wagons. If there was china, crockery that belonged to the woman or the man, they'd do the same thing at night, go off and bury the crockery, so it was gone forever, so they could start again. New life begins. I suppose that died out in the forties and fifties, after the war.

According to the Romani view, whatever the personal circumstances in life, all become equal in death. Maggie remembered the response from those around upon the death of a cousin.

Maggie:

I had a cousin called Joe and he died penniless. We all clubbed together when we heard he died. He died in a pub talking about death, 'cos he was like that – and I made one phone call, and from that phone call, within four or five days, I had over three thousand pounds here in cash, and we buried him. That is the Gypsy way – if somebody dies in poverty, they're put away the same as everybody else.

Along with this sense of egalitarianism, there is a rejection of materialism.

Rodney:

I've been to some big Gypsy funerals. There's been so many, to be honest with you. When you're in your teens there's nobody you really know that's gone on, but now – there's just loads gone on that you knew quite well. You do a lot of walking behind up to the graveyard. A lot don't believe in cremation. And down in the hole has to be all blocked up, or boarded up, like a tomb, so no dirt touches that person. Paving slabs, like a lining, and slabs on top. They treat that person like they're alive still. If it's pouring with rain they don't want to see a load of water where their loved one is going down. I remember my Aunt Paula – when she was buried they put money in her hand – she had handfuls of money. She loved her money, so she had some to take with her! And they loved her money, so for her to be buried like that, they were saying how much they loved their mother by not keeping it.

Although now growing rare, amongst Gypsies the traditional way has been to burn possessions after a death, including the wagons – normally a private ceremony. The belongings of the deceased are put inside the wagon, which is set alight. Afterwards, the shell of the wagon is broken up and buried. Robert connects the custom to Gypsy survival.

Robert:

Part of the reason we have survived so long is because we're non-materialistic. I've got nothing that belonged to my great-great-grandfather. None of the family have, so all those things were put in the grave. What I'd love now is some of the old-fashioned whips to go with my collection. I can't find any but I know a coffin with at least four in there. They would put all their worldly goods in the coffin.

We wouldn't survive as Gypsies if we'd clung to things all the way down through. No doubt that's part of the culture that's gone now. I've got a pair of old-fashioned weights out on the wheels that my father used to use – nothing personal of his. I don't want anything. He's in my heart, in my mind. If you love that person, they'll always be with you, anyway.

His sister, Maggie, yearns for that contact with their parents.

Maggie:

The only spirit I've ever seen was me dad, since I lived here. He used to come out to Maggie and Storm, his horses. He never looked this way – he was too intent on sorting them out then going back to whatever he had parked at the gate. I've looked drastically for me dad and me mum, but I've never seen anything.

For Tom and Jean Orchard, however, the presence remains strong of the two sons they lost in a car crash.

Tom:

> Up above us there's Anthony and Nathan's faces as clear as day in the clouds. One old aunty and granny is with the two boys. Sometimes – you don't see them very often – but out the corner of your eye, you see two heads going down the path. It was that strong the other day I went out and I thought there was somebody outside. Ashley came home on his bike in the winter – it was dark – Jean'll tell you. There were two shadows behind Ashley, still protecting him and seeing he got home safely. There is life after death. The two boys didn't believe in any of it…
>
> Jean went and saw a spiritualist. The two boys were talking through her to Jean. I was dead against it, but it is so. She said exactly what we put in the coffins. That was strangers to us. Jean's niece went to a spiritualist, in the Midlands. She said, 'You've had some tragedy in your family. Two cousins died in a car accident.'
>
> 'That's right.'
>
> 'Well, I've got the two boys here telling me this.' Told her the red car they died in, the Escort, and, 'Tell Dad, I'm sorry that we couldn't stay. The wheel touched me heart.' That's what the woman said. That's what did happen. They were crushed. They weren't cut or marked. There's definitely something in it… When I'm playing that music on stage with Jean, the boys are there…

As a fortune teller, Anna has encountered many seeking to come to terms with illness and death.

Anna:

> When I'm at the fairs I've got a queue all day. I try to let troubled people go by. But if they come in, I'd like to put them on the right route. I try me hardest to help them. People that's dying come in really to be helped. I give them peace of mind. I explain to them in my way. I ain't going to just say, 'You're going to die', 'cos I wouldn't do that. I've got a heart. I'll help them.

Perhaps it is something to do with the precarious nature of Romani existence over the centuries that death seems to hover in the background as a presence, not actually malign, just part of life. Some people have been known to predict the amount of time left to them; others will say that they have known when a family member has died, even though they were miles away at the time. Some just seem to be particularly attuned to a world of spirits.

Maggie:

> I knew how many days we had left with me mam. When her dad died, we

knew. This is why we gather so much because we know the time we've got. The doctors say this and that – 'We can give you longer' – but it don't stop your instinct or your knowledge. The look of you, the way you're behaving, the way you're breathing. Even the way you're laying. Is he making his nest? Is he getting ready to go? We go looking for these things.

Me dad always knew there was something funny about me, and our Alfie seen his first spirit after Jesse died. We went down to Devon to me mum's people, and we pulled in this little spinney. Me grandad wouldn't have us in because me dad was a peg maker. Me grandad owned his paddock, and he thought me dad would cut his hedges. We pulled in at Drum Bridges. Me mum and dad had to borrow money to bury me brother off me dad's brother because they didn't have any money. We had to earn money to pay this debt back. We never had nothing. She put us into school at Drum Bridges. The first day we was dragged to the school, but we was allowed to walk home down the path, and our Alfie picked up a postal order – I think it was for twenty-five shillings. That put them on their feet. That same night he and Robert had to sleep in the tent. How he described it was [that] he seen a waiter with a tray, dressed in black and white. Then he went down under the bedclothes!

Me mum and dad was going to buy a house and we was going to have a nose round. Alfie happened to come down and he stood outside and said, 'Oh, Mum don't buy this place – it's unlucky. There's a bedroom there, and a man that died in that room was took out that window on a piece of galvanised.' We smiled. We thought, 'What the hell?' He kept on that much she lost interest. We went back to the family just for nosiness.

We said, 'Anybody ever die up there?'

They said, 'Yes.'

'How did you get him out?'

'What we had to, because we couldn't get 'un down the stairs, we had to put him on a piece of galvanised and lower him out the window.' How would he see that? He knew! He seen that!

Many Gypsies are ever wary for signs of impending death. As Dorothy remarks, 'If we sees a robin, a little bird outside, we know there's going to be a death.' Amongst a people who have had to live for generations with the shadowy presence of death amongst them, it is as well to be prepared. Meanwhile, somewhere in a clearing, in an overgrown wood, on a hill, not far from a road where the world rushes by, all is still.

THE ROAD

IN SEARCH OF OLD CHILDHOOD LANES

The tatcho drom to be a jinnimengro is to dik and rig in zi.
(The true way to be a wise man is to look and remember.)

Romani proverb

Robert:

One of the misconceptions *gadjes* – non-Gypsies – have is the romantic idea about Gypsies. I've been to so many meetings where the local people are against this family living in such a place: they don't associate them with the old traditional horse and wagon; they say they're not real Gypsies. They are; they're our people – pure blood, Romani Gypsies. They say, 'These aren't the people that we knew as children, going round on the horses!' What they don't take on board is that we've been forced out of that way of life. It's only a small minority living the traditional life. It's so different now. They've got thousands of pounds worth of vehicle, thousands of pounds worth of caravan – money that our people never had in the past. A lot of our people are

A beautiful example of a Ledge wagon, with a chicken pecking at the soil and a campfire burning in the background.

millionaires now. It was an unknown thing for the older generation – though we had our posh rats. My great-grandfather was a posh rat. How I know that's from the photograph there: that's a posh rat's wagon. I've got one of those outside.

Maggie:

We're phased out of a lot of traditional stopping places. I'd love to take a trailer for a weekend and go up on Chapel Plaister, or Maidendown, or Dartmoor, but you can't do it. They're blocked off. You can't use them any more. There's these Section 61 [legislation related to trespass] – if you stop on any of our old stopping places, like Ember Pond Lane, the police come up and see that you're Gypsies, and you're gone. You can't have any of your old life. The only way you can do it is by horse and wagon, but you're taking your life in your hands by being out there on that road. The police tell you, for your own safety, not to use a horse and wagon on the roads. It's disappearing. That's why it should all be written down.

During their five centuries of residence in England, Gypsies have survived, through their wits, on the margins. They have inspired a mixture of fear and fascination among their sedentary neighbours. They have been restricted in their movements, and also thrown off land when they have stopped. They have been enslaved, deported and branded. Their possessions have been confiscated, and their children taken away into care.

For all that, and in spite of legislation, such as the Moveable Dwellings Bills of the late-nineteenth century, their nomadic way of life was never completely erased. Despite the Children's Act (1908) and the Education Act (1944), many Gypsy children continued to grow up with no, or barely any, formal schooling. Yet over the past half-century, forces both from within and without have made this separate, and distinctive, existence increasingly problematic. The old stopping places, the *atchin tan*, have disappeared. The Criminal Justice and Public Order Act of 1994 has made the very act of roaming the land illegal. While Gypsies can buy land, they are not allowed to develop it in a manner that would allow family members to stay together. Local authorities have resisted pressures to provide sites, and those that do exist are often on land that would be deemed unfit for habitation by any other group, often without basic facilities, such as hot and cold water, and infested by rodents. Such sites are generally concealed from the public eye: on urban industrial sites, alongside railway tracks, dual carriageways or motorways; next to air bases, factories and refineries; by power stations, chemical plants, refuse tips or sewage works. An extreme instance was of an official site, occupied by Gypsy families for two decades, near an old rubbish dump in Plymouth. Allegedly, this was deemed by the authorities as unsuitable for a golf course, for which there had been a planning application. The application was rejected on the grounds that there was too much toxicity in the atmosphere. Yet it appears to have been considered sufficiently safe for Gypsy children to be left growing up there. Indeed, in the last few years an official site has been constructed near the Chelson Meadow tip.

Those contributing to this book have alluded to some of these factors, referring to hostility from authorities and violence from bailiffs and hired thugs brought in to break up sites, while the *gavvers* (police) have looked on. In theory, evictions can take place at any time of day or night. Most typically, a large police presence builds up from around five o'clock in the morning, for a clearing-out due to start at nine. The water and electricity will have been cut off. Before six, the bailiffs will have begun with pickaxes, smashing up trailers, and beating people who obstruct them. Anyone who gets caught in the melée is liable to be hit – including children, grandparents and pregnant mothers. Older people are reminded of the events from past days, when police would suddenly appear, kicking over the pots of broth and ordering families to move on.

At the same time, internal reasons for the decline of the old lifestyle have been identified. Not least significant is the demise of seasonal farm work, due in part to mechanisation, but also to the importation of cheap labour from Eastern Europe. To some, it seems a little strange to feel such nostalgia at the thought of being hunched over in fields, picking sprouts, on frosty mornings.

There are other factors that have been mentioned: the loss of autonomy through reliance on social security; the growth of a youth culture dominated by drug and alcohol abuse; even the *dinnilos dikkamuktar* (TV set – literally, 'fool's looking box').

To some extent, time has caught up with them, in a world that has embraced all modern evolution as 'progress'.

Robert:

People like me can remember going around with the horses as an everyday part of life – that pace – you can't go further back than the horse-drawn days. It's not only the animals and affinity with the animals – it's the pace of life. Nothing moved faster than that pace. That's a natural pace. The pace that was dictated by the horse was also reflected through the people. They had more time for each other.

All life is controlled by speed – the speed of going somewhere or getting something to you. The horse-drawn days were the speed of life. If you wanted something from Bridgwater, you're talking perhaps a whole day. Six hours there, six hours back with a wagon or a flat cart. I can be down there now in twenty minutes in my car.

Amy:

Travellers did what they had to do to make a living and survive beside the road. The farmers would say, 'You can stay there for a little while.' Going way back, nobody bothered them. But as time went on, there's different legislation, different planning circumstances and you couldn't stay anywhere. Up until ten or twelve years ago you had people come in to do all the pea picking, all the potato picking, then as the years went on there were machines to do that. But it was much cheaper to have labour, to have the Gypsies, than it was to find all that money to buy those machines that could do half the job that people could do – because people would clear it, but a machine would go over it and over it and over. At the end of the day they did get better mechanical things.

Dorothy:

In time – knocking on the doors, people's not going to come out. The old ways is gone.

Some have managed to adapt to a new life; yet almost all seem to yearn for the old ways.

Dorothy:

In the house, some of the neighbours was nice and some of them weren't. What with the animals and calling the kids Gypsies, we had enough of it. This bit of ground come up here – nearly four acres. We moved down here nearly twenty years ago. The council came down and said, 'You've got to go,' and asked why we left the house.

So I said, 'Really and truly, we was like animals in cages. We couldn't go outside the house where people wanted to know what we were doing and what we wasn't doing!'

The council said, 'You gotta go.'

We said, 'Why have we got to go when we own this land and we just have caravans?'

He said, 'You're not allowed to buy property and come down here without planning permission. It will not pass.'

We said, 'We was going to try.'

We got a form, filled it out, and no problems at all. Apart from the man up the road. He didn't want Gypsies near. So we came down here, been here ever since and been very happy. There were all these snowdrops down the bottom – me and me daughter, with the old digger, took the snowdrops off and with the hoe, put the snowdrops up here.

Lisa:

I am a Gypsy and I'm proud to be one. There's good and there's bad in everybody. I am in a house now with my four children; we have settled down nearly seven years; my children go to school; we do miss the travelling life. There's nowhere for Gypsies to live. As soon as you pull on a bit of land, the police move you. At the end of the day we are no different 'n nobody else. We go the same way; we's made the same way.

When Gypsies pull on with good tackle, clean and respectable – we look after our children, we're not allowed to stay… We are full-bred Gypsies… We've travelled all our lives, all over the country from top to bottom.

We really do look after our children. You don't hear about Traveller children get picked up, or get lost, raped or murdered.

My children would go back on the road tomorrow. But where is there to go?

Partly, what is missing is the sense of community.

Lisa:

In the house on my own, I get my odd days and I get fed up. I do get itchy feet, especially in the spring.

Robert:

A lot of the old traditions are gone. Like the language, it's gradually been watered down. Society has changed vastly in the last fifty years. When you look back – no electricity, no water, the old wells. Nowadays the young people wouldn't live like that. All society has changed and we've gradually changed with them – to our detriment, I say. I go to many sites and I've met a lot of our people, and I'm not happy how it is. The old way was, if one was in trouble, the rest would gather round and do something...

Sometimes, it seems that things have been lost almost before they were recognised – skills passed down from one generation to the next, a harmony with the surrounding landscape.

Maggie:

When I look at a hedgerow I see...blackthorn...a good-luck charm...young white ash...hazel for pegs. We lived out of hedges...boiled up bark, important for wax flowers...

I am only just beginning to realise how skilled we were; hedge...stone-walling, shoeing, gelding...

And amongst almost all whose voices are included here, the hope has never been completely relinquished of a return to another way of life, and while links may be broken, the chain persists, an aspect encapsulated in Pat's story.

Pat:

They are two different worlds. My memories are very few in the Romani world because I was brought up in the town in the shop. My mother had a shop and my father had a business. Now old Gypsy men would say to me, 'I can remember you playing by the wagons.' And Big Joe said, 'I remember you when you was a little one.' So there were times I must have visited. My mother must have visited a few times.

Our origins were concealed. She (my mother) would go into a house. There's apartment blocks in London built for people to live in; to be close to the ammunition factories, they built these small apartments. She could cope in a small apartment because she'd managed with a wagon and the kids underneath, so she could do that. The farmer would look after the wagon for having the horse to help on his farm, so she could leave it at some farm, and she could lemon juice the kids' hair so it wasn't so black, and she could get clothes. She could beg clothes. The thing was to make them look like ordinary kids.

However as time went by the kids are remembering and saying, 'Look mum! There's a Gypsy wagon there!'

And she'd say, 'Look, we don't have anything to do with them.'

She still didn't know if they were going to have that threat. If she didn't talk to them in their own language, they couldn't give themselves away, if they were picked up by somebody. That was one way of making sure your family was safe. You've got the little child who says, 'There's a wagon and a horse.' And she says, 'Don't have anything to do with them; just forget it; nothing to do with you. Come on. We're going to go shopping.' The child grows up thinking, 'Better not have anything to do with them.' So you've actually got Gypsies now who are prejudiced against Gypsies.

Then they grow up and bring their children up and their children are thinking, 'I just can't help it. I want to travel. I want to be out,' and Mum says, 'No! No!' But these youngsters are thinking, 'I've gotta get out there.' They've lost all the know-how of being on the road and how to handle yourself on the road, so they do it all wrong, but they still go out there because they've got that innate sensitivity that they want to do this travelling...

As we have seen, Pat's son, Mark, was drawn back, instinctively, into the Romani world through his love of horses. Indeed, there would seem to be something about the horse and wagon, crisscrossing memory in some subtle way, leaving an invisible patteran for the soul to follow. A house, a mortgage, a car – how could these ever amount to the same?

Maggie:

It's very hard to conform to livin' in an 'ouse... In fact, me grandad always had a bit of land called the Princes Lane, at Peasedown St John. There was an old Roman road. He and this other lad, Jonnie Ayres, 'ad bought this lane years ago, 'e owned, 'e bought it, I think. 'E got the paperwork somewhere; 'e give £30 for Poulton tall house, it was called; it 'ad five or six acres with it.

Now we'd use that for winter quarters sometimes, and we'd go back and pull the wagons round the Poulton tall house and the 'orses would be in the 'ouse. They'd be fed in the downstairs rooms, out of the cold. That's what 'ouses meant to us...

We started dealing in horses again, breaking in 'orses, and I've lived in quite a few 'ouses, but can honestly say, I've never been 'appy. I've always entertained the neighbours by 'avin' a fire outside with me cooking pots. I've hated sleeping; all the windows 'ave 'ad to be open.

When she was a very old woman, her body succumbing to illness, Polly Small took her niece, Maggie, on a rather strange journey around some narrow lanes by the villages surrounding Newton Abbot. It was one of those journeys where you spend as much time reversing as driving forwards, and during which one begins to lose sense of time and direction. Finally, they stopped at a rather 'posh' bungalow. 'I want to show you this place,' Polly remarked. 'It's part of your history. It belonged to Aunt Tiny.' The property and its land had been owned by the family for many years before the war. When the owner appeared, far from throwing these uninvited guests off his land for trespassing, he invited them in. Polly Small, however, told him that all she wanted was to walk around the grounds, pointing things out.

> 'That's where me Uncle Jim had his rod tent; now there should be a gap in the hedge down there, where we used to pop over to have a pee! And either side of the paddock there was a gap in the hedge for the men to go on the left, and one on the right for the women. That's where so-and-so had her baby, down there... That was where the wagon was pulled in...'. She talked about simple things – where the fire was lit, where they cooked, seemingly able to conjure up even the most mundane events from her childhood memory, re-playing them, as if on film.
>
> When the owner returned, he had remembered something, an item owned by Tiny Small. He led the way to a beautiful rhododendron bush, in flower at the time, over fifty years old and mused, 'Around these parts people say that was a stick that your Aunt Tiny pushed in the ground, and that's the result.'

And in a way, that sums up the feelings of almost all whose words appear in this book. A Gypsy childhood was often harsh, a struggle to take root and flourish in the face of an unforgiving environment, an external world that was, at best indifferent, and more often hostile. This is a world that has almost vanished, one in which what

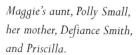

Maggie's aunt, Polly Small, her mother, Defiance Smith, and Priscilla.

was once commonplace seems now to be imbued with something magical.

Anna:

I feel like a prisoner…because when that blossom comes and you can see the buds on the trees, it's time for your wings to spread, and I'm missing where I'm used to going…

If we've got something, a shilling we're 'appy. If we've got nothing, we're 'appy, 'cos you don't expect something every day. Every hour, every day, is a special day.

I've got loads of clocks in 'ere, but 'onestly, none of them don't work, none of them. And if you feel outside, you know what time to get up, you're pretty judged by the time of day, and you're pretty judged in the mornings, because we're up for 4 o'clock, 5 o'clock, but that is only for one reason: we hear them birds singing. I don't want to sleep my life away; every hour is precious.

Day's a day, it's not going to change, if they turn clocks backwards or forwards… If I could turn time back, I'd be free and 'appy…

Maggie:

Sometimes I go ten mile out of me way to go up a certain lane I went up as a child… I want all my old life back!

Almost imperceptibility, like pieces of some intricate but fragile formation, once-treasured customs have been allowed to slip away. Yet it is not only the Romani perspective that is threatened by such erosion.

Robert:

We've lived in amongst *gadjes* for so many centuries. We've changed your landscape. We've changed your psyche. Very gradually over time we're with you. When you look at the fair – all those bright lights, you don't think of us. All those beautiful decorations, such as in the wagon, those Burroughs steam engines, dynamos for the show people. It was us again. We've influenced and brought so many things down with no credit ever. No one will ever say, 'Gypsies have been with us for so many centuries in a part of our culture; they've made the way we are, how things are, not for the bad, but for good.'

This atmospheric image showing a Gypsy couple, their bender tents and a donkey and cart is part of the Miss Wight Collection, housed at the Museum of English Rural Life. (Used by kind permission of the University of Reading)

Glossary

Atchin / atchen / atching tan – stopping place

Bavolengro – ghost (literally, wind-fellow)

Canni / kanni – chicken
Chavvies – children
Chaw – grass
Chir – to sing
Chiriko / chirilo – bird
Chor – steal
Chopping – dealing
Cuskti / kushti – good

Dicklo – neck scarf
Didikoi / didikai / diddikoi / diddikai – The meaning seems to vary slightly according to the social position of the speaker. To those who consider themselves of pure Romani descent, it is often used rather disparagingly to denote those of part Romani descent, perhaps those having one Romani parent. That group, in turn, sometimes use the term to refer to someone with some, but very little, Romani blood. Some non-Gypsies use the term to refer to all those of non-Gypsy background. It has been suggested that, originally, the word denoted a low-caste group in India.
Dinnilos dikkamuktar – TV set (literally, fool's looking box)
Drom – the way
Dukkering – fortune telling (originally *dukker* meant to bewitch)

Gadje / gadze / gauje / gorgio – non-Gypsy
Gav / gavvers – police (the less polite term is *baulo*, which translates as 'pig')
Grai / gry – horse
Gryengro – horse dealer

Gubb – old woman with the ability to curse

Hotchi – hedgehog
Hotchimengri – frying pan
Jukkles / juckal – dogs

Kel the bosh – play the fiddle
Kharvi / kavvi / kekkavvi – kettle
Kharvisaster / kavvisaster / sasterkabakosh – kettle-iron (the metal bar that holds the kettle over the fire)
Kooli – soldier
Kor – to fight
Kosh / kosht – stick
Kris – the law (Gypsy law and custom)

Lav – name, word
Lil – book

Mandi – man, me or I
Mouth tuning – accompanied singing, giving the beat for step dancing
Mulo – ghost
Mush – man

Nash – to race and, also, to hang
Nashimescro – racer and hangman

Patteran / patrin – an arrangement of sticks or stones to indicate direction taken
Pattriensis – herbs used in cures
Petulengo – horseshoe maker / farrier
Pikie – a Gypsy expelled from the group
Pucker / pooker – to ask or tell (hence the *kosht that pookers the drom* or the *pookering-kosh*, both meaning signpost or, literally, telling-stick)
Pouffing / pooving – grazing

Pouff the grai / poov the gry – sneak a horse into a field in the darkness for illicit grazing

Rai – man, gentleman

Rawnie – a lady

Rokker – to talk

Rokker shoonengri – telephone (literally, talking thing)

Rom – Gypsy man

Roma – a member of the Gypsy people (singular) or the Gypsy people (plural)

Romani chi – Gypsy girl

Romano chal – Gypsy boy

Roozlums / rustlers / iouzers – flowers

Ruk / rukh / rooker – tree

Rukkersamengri – squirrel (literally, treefellow)

Shussi / shooshi / shoshi – rabbit

Shussyin' / shooshying – rabbiting

Skit – taunt

Spleeder – a long wooden stick, similar to a skewer, on which to cook meat

Step dancing – dancing on a board – similar to tap dancing or clog dancing

Tardra – to pull

Tardramengri – hop pickers

Tem – country

Tober – the road

Vardo – wagon, caravan

Welgora – fair

Yog – fire

BIBLIOGRAPHY

Borrow, G. (1851): *Lavengro*, London, John Murray.

Borrow, G. (1857): *The Romany Rye*, London, John Murray.

Borrow, G. (1883): *Romano Lavo-Lil* – Handbook of the Romany, or English Gypsy Language, London, John Murray.

Bowness, C. (1973): *Romany Magic*, Dartford, Aquarian Press.

Burgess, P. (2000): Wiggy Smith and other members of the Smith family, 'Band of Gold', http://www.mustrad.org.uk

Davies, J. (1999): *Tales of the Old Gypsies*, Newton Abbot, David & Charles.

Dickens, C. (1840): *The Old Curiosity Shop*, London, Chapman & Hall.

Elliott, C. (1997): 'Rash Encounters', *Horticulture*, vol. 94, pp. 30.

Ezard, J. (1976): Gypsy children write of life on the road, the *Guardian*, 27.09.76

Fraser, A. (1995): *The Gypsies* (Second Edition), Oxford, Blackwell.

Garmston, D. (2001): 'Surviving World War Two: The Bristol Evacuees', http://www.bbc.co.uk/history.

Goldsworthy, E. (1883): *Recollections of Old Taunton*, Taunton, Books of Wessex.

Gorman, B. & Walsh, P. (2003): *King of the Gypsies: Memoirs of the Undefeated Bareknuckle Champion of Great Britain and Ireland*, Preston, Milo Books.

Halliday, R. (1997): *Criminal Graves and Rural Crossroads*, British Archaeology, 25:6.

Hancock, I. (1987): *The Pariah Syndrome: An Account of Gypsy Slavery and Persecution*, Ann Arbor, Karoma Publishers.

Harvey, D. (1979): *The Gypsies: Waggon time and after*, London, Batsford.

Hayward, J. (2003): *Gypsy Jib: A Romany Dictionary*, Wenhaston, Suffolk, Holm Oak Publishing.

Huth, F.G. (1940): Gypsy caravans, Journal of the Gypsy Lore Society, 19 (4), pp114–146

Kilvert, R.F. (1947): *R.F. Kilvert's Diary, Selections from the Diary of the Rev. Francis Kilvert*, New York, Macmillan.

Leland, C.G. (1891): *Gypsy Sorcery and Fortune Telling*, London, T. Fisher Unwin.

Liegeois, J.P. (1986): *The Gypsies: An Illustrated History*, London, Al Saqi Books.

Matthews, R. (1995): 'A Farmer's Story: My life at Roncombe Farm', Bridport: [n.p.].

Mayall, D. (2004): *Gypsy Identities, 1500–2000: From Egipcyans and Moon-men to the Ethnic Romany*, London, Routledge.

Paspati, A.G. (1870): *Etudes sur les Tchinghianes ou Bohemiens de L'Empire Ottoman*, Constantinople, Antoine Koromela.

Price, F. (2005): *The Way of the Romany*, published by Robert Dawson on behalf of Derbyshire Gypsy Liaison Group.

Quelch, M.T. (1941): *Herbs For Daily Use*, London, Faber & Faber.

Sampson, A. (1997): *The Scholar Gypsy*, London, John Murray.

Sampson, J. (1926): *The Dialect of the Gypsies of Wales*, London, Clarendon Press.

Sibley, D. (1995): *Geographies of Exclusion*, London, Routledge.

Simson, W. (1865): *A History of the Gipsies*, London, Sampson Low, Marston & Co.

Smith, C. (1911): *Gypsy Smith: His Life and His Work*, By Himself, New York, Fleming H. Revell Company.

Thompson, T.W. (1924): *English Gypsy Death and Burial Customs*, Journal of Gypsy Lore Society, 3:3, pp. 5–38; 60–93.

Tongue, R. (1965): *Somerset Folklore*, (edited by K. Briggs), County Folklore, The Folklore Society, vol. viii, pp.43–5.

Tongue, R. (1968): *The Chimes Child*, London, Routledge and Kegan Paul.

Travell, I. (2005): National Fairground Archive, The University of Sheffield, http://www.nfa.dept.shef.ac.uk

Uplyme Records of Churchwardens (1650): Dorset History Centre, Dorchester.

Walsh, T. (2003): *Musical Traditions*, internet magazine.

Ward-Jackson, C. & Harvey, D. (1972): *The English Gypsy Caravan*, Newton Abbot, David & Charles.

Williamson, H. (1945): *Life in a Devon Village*, London, Faber & Faber.

Wilson, C. (2004): *Gypsy Feast: Recipes and Culinary Traditions of the Gypsy People*, New York, Hippocrene Books.

Wood, M.F. (1973): *In the Life of a Romany Gypsy*, London, Routledge and Kegan Paul.

Websites visited during research

Patrin Web Journal, http://www.geocities.com

University of Liverpool, http://sca.lib.liv.ac.uk/collections/gypsy/links.htm

The Romani Archives and Documentation Center, University of Texas, http://www.radoc.net

INDEX